LEAVES
FROM A
SPIRITUAL
NOTEBOOK

 A B I N G D O N   P R E S S — NEW YORK   •   NASHVILLE

LEAVES

FROM A

SPIRITUAL

NOTEBOOK

THOMAS S. KEPLER

LEAVES FROM A SPIRITUAL NOTEBOOK

Copyright © 1960 by Abingdon Press

All rights in this book are reserved.

Library of Congress Catalog Card Number: 60:10910

PRINTED IN THE U.S.A.

Special acknowledgment is made to the following who have granted permission for the reprinting of copyrighted material from the books listed below:

ABINGDON PRESS for "How to Pray" by E. Stanley Jones, copyright 1943 by Whitmore & Stone; extract from *An Approach to the Teachings of Jesus* by Ernest Cadman Colwell, copyright 1947 by Stone & Pierce; extract from *The Beginnings of Christianity* by Clarence T. Craig, copyright 1942 by Whitmore & Stone; extract from *Come as You Are* by Orval H. Austin, copyright 1956 by Pierce & Washabaugh; extract from *Dark Night of the Soul* by Georgia Harkness, copyright 1945 by Whitmore & Stone; extract from *The Methodist Heritage* by Henry Carter; extract from *The Spiritual Life* by Edgar S. Brightman, copyright 1942 by Whitmore & Stone; extract from *Criticism and Faith* by John Knox, copyright 1952 by Pierce & Smith.

ASSOCIATION PRESS for extract from *From Experience to Faith* by E. P. Booth.

THE ATLANTIC MONTHLY for the William James letter; for article, "Twenty Minutes of Reality," by Margaret Prescott Montague; for extract from "The Anatomy of Courage" by Charles E. Wyzanski, Jr.; for "These I Love" by Edward Weeks; for "As I Grow Older I Grow Calm" by Oliver Wendell Holmes, Jr.

THE BOBBS-MERRILL COMPANY, INC. for extract from *Letters from Joseph Conrad* by Edward Garnett, copyright 1928, 1955, by David Garnett, used by special permission of the publishers, The Bobbs-Merrill Company, Inc.

DODD, MEAD & COMPANY for prayer from *A Book of Prayers* by Samuel McComb, reprinted by permission of the publisher; extract from "The Great Lover" by Rupert Brooke, reprinted by permission of Dodd, Mead & Company from *The Collected Poems of Rupert Brooke*, copyright 1915 by Dodd, Mead & Company, Inc., and by permission of McCLELLAND & STEWART.

DOUBLEDAY & COMPANY, INC. for extract from *Madame Curie* by Eve Curie, copyright 1937 by Doubleday & Company, Inc., and reprinted by permission of the publishers; extract from *His Eye Is on the Sparrow* by Ethel Waters and Charles Samuel, copyright 1950, 1951 by Ethel Waters and Charles Samuel and reprinted by permission of Doubleday & Company, Inc.; extract from "Twelve Rules for Poise" from *Happiness Through Creative Living* by Preston Bradley, copyright, 1955, by Preston Bradley and used by permission of the publishers, Doubleday & Company, Inc.; for extracts from *The Story of My Life* by Helen Keller, copyright 1902, 1903, 1905, by Helen Keller, reprinted by permission of Doubleday & Company, Inc.

E. P. DUTTON & CO., INC. for seven prayers from the book *The Temple* by W. E. Orchard, copyright, 1918, by E. P. Dutton & Co., Inc., renewal 1946, and reprinted by permission of the publishers; extract from the book *Selected Letters 1896-1924* of Baron Friedrich Von

4

Hügel and reprinted by permission of the publishers, E. P. Dutton & Co., Inc., and J M Dent & Sons, Ltd; extract from *The Crisis of Our Age* by Pitirim Sorokin.

The Fellowship of Reconciliation for extract from *With the Master* by Philippe Vernier.

Funk & Wagnalls Company for extract from *Albert Einstein, Maker of Universes* by H. Gordon Garbedian.

Harcourt, Brace and Company, Inc. for extract from *History of Christianity in the Light of Modern Knowledge* by Francis C. Burkitt; extract abridged from *Abraham Lincoln: The War Years*, copyright 1936, 1937, 1938, 1939, by Carl Sandburg; copyright, 1939, by Harcourt, Brace and Company, Inc. and reprinted with their permission.

Harper & Brothers for extracts from *A Diary of Private Prayer* by John Baillie; extract from *Mr. Smith* by Louis Bromfield; extract from *Death Be Not Proud* by John Gunther; extracts from *From My Journal* by André Maurois, reprinted by permission of Harper & Brothers, copyright 1947, 1948, by André Maurois; extract from *The Inner Life* by C. F. Andrews, copyright by Harper & Brothers, used by permission; extracts from *A Testament of Devotion* by Thomas R. Kelly, copyright by Harper & Brothers, used by permission; extracts from *On Beginning from Within* by Douglas V. Steere, copyright by Harper & Brothers, used by permission; extracts from *Strengthening the Spiritual Life* by Nels F. S. Ferré, copyright by Harper & Brothers, used by permission; extract from *Purity of Heart* by Sören Kierkegaard, translated by Douglas V. Steere, copyright by Harper & Brothers, used by permission; extracts from *American Spiritual Autobiographies*, edited by Louis Finkelstein, copyright by Harper & Brothers, used by permission; extract from *Life Together* by Dietrich Bonhoeffer; extract from *Authority of the Bible* by C. H. Dodd; extract from *Insights from the Diary of Bishop Charles H. Brent* by Charles Brent; extracts from *Prayers and Meditations* by Gerald Heard; extract from *History and Interpretations in the Gospels* by Robert H. Lightfoot; extract from *Start Where You Are* by A. H. Lowe; extract from *Unfinished Business* by Halford E. Luccock; extract from *Alternative to Futility* by D. Elton Trueblood; extract from *New Testament Faith for Today* by Amos Wilder; extracts from *Meditations on the Cross* by Toyohiko Kagawa; extract from *Oberlin: Protestant Saint* by Marshall Dawson; extract from *God* by J. Middleton Murry; extract from *My Gandhi* by John H. Holmes; prayers from *Dr. Johnson's Prayers* by D. Elton Trueblood; extract from *Let Your Soul Catch Up* by Muriel Lester; extract from *Memoirs of a Superfluous Man* by Albert Jay Nock; extract, "Illusions About Leisure," by L. P. Jacks.

Henry Holt and Company, Inc. for extract from *Out of My Life and Thought* by Albert Schweitzer.

The Hibbert Journal for article by Claude G. Montefiore.

Houghton Mifflin Company for extract from *Accepting the Universe* by John Burroughs.

The Hutchinson Group for extracts from *The Diary of a Dean* by W. R. Inge.

The John Day Company, Inc. for extract from *If This Be Religion* by Frederick K. Stamm.

Alfred A. Knopf, Inc. for extracts reprinted from the *Journal of Katherine Mansfield* by Katherine Mansfield, copyright 1927 by Alfred A. Knopf, Inc.; for extracts reprinted from *The Journals of André Gide* by André Gide, copyright 1949 by Alfred A. Knopf, Inc.

Little, Brown & Company for extract from *Adventures in Two Worlds* by A. J. Cronin.

Longmans, Green & Co., Inc. for extract from *Selected Poems* by Evelyn Underhill.

McGraw-Hill Book Company, Inc. for extracts from *Life Begins at 40* by Walter B. Pitkin, copyright, 1932, by Walter B. Pitkin.

Macmillan & Co. Ltd. for four lines from *Collected Poems of Thomas Hardy*, by permission of the Trustees of the Hardy Estate and by permission of the publisher.

The Macmillan Company for extract from *Mahatma Gandhi's Ideas* by C. F. Andrews and reprinted by permission of the publisher, and by George Allen & Unwin Ltd.; extract from *Jesus of Nazareth* by Joseph Klausner, reprinted by permission of the publisher; extract from *Religion in the Making* by Alfred North Whitehead, reprinted by permission of the publisher; extract from *Finding the Trail of Life* by Rufus Jones; for two prayers from *Collected Poems and Plays* by Rabindranath Tagore, by permission of the publisher and Macmillan & Co., Ltd.

Oxford University Press for extract from *The Idea of the Holy* by Rudolf Otto, translated by John W. Harvey, 1923, a Galaxy Book, and reprinted by permission of Oxford University Press, Inc.

Pantheon Books, Inc. for extract from *Gift from the Sea* by Anne Morrow Lindbergh.

The Pilgrim Press for prayer from *Book of Church Services*; four prayers from *Prayers of the Social Awakening* by Walter Rauschenbusch.

Princeton University Press for extract from *The Christ of the New Testament* by Paul Elmer More.

5

G. P. Putnam's Sons for extract from *What Is Christianity?* by Adolf Harnack; extract from *Lou Gehrig: A Quiet Hero* by Frank Graham, copyright, 1942, by Frank Graham, published by G. P. Putnam's Sons and used by their permission; extracts from *Alone* by Richard E. Byrd, copyright, 1938, by Richard E. Byrd, published by G. P. Putnam's Sons and used by their permission; extract from *Outline of Science* by Sir John A. Thomson.

Random House, Inc. for extract from William Faulkner's Nobel Prize Acceptance Speech, reprinted from *The Faulkner Reader*, copyright 1954.

The Reader's Digest for extracts from "Ethel Barrymore, Queen Once More" by Adela Rogers St. John; extract from "Prayer Is Power" by Alexis Carrell; extracts from "Your Next 12 Hours" by Kenneth L. Holmes.

Fleming H. Revell Company for extract by G. Bromley Oxnam.

Rivingtons for prayer from *The Sanctuary* by Percy Dearmer.

SPCK for two prayers from *A Book of Prayers Written for Use in an Indian College* by J. S. Hoyland, by permission of Mrs. J. S. Hoyland.

Charles Scribner's Sons for extract from *Theology of Crisis* by Emil Brunner; extract from *The Search for the Real Jesus* by Chester C. McCowin; extract from *Jesus the Unknown* by Dmitri Merejowski; extract from *Human Nature and Its Gospel* by William Lyon Phelps; extract from *The Spirit of St. Louis* by Charles Lindbergh, copyright, 1953, by Charles Scribner's Sons; extract from *Beyond Tragedy* by Reinhold Niebuhr, copyright, 1937, Charles Scribner's Sons; extract from *My Host the World* by Santayana; extract from *On Justice Holmes* by Francis Biddle; extract from *Twice Thirty* by Edward W. Bok; extracts from *The Sermon on the Mount* by Martin Dibelius; extracts from *Jesus and the Word* by Rudolf Bultmann, reprinted with the permission of Charles Scribner's Sons, copyright, 1934, Charles Scribner's Sons; prayer from *Prayers for Services* by Morgan P. Noyes; extract from *From Immigrant to Inventor* by Michael Pupin, reprinted by permission of Charles Scribner's Sons, copyright, 1922, 1923, Charles Scribner's Sons; renewal copyright 1950, 1951.

Simon and Schuster, Inc. for extract from *The Organization Man* by William H. Whyte, Jr.; extract from the *Story of Philosophy* by Will Durant; extracts from *Reading I've Liked* by Clifton Fadiman; extract from *The Art of Thinking* by Ernest Dimnet.

This Week for "Your Next 12 Hours" by Kenneth L. Holmes, reprinted from *This Week* magazine, copyright 1953 by the United Newspapers Magazine Corporation.

The University of Chicago Press for six prayers by Sören Kierkegaard, reprinted from *Prayers of Kierkegaard*, edited by Perry D. LeFevre by the courtesy of The University of Chicago Press, copyright 1956 by The University of Chicago.

The Viking Press, Inc. for extract, "Heroism, the Mystery of Happiness," from *Humanity and Happiness* by Georg Brochmann, copyright 1950 by The Viking Press, Inc., and reprinted with their permission.

A. Watkins, Inc. for extract "The Dogma Is the Drama" from *Creed or Chaos* by Dorothy L. Sayers, copyright, 1947, by Dorothy L. Sayers.

Zondervan Publishing House for extract from *The Kingdom of God and the Son of Man* by Rudolf Otto.

Special acknowledgment is also made to the following persons and organizations for permission to reprint the materials indicated:

Robert Merrill Bartlett for prayers from *Ascending Trail*.

Bill Cunningham for *A Tribute to Bill Stidger*.

Donald M. R. Cameron for prayers of Hugh Cameron.

Central Conference of American Rabbis for six prayers from *The Union Prayerbook for Jewish Worship*.

Stuart Chase for essay "Are You Alive?" written for the *Nation*, July 19, 1922, and reprinted in *Reader's Digest* for April, 1927.

The Estate of Albert P. Fitch for prayers by Albert P. Fitch.

The Trustees of the Estate of the Late J. E. C. Flitch for extract from *The Tragic Sense of Life* by Miguel de Unamuno.

Granville Hicks for extract from *Eight Ways of Looking at Christianity*.

Holiday Magazine for "What Is an Aristocrat?" by H. L. Mencken, March, 1958.

Frank Laubach for extract from *Letters by a Modern Mystic*.

Mrs. William L. Stidger for articles by William L. Stidger.

Chad Walsh for extract from *Stop Looking and Listen*.

W. L. White for "Mary White" by William Allen White.

PREFACE

In assembling these "leaves from a spiritual notebook," I realize that such an anthology or "notebook" is never completed. There are many more excerpts from many writers which I would like to enter into these pages. But I have found it necessary to observe space limitations; and from a larger scope of readings these are the ones which I have really enjoyed the most.

I have not had strict norms for selecting the materials in this volume; nor have I tried to thread the articles together around any school of religious thought. Most of these pages contain nonfictional prose and prayers from a wide range of writers whose ideas I have found to be of real worth. They have expressed a note of inspiration for me in my own thinking and living. Hence the main norm for the selection of these writings has been a personal, experiential one, which can be expressed in one phrase, "They appeal to me." I have also included within these pages some of my own writings, mainly from "leaves" which I have used both in a written and oral fashion in trying to communicate my ideas to others.

This "spiritual notebook" thus possesses two kinds of articles: those written by others, which compose 85 per cent of the volume; and those from my own pen. The former are followed by the names of the authors; mine are left without signature, although I am sure that in most of my own thoughts I am greatly indebted to others' writings. "Originality" is oftentimes but a rephrasing of an idea written earlier—and sometimes many times—by other persons.

Some of these selections are short; a few are rather long. While some of the prose selections lie within the area of "secular" writings and others within the area of "devotional" literature, the purpose of all the selections is one of an inspirational-religious significance, with the term "religion" defined in a broad sense.

The prose selections of Parts I and III are largely nonfictional, most of them lying in the areas of biography and autobiography and containing excerpts from diaries, evaluations of persons by those who knew them well, confessions of persons regarding their insights into the spiritual life and the meaning of life and its problems, letters from great souls to friends on the verities of life.

There is some similarity in the articles of Parts I and III; yet there is a difference. The selections in Part III can be labeled "devotional," most of the articles coming from devotional classics and books on prayer and worship. Those in Part I can be called "inspirational," as they consist mainly of biographical and autobiographical excerpts. Both sections are excellent aids for any reader who wishes to understand the meaning of life and who also wishes some insights into a solution of many of life's perennial problems. Either section will give aids to daily devotions.

The prayers in Part II are selected from a wide reading of many prayers and are the ones which I have found to be of real depth. There are 130 of them. These prayers, like the Psalms, touch most of the moods of life.

The "leaves" of this spiritual notebook are intended for several purposes: for personal daily devotions, where an individual can select prose and prayers for day by day use; for leaders of devotional services, as a resource for selections to key around a certain theme; for ministers and other public speakers who wish illustrative materials and/or stimulation for their own needs; for general perusal as an aid to reflection and inspiration. I am confronted constantly by people—laymen, students, ministers—who wish a source book of this nature. These "leaves from my spiritual notebook" are an answer to their request.

Three indexes at the back of this volume will guide readers in the use of the materials: The "Index of Titles" gives the title of each of the 327 articles. The "Topical Index" is a guide to 586 topics, with several thousand ideas on a variety of subjects. The "Index of Authors" is a "Who's Who" of the 227 contributors to this volume. The correlation of these indexes will be of inestimable value to the person who uses this book for almost any purpose.

8

I am deeply indebted to the following persons for aiding me in the preparation of this manuscript: to Juanita Schramm for her typing; to Connie Kock Pipok, David Shannon, and Robert Arnold for helping me in the preparing of the indexes, the checking of references, and the obtaining of permissions; to the library staff of Oberlin College, to my wife Florence who, as usual, has given me her helpful criticisms and evaluations; and to the acknowledged publishers and individuals who have given me permission to use their writings.

THOMAS S. KEPLER

This anthology is dedicated
to
Deborah and Tom
Ann and Felix
Lyn, Tom III, Jon, David, Marc

CONTENTS

PROSE

 WHICH SPEAKS TO LIFE SITUATIONS

[1] The Secret of Michael Pupin

WHEN I landed at Castle Garden, forty-eight years ago, I had only five cents in my pocket. Had I brought five hundred dollars, instead of five cents from Serbia, my immediate career in the new, and to me a perfectly strange, land would have been the same. A young immigrant, such as I was then, does not begin his career until he has spent all the money which he has brought with him. . . .

He who has never crossed the stormy Atlantic during the month of March in the crowded steerage of an immigrant ship does not know what hardships are. Many a night I spent on the deck of that immigrant ship hugging the warm smoke-stack and adjusting my position so as to avoid the force of the gale and the sharpness of its icy chilliness. All I had was the light suit of clothes which I carried on my back. Everything else I had converted into money with which to pay my transportation expenses. I could not rest during the cold nights of March without shivering and unbearable discomfort. If it had not been for the warm smoke-stack I should have died of cold.

A blast of the everlasting gales had carried away my hat, and a Turkish fez such as the Serbs of Bosnia wear was the only head-gear I had. It was providential that I had not succeeded in selling it at Prague. Most of my fellow emigrants thought that I was a Turk and cared little about my discomforts. But, nevertheless, I felt quite brave and strong in the daytime: at night, however, when, standing alone alongside

15

of the smoke-stack, I beheld through the howling darkness the white rims of the mountain-high waves speeding on like maddened dragons toward the tumbling ship, my heart sank low. It was my implicit trust in God and in his regard for my mother's prayers which enabled me to overcome my fear and bravely face the horrors of the angry seas.

—MICHAEL PUPIN, 1858-1935

[2] Alone

THE first days of May carried no hint of the calamities that would overtake me at the month's end. On the contrary, they were among the most wonderful days I had ever known. The blizzards departed, the cold moved down from the South Pole, and opposite the moon in a coal-black sky the cast-up light from the departed sun burned like a bonfire. During the first six days the temperature averaged —47.03°; much of the time it was deep in the minus forties and fifties. The winds scarcely blew. And a soundlessness fell over the Barrier. I have never known such utter quiet.

It was a queer business. I felt as though I had been plumped upon another planet or into another geologic horizon of which man had no knowledge or memory. And yet, I thought at the time it was very good for me; I was learning what the philosophers have long been harping on—that a man can live profoundly without masses of things.

For all my realism and skepticism there came over me, too powerfully to be denied, that exalted sense of identification—or oneness—with the outer world which is partly mystical but also certainty. I came to understand what Thoreau meant when he said, "My body is all sentient." There were moments when I felt more *alive* than at any other time in my life.

—RICHARD E. BYRD, 1888-1957

[3] Who Could Believe that Rome Is Fallen?

"The wolves of the North have been let loose."
I SHUDDER when I think of the calamities of our time. For twenty years the blood of Romans has been shed daily between Constantinople and

16

the Alps. Scythia, Thrace, Macedon, Thessaly, Dacia, Achaea, Epirus—all these regions have been sacked and pillaged by Goths and Alans, Huns and Vandals. How many noble and virtuous women have been made the sport of these beasts! Churches have been overthrown, horses stalled in the holy places, the bones of the saints dug up and scattered

Indeed, the Roman world is falling; yet we still hold up our heads instead of bowing them. The East, indeed, seemed to be free from these perils; but now, in the year just past, the wolves of the North have been let loose from their remotest fastnesses, and have overrun great provinces. . . . Well may we be unhappy, for it is our sins that have made the barbarians strong; as in the days of Hezekiah, so today is God using the fury of the barbarian to execute His fierce anger. Rome's army, once the lord of the world, trembles today at sight of the foe.

Who will hereafter believe that Rome has to fight now within her own borders, not for glory but for life? and, as the poet Lucan says, "If Rome be weak, where shall strength be found?"

And now a dreadful rumor has come to hand. Rome has been besieged, and its citizens have been forced to buy off their lives with gold. My voice cleaves to my throat; sobs choke my utterance. The city which had taken the whole world captive is itself taken. Famine too has done its awful work.

The world sinks into ruin; all things are perishing save our sins; these alone flourish. The great city is swallowed up in one vast conflagration; everywhere Romans are in exile.

Who could believe it? Who could believe that Rome, built up through the ages by the conquest of the world, had fallen; that the mother of nations had become their tomb? who could imagine that the proud city, with its careless security and its boundless wealth, is brought so low that her children are outcasts and beggars? We cannot indeed help them; all we can do is sympathize with them, and mingle our tears with theirs.

—SAINT JEROME, 340?-420

[4] Christopher Columbus on "The Islands"

YET when they perceive that they are safe, putting aside all fear, they are of simple manners and trustworthy, and very liberal with everything they have, refusing no one who asks for anything they may possess, and even themselves inviting us to ask for things. They show greater love for all others than for themselves; they give valuable things for

17

trifles, being satisfied even with a very small return, or with nothing; however, I forbade that things so small and of no value should be given to them, such as pieces of plate, dishes and glass, likewise keys and shoestraps; although if they were able to obtain these, it seemed to them like getting the most beautiful jewels in the world . . . .

In all these islands there is no difference in the appearance of the people, nor in the manners and language, but all understand each other mutually; a fact that is very important for the end which I suppose to be earnestly desired by our most illustrious king, that is, their conversion to the holy religion of Christ, to which in truth, as far as I can perceive, they are very ready and favorably inclined . . . .

Let the king and queen, the princes and their most fortunate kingdoms, and all other countries of Christendom give thanks to our Lord and Saviour Jesus Christ, who has bestowed upon us so great a victory and gift. Let religious processions be solemnized; let sacred festivals be given; let the churches be covered with festive garlands. Let Christ rejoice on earth, as he rejoices in heaven, when he foresees coming to salvation so many souls of people hitherto lost. Let us be glad also, as well on account of the exaltation of our faith, as on account of the increase of our temporal affairs, of which not only Spain, but universal Christendom will be partaker. These things that have been done are thus briefly related. Farewell. Lisbon, the day before the ides of March.

—CHRISTOPHER COLUMBUS, Admiral of the Ocean Fleet, 1451-1506

[5] Nobel Prize Speech

OUR tragedy today is a general and universal physical fear so long sustained by now that we can even bear it. There are no longer problems of the spirit. There is only the question: When will I be blown up? Because of this, the young man or woman writing today has forgotten the problems of the human heart in conflict with itself which alone can make good writing because only that is worth writing about, worth the agony and the sweat.

He must learn them again. He must teach himself that the basest of all things is to be afraid; and, teaching himself that, forget it forever, leaving no room in his workshop for anything but the old verities and truths of the heart, the old universal truths lacking which any story is ephemeral and doomed—love and honor and pity and pride and compassion and sacrifice. Until he does so, he labors under a curse. He writes

18

not of love but of lust, of defeats in which nobody loses anything of value, of victories without hope, and, worst of all, without pity or compassion. His griefs grieve on no universal bones, leaving no scars. He writes not of the heart but of the glands.

Until he learns these things, he will write as though he stood among and watched the end of man. I decline to accept the end of man. It is easy enough to say that man is immortal simply because he will endure: that when the last ding-dong of doom has clanged and faded from the last worthless rock hanging tideless in the last red and dying evening, that even then there will still be one more sound: that of his puny inexhaustible voice, still talking. I refuse to accept this. I believe that man will not merely endure: he will prevail. He is immortal, not because he alone among creatures has an inexhaustible voice, but because he has a soul, a spirit capable of compassion and sacrifice and endurance. . . . The poet's voice need not merely be the record of man; it can be one of the props, the pillars to help him endure and prevail.

—WILLIAM FAULKNER, 1897-

[6] The Tower of Babel

THE Tower of Babel myth belongs to the same category of mythical fancies as the Promethean myth. . . . They both picture God as being jealous of man's ambitions, achievements and pretensions. The modern mind, which has exchanged the wooden-headed literalism of orthodoxy for a shallow rationalism, can find no validity in the idea of a jealous God. It does not believe in God at all, or the God of its faith is so very kind and fatherly as to be grandmotherly. A jealous God expresses the primitive fear of higher powers from which the modern man feels himself happily emancipated. Yet the idea of a jealous God expresses a permanently valid sense of guilt in all human strivings. Religion, declares modern man, is consciousness of our highest social values. Nothing could be further from the truth. True religion is a profound uneasiness about our social values. Its uneasiness springs from the knowledge that the God whom it worships transcends the limits of finite man, while this same man is constantly tempted to forget the finiteness of his cultures and civilization and to pretend a finality for them which they do not have. Every civilisation and every culture is thus a Tower of Babel.

—REINHOLD NIEBUHR, 1892-

19

[7] The University

THERE are few earthly things more splendid than a University. In these days of broken frontiers and collapsing values, when the dams are down and floods are making misery, when every future looks somewhat grim and every ancient foothold has become something of quagmire, wherever a University stands, it stands and shines; wherever it exists the free minds of men, urged on to full and fair enquiry, may still bring wisdom into human affairs.

There are few earthly things more beautiful than a University. It is a place where those who hate ignorance may strive to know, where those who perceive truth may strive to make others see; where seekers and learners alike, banded together in the search for knowledge, will honour thought in all its finer ways, will welcome thinkers in distress or in exile, will uphold ever the dignity of thought and learning and will exact standards in these things. They give to the young in their impressionable years, the bond of a lofty purpose shared, of a great corporate life whose links will not be loosed until they die. They give young people that close companionship for which youth longs, and that chance of the endless discussion of the themes which are endless, without which youth would seem a waste of time.

—JOHN MASEFIELD, 1878-

[8] Echatology and History

THIS cosmic drama for most people is heavily weighted with tragedy. Jesus at Golgotha, Kagawa in Kobe, Milton gone blind, Beethoven deaf, Nietzsche insane—even the great actors bring little more than heartaches tempered with inspiration to those who admire them. Life so often is a perplexing, baffling dilemma. Yet in spite of the bruises it leaves on man's soul, he cannot but feel—or hope—that some day the real will become the ideal. Even one like Thomas Hardy, steeled almost to despair for a grinding universe, could pen a tone of hope,

> And they shall see what is, ere long
> Not through a glass but face to face,
> And Right shall disestablish Wrong;
> The Great Adjustment is taking place.

[9] In the Heavens

ONE of the nearest stars to the earth that we know of is Alpha Centauri, estimated to be some twenty-five million millions of miles away. Sirius, the brightest star in the firmament, is double this distance from the earth. . . .

The Earth, the planet on which we live, is a mighty globe bounded by a crust of rock many miles in thickness; the great volumes of water which we call our oceans lie in the deeper hollows of the crust. Above the surface an ocean of invisible gas, the atmosphere, rises to a height of about three hundred miles, getting thinner and thinner as it ascends. . . .

In addition to this the earth revolves around the sun at a speed of more than a thousand miles a minute. Its path around the sun, year in year out, measures about 580,000,000 miles. The earth is held closely to this path by the gravitational pull of the sun, which has a mass 333,432 times that of the earth. If at any moment the sun ceased to exert this pull the earth would instantly fly off into space straight in the direction in which it was moving at the time, that is to say, at a tangent. This tendency to fly off at a tangent is continuous. It is the balance between it and the sun's pull which keeps the earth to her almost circular orbit. In the same way the seven other planets are held to their orbits.

If we could be transported in some magical way to an immense distance in space above the sun and could see our Solar System, say trillions of miles away, the planets would fade entirely out of view, and the sun would shrink into a point of fire, a star. And here you begin to realize the nature of the universe. *The sun is a star. The stars are suns.* Our sun looks big simply because of its comparative nearness to us. The universe is a stupendous collection of millions of stars or suns, many of which may have planetary families like ours.

—SIR JOHN ARTHUR THOMSON, 1861-1933

[10] Illusions About Leisure

THE commonest error is the idea of leisure as always pleasant. This, of course, is not so. Whether leisure is pleasant or not depends on circumstances, and still more on the kind of man who has it. There is all the difference in the world between the leisure of wise men and the leisure of fools. Leisure is not pleasant—at least as a rule—when it has to be spent in gaol or on a sick-bed or in listening to the conversation of a bore. Which leads, by the way, to an important rule about the use of leisure, one of the very few that can be laid down. "Don't spend your leisure in ways that spoil the leisure of your friends." . . .

Even playing games is not always a pleasant occupation for leisure, especially if one plays them badly. Pleasure resorts where this kind of recreation is catered for often turn out very disappointing. At Monte Carlo, for example, there are many unhappy faces and suicides are not uncommon.

Another common mistake is to draw a sharp line between labor and leisure, putting labor occupations into the left-hand column and leisure occupations into the right; or treating leisure as though it began where labor left off. This clearly will not do, because the labor occupation of one man is often the leisure occupation of another. A country walk is a leisure occupation for many of us, but not for a country postman who walks fifteen miles every day in delivering his letters. But on the highest levels of life the distinction between labor and leisure or between work and play fades out. A great artist finds his play in his work. Play becomes art when raised to its highest excellence, its highest beauty, and its highest power. Anything that one does, from cooking a dinner to governing a state, becomes a work of art if motivated by the passion for excellence and done as well as it can be. A man who does his job in that spirit will be the one who gets the most satisfaction out of life.

—L. P. Jacks, 1860-1955

[11] Life Is Too Short

Although the duration of the life of man is one of the longest amongst mammals, men find it too short. Ought we to listen to the cry of humanity that life is too short, and that it will be well to prolong it? If the question were merely one of prolonging the life of old people, without modifying old age itself, the answer would be doubtful. It must be understood, however, that the prolongation of life will be associated with the preservation of intelligence and of the power to work. When we have reduced or abolished such causes of precocious senility as intemperance and disease, it will no longer be necessary to give pensions at the age of sixty or seventy years. The cost of supporting the old, instead of increasing, will diminish progressively. We must use all our endeavors to allow men to complete their normal course of life, and to make it possible for

22

old men to play their parts as advisers and judges, endowed with their long experience.

—ÉLIE METCHNIKOFF, 1845-1916

[12] Thoughts in a Cathedral Town

READER, have you ever lived in the moral and intellectual atmosphere of a cathedral town? Have you ever experienced the strange sensations arising from the living presence of events dead and gone; of shadows of history that haunt the lives of the men and women of to-day; of long-vanished rituals and ceremonies that revisit the glimpses of the moon; the conventions of a community which play with mysteries and moralities sacred and profane, the autocracy of a building that has weathered the centuries, outlived creeds, survived reformations, convocations; a Work of Man and a Work of Art that is honourable and venerable and beautiful; which enshrines God in the past, the present, the future "as He was in the beginning, is now, and ever shall be . . ." A cathedral with its trim precincts, cloisters, green lawns; prim Georgian houses with neat white steps, polished knockers and drawn curtains; the sanctuaries and strongholds of the ecclesiastical proprieties—and of men, women, children; some ghosts of to-day and yesterday and the day to come . . . And do you think . . . Are there any secrets and heartburnings and tragedies behind those polite barricades of theological austerity? Listen.

—HUGH WALPOLE, 1884-1941

[13] The "Leaves" Begin on a Fall Evening in 1936

A DECADE OF THEOLOGY

October 18, 1936

I AM glad to be alone this evening. Outside it is cool; the streets and sidewalks are partly covered by fallen yellow leaves, and it is raining gently. I can see the reflection of the street light on the shiny, wet, leaf-covered pavement. Indoors, it is too chilly to sit comfortably without a lighted fireplace. Somehow the feel and odor of the burning logs temper with a realistic serenity the melancholy which always comes over me at this time of year. It is fun to look into the flames, to see an ember break off, shoot a bit into space, and then fall, to hear the cracking of the fire.

I have been reading *The Fool Hath Said* by Beverley Nichols, but it is difficult to keep my attention steady upon the book. I am restless: my eyes wander about my study; they fall upon my bookshelves and linger especially on those books written in the last ten years. These are a stimulating fellowship; had I not met them I wonder what my own thoughts might be. I begin to realize that I belong to a thought era, and the ideas of this recent library are weaving themselves together as a pattern for an age. I say to myself: "What a decade it has been! I am living in the most virile moment of history. Was there ever a time in which so much happened so intensively as these last ten years depict?"

I find my mind retracing the religious thinking of this decade as it has touched me.

HUMANISM'S INITIAL ATTRACTION

My first awakening to the import of religious movements was occasioned years ago as I saw centuries of Greek thought meet longer periods of Jewish revelation and become Christianity. It was then that I began to "feel" religious-historical movements. Religious expression ought to be well rounded; when it becomes biased or partial, movements arise to supplement its weaknesses. If religious events are expressions of man's search for truth, they are simultaneously correctives of each other in the common inquiry for truth.

I have been deeply impressed by certain religious schools in these last ten years and have almost tied myself vitally to several of them at different times. Humanism was attractive to me for a while. I had been irked by careless religious thinking, so often "armchair," unrelated to life; so much theology has talked about God in a smug way, but has forgotten man. Humanism savored of the scientific method in a scientific age; it stressed primarily the betterment of humanity; it seemed unselfish, noble. Yet, humanism took mystery and awe away from me; it wanted too definite an answer to profound problems; it gave me no impelling dynamic, no *elan*. The more I surveyed its possibilities, the more I felt that the world would not be saved by "tired radicals." From the psychological angle at least it seemed highly important that the religious man have an "alternation" from society to God and from God to society. That is, humanism was partial; it did not offer a proper means of worship whereby I could integrate my tensions. Much that it stressed appealed to my religious sensitivities, but I wanted a real God in my worship, as well as a real humanity for testing the fruits of my religious devotion. Humanism seemed to give me only the latter.

24

CRISIS MOVEMENT SUGGESTS A CORRECTIVE

In 1928 I was stimulated by the crisis movement, this being due somewhat to my associations in Germany, where I studied with Rudolf Bultmann and assimilated the viewpoint that crisis exponents were printing in *Zwischen den Zeiten.* Bultmann helped me to realize that liberal biblical criticism, which has always attracted me, could go hand in hand with a certain type of constructive theology. The crisis viewpoint supplied me with a tremendous lift, and it still serves as a needed corrective. Sometimes I am frank enough to admit that it saved me from being a humanist. Conversely, however, I would never have been a crisis devotee, even if I had not been so deeply attracted by humanism.

Deism, the approach apparently stressed by the crisis group, is a monstrosity which has no place in contemporary cosmology. It takes away both the dynamic of worship and the hope for alleviating social wrongs. God to me is either identified with my universe as omnipresent, with whom I co-create, or he is not existent. My universe which includes him and us in an organism in which God exists for my Hindu and Buddhist friends as well as for Christians who have faith in Christ, even though God relates himself differently to these various groups due to human divergences.

Nevertheless, I am grateful that the crisis movement has been stressed in recent years. When I read from Karl Barth I get a new poise, for I begin to see my temporality as but a momentary part of my eternal nature; I regain an awesome approach to the Scriptures which reminds me that revelation as well as reason (even though Barth would rule out reason) has played a vital role in man's understanding of religious truth; I contemplate the central place of Jesus, not merely as a historical genius but as *the* cosmic event in religious history; I recenter my consideration of God as the pivotal place from which religious truth radiates and save myself from a primarily homocentric approach. I want both God and man at the center of my religion, and both the crisis movement and humanism have helped me to acquire equilibrium. Also, the crisis movement reminds me that there is a divine impact behind the beautiful literature of the Bible, and this rekindles the enthusiasm I have always had for Bible reading.

A mystical moment comes over me as I look again into the fire before me—the printed names on my books become a fellowship of real spirits. I am grateful to Edgar Brightman, Paul Tillich, Karl Barth, Edward Scribner Ames, John Dewey, Emil Brunner, Eustace Haydon, and many others for allowing me to have comradeship with them in these searching years.

THE SACRAMENTARIAN STRESS

It was Easter vacation, 1934, in Philadelphia. I lunched with an English author and clergyman on a Tuesday. Queer, but it was raining that day —a warm rain—and I recall driving with him along a river where "Rusty" Callow was training a Penn crew. During our conversation at lunch he told me that if he were starting his ministry again (he is now sixty) he would join the Anglo-Catholic movement for he felt it offered both a religious certainty and a mysticism in the sacraments which sterile Protestantism had lost. But I told him that I could sympathize very little with him in that expression. I want a profound religion, but I doubt if it will ever have a sacramental stress.

There have been moments when I have yearned for the awe and immensity of the mass in the Anglo-Catholic movement, and occasionally I have desired the certainty which its exponents seem to have; but usually I want my religious expression to savor of adventure, to be in quest of truth. I would rather be a prophet mistaken, living dangerously, than a priest with his dole of truth. I do not have the training nor the sensitivity to find meaning in the statement that the material never reaches its fullest reality until it wears the cloak of the spiritual; the sacraments will never be more to me than symbols of a remembered idealism. I presume that I am not a sacramentarian, not because I do not want to be, but because I do not know how to be. Perhaps this is so since I am too much a Protestant won to the prophetic appreciation rather than the priestly interpretation.

THE RESURRECTION OF THOMAS AQUINAS

"I am too much a Protestant won to the prophetic appreciation." I do not mean I am dogmatically so, because I try to evaluate the sacramentarian viewpoint of Anglo-Catholic, Lutheran, and Roman Catholic. How much we are influenced in our religious views by birth! I might have been born a Roman Catholic. Had I been, I would probably be studying today with renewed interest Thomas Aquinas' *Summa Theologica,* due to the emphasis Jacques Maritain and others have given recently to the Neo-Thomist movement. I realize the enormous contribution Aquinas made to the church in stressing Aristotle as her second standard. In so doing he established a philosophic criterion for religious truth and at the same time stimulated a taste for science as the foundation for metaphysics. He revived intellectual religion, made decadent in the Middle Ages.

Neo-Thomism, which analyzes society as having neither depth nor sense of destiny in its disintegrated state, is an attempt to stem the tide

26

of bourgeois nationalism. It sees a world trying to find the verities of religion in naturalism, half-shod intellectualism which lacks both thoroughness and clarity, dominated by an anthropocentric note. It perceives intuitive certainty as the abiding ground for faith and furthermore, views this faith as related to a permanent ground of existence in a world of apparent change and upheaval.

Protestants as well as Roman Catholics can well benefit by regaining an intellectual structure in order to win self-respect from many of its adherents. What a dominant place Neo-Thomism must have in the religious experiences of Roman Catholics who want to wed the intellectual with the aesthetic and the mystical in a triune manner! How could I avoid the attraction of this movement were I a Roman Catholic?

AN ETHICAL MYSTICISM

I want to live dangerously, vitally, unselfishly, courageously. I cannot provoke myself with a religion that I must toy with in its little externalities or defend with frail doctrines. It must support me in such a way that I can chorus with Ibsen's Dr. Stockmann: "I have made a great discovery. . . . It is this, let me tell you—that the strongest man in the world is he who stands alone." My religion makes me want moral courage like that. Should Christianity offer less? Furthermore, can it?

Yet I find it difficult to be deeply religious long apart from my fellows. In solitude I pray; I read Hebbel, Chateaubriand, Tolstoi, Dostoevski; I saturate my soul with Wagnerian music; I look oftimes with moistened eyes at the lonesome stars above; I search through the words of Maurice, Kingsley, Rauschenbusch, Josiah Strong, and contemporary men of similar impulse; I contemplate the significance of Jesus and his Via Dolorosa. And what do I find? A sense of fellowship; yes. But I obtain further a drive as well as a feeling of the tremendous pull of destiny, which I can bring to realization only as I relate such individual experiences to the larger pattern of humanity. When I make effective in society the urges and impulses I experience in my solitude, I find ecstasy—but not until. Ecstasy is never complete until the results of worship are made active in the social group. I call it an ethical mysticism.

I am thinking tonight of my universe as an organism in which the independent, free, purposive members are as sensitive to one another as the members of my body. The life of this organism is God with whom my relationships are personal. The experiences of my fellows are also related to God in a similar manner; in order to complete my fuller kinship in my universe I am obliged to treat my fellow men as members of the same "body" or "family." Thus, sin is not only individual; it is social and cosmic as well.

27

I owe much to all religious movements for what they have added to my culture. They have kept me tolerant, alive to the fact that growth is the secret purpose and that all men are searchers after, rather than finders of, truth. Some movements make me very humble, for I am impressed by their profundity; they cause me to realize the immensity of religion. They remind me that religious interpretations must have touch with all realms of life, or else lose much of their import. They keep telling me that religion must grow or become a curiosity.

Only a few embers are now in my fireplace; little did I realize how late it had become. I go to the window and raise the shade. It has ceased raining; the moon has been hiding behind a cloud and is now slowly floating out to join the stars. I open the door to my study and breathe in the air freshened by the rain. Then I climb slowly up to my chamber, for I am ready to sleep.

[14] There Is So Much Ahead!

OUR civilization is very young, when we compare the history of man's search for truth with man's life upon this planet. About five thousand years ago came "the dawn of conscience," when man began to distinguish right from wrong and say to himself, "I ought!" It was 350 years ago that Francis Bacon, carrying further the work of Roger Bacon (1214-1294), propounded the scientific method for finding truth. In September, 1452, Gutenberg invented and first used the movable type, printing with this type the Holy Bible. Less than one hundred years ago the emancipation of the Negro slave in the United States became a reality. For less than thirty-five years we have been putting forth our enthusiastic efforts for world peace. If great truths have been unfolded in the last five thousand years, what tremendous discoveries of further truths lie in the centuries ahead!

[15] Time Discovers Truth

I VIVIDLY remember the "modern" conveniences of my early boyhood days —oil lamps, a coal heater in the living room, the kitchen stove for which I split wood each fall, my "horse-and-buggy doctor" grandfather with his dapple-gray horse "Fanny," the first scratchy Graphophone with its "Josh Billings" cylinder records.

Today I watch the coronation of Queen Elizabeth in my living room as I sit before my television set. With the mere touch of my finger I regulate the thermostat which determines the amount of heat which I wish from my gas furnace. I eat breakfast in my Oberlin home at the regular hour, drive twenty-five miles in my car to the airport, and find myself lecturing at four o'clock that afternoon in southern Alabama. "Time discovers truth," I say to myself—fifty years show the results! "What will the next five thousand years bring forth in scientific discoveries?" I further ask. My imagination fails to tell me!

[16] Seeing Life at Middle Age

WHEN a man surveys his past from middle age he must surely ask himself what those bygone years have taught him. If I have learned anything in the swift unrolling of the web of time . . . it is the virtue of tolerance, of moderation in thought and deed, of forbearance toward one's fellowmen.

I have come also to acknowledge the great illusion which lies in the pursuit of a purely material goal. What slight satisfaction lies in temporal honour and worldly grandeur! . . . All the material possessions for which I strove so strenuously mean less to me now than a glance of love from those who are dear to me.

Above all am I convinced of the need, irrevocable and inescapable, of every human heart, for God. No matter how we try to escape, to lose ourselves in restless seeking, we cannot separate ourselves from our divine source. There is no substitute for God.

—A. J. CRONIN, 1896-

[17] One Page at a Time

THOMAS CARLYLE had finished his tremendous manuscript on the French Revolution. He gave it to his neighbor, John Stuart Mill, to read. Several days later Mill came to Carlyle's home, pale and nervous; Mill's maid had used the manuscript to start a fire. Carlyle was in a frenzy for days.

29

Two years of disciplined labor were gone; he could never write again. Then one day he observed a mason building a wall, laying one brick at a time. From this sight Carlyle took new courage; he could rewrite *The French Revolution* one page at a time.

[18] The Advantage of a Handicap

HANDICAPS come to all types of persons. Two men, Charles Darwin and Abraham Lincoln, were born on the same day, February 12, 1809, each with his handicap. Darwin was born into a privileged home in Shrewsbury, England. Forced to study medicine and theology, he turned to natural science. But he never had good health. "If I had not been so great an invalid," he said, "I should not have done so much work as I have accomplished." Lincoln, born in poverty in Hardin County, Kentucky, learned sympathy toward all men and later wrote the finest phrase in the human language: "With malice toward none; with charity toward all." For Darwin and Lincoln, their lives illustrate "the advantage of a handicap."

[19] Hold Fast to Morality

THE words of Dr. Frederick W. Robertson, a great British preacher who was going through terrible spiritual conflict in solitude in the Tyrolean Alps, speak to our needs today:

"I know but one way in which a man may come forth from his agony scathless; it is by holding fast to those things which are certain still—the grand, simple landmarks of morality. In the darkest hour through which a human soul can pass, whatever else is doubtful this is at least certain: If there be no God and no future state, yet, even then, it is better to be generous than selfish; better to be chaste than licentious; better to be true than false; better to be brave than a coward. Blessed beyond all earthly blessedness is the man who in the tempestuous darkness of the soul has dared to hold fast these venerable landmarks. . . . Thrice blessed, because his night shall pass into clear, bright day."

30

[20] The Hope of the World

A MAMMOTH statue of Christ with outstretched arms stands between Chile and Argentina. Built at a cost of $250,000 it is 125 feet in height and 92 feet in breadth from finger tip to finger tip. The words chiseled at the base of the statue are: "As long as the living Christ stands guard over us, Chile and Argentina shall never go to war." Not only for Chile and Argentina is Christ the hope for peace; he is the hope of the world.

[21] The Tragic Folly of Sensate Man

INVESTING all his energies in the control of nature, sensate man achieved a conspicuous degree of success. But in this process he lost his *self-control*. Becoming—like a child toying with a bomb—infatuated with the physical forces at his disposal, in an access of madness he directed them against himself and his own achievements. In his eagerness to serve mammon he forgot to serve God, and he now pays the tragic price of his folly.

—PITIRIM A. SOROKIN, 1889-

[22] What Is Man?

A BASEBALL stadium is one of the finest laboratories in which to study mankind. Recently I sat in an upper deck of the Cleveland Stadium among 65,000 fans, watching a game between the Cleveland Indians and the New York Yankees. As I watched the players on the field and the crowds in the stands, I asked myself the question, "What is man?" As I watched some of the finest baseball players in the world making almost perfect plays, making quick, automatic decisions when the play was close, I marveled that a group of men could correlate individual action and collective action into such an activity. As I sat there amidst the enthusiastic noise of the crowd, I asked myself several questions: How did man come into existence? Of what stuff is he made? What are the various motives within the breasts of the individuals assembled here? Is man eternal or temporal?

31

[23] Life Begins at Forty

Now we come to the one serious decline at forty. It is the waning of free energy. To belittle this would be folly; for it changes the entire pattern of life. And rare the man who rearranges his affairs and his outlook in harmony with this profound transformation!

Shall we settle at ten cents on the dollar and go out of business? Not in the least! I maintain that the loss of free energy for strenuous activities need not cramp our style at all. On the contrary, it may be turned to profit by anybody who can keep on using his brain. For his brain can improve with use almost as long as he lives; and it can be used to manage all activities of the body, to the end of more health and happiness. Above all, it is the past master of economy, it makes the least energy deliver the greatest possible results; hence it serves man best of all after forty, when he must watch his horsepower.

So in a fresh sense, life begins at forty. For the brain requires most of the years before forty to perfect the art of managing its body. The better the brain, the earlier it masters all the tricks of economy and accomplishment. But, be it good or bad, it requires much time, especially in these days of baffling complexity. I think it highly probable that the very year which brings the first marked decline in physical energy—namely the thirty-seventh or thirty-eight—normally lifts our practical intelligence to its final high level. As forty draws near, a man manages himself about as well as he ever can.

—WALTER B. PITKIN, 1878-1953

[24] What Books Shall I Read?

READING, to most people, means an ashamed way of killing time disguised under a dignified name. Trifling with print in that manner quickly diminishes the resilience of the intellect. It goes directly against the Art of Thinking.

If you wish to use books as an adjuvant to thought, they must be books that will not merely amuse or put your mind to sleep, but, on the contrary, will keep it wide awake and alert.

What are those books?

What they are *you* know best, and I do not know in the least. A book, like a landscape, is a state of consciousness varying with readers. There

32

exists some book, pamphlet, article in an encyclopaedia, or possibly an old clipping from a newspaper that once set you thinking; there may be many; indeed you may be one of those rare beings with whom a few lines of print are food enough for thought because, as Lamartine says, their thoughts think themselves. The something evocative for you may be poetry, history, philosophy, the sciences, or moral sciences, i.e., the progress of mankind.

And what books should we so read?

The principle which has never failed to confer superiority on a man's thinking activity is the well worn precept: DO NOT READ GOOD BOOKS—life is too short for that—ONLY READ THE BEST.

—ERNEST DIMNET, 1869-1954

[25] Mary White

THE Associated Press reports carrying the news of Mary White's death declared that it came as a result of a fall from a horse. How she would have hooted at that! She never fell from a horse in her life. Horses have fallen on her and with her—"I'm always trying to hold 'em in my lap," she used to say. But she was proud of few things, and one was that she could ride anything that had four legs and hair. Her death resulted not from a fall, but from a blow on the head which fractured her skull, and the blow came from the limb of an overhanging tree on the parking.

The last hour of her life was typical of its happiness. She came home from a day's work at school, topped off by a hard grind with the copy on the High School Annual, and felt that a ride would refresh her. She climbed into her khakis, chattering to her mother about the work she was doing, and hurried to get her horse and be out on the dirt roads for the country air and the radiant green fields of the spring. As she rode through the town on an easy gallop, she kept waving at passers-by. She knew everyone in town. For a decade the little figure with the long pigtail and the red hair-ribbon has been familiar on the streets of Emporia, and she got in the way of speaking to those who nodded at her. . . . A *Gazette* carrier passed—a High School boy friend—and she waved at him, but with her bridle hand; the horse veered quickly, plunged into the parking where the low-hanging limb faced her, and, while she still looked back waving, the blow came. But she did not fall from the horse; she slipped off, dazed a bit, staggered, and fell in a faint. She never quite recovered consciousness. . . .

Her funeral yesterday at the Congregational Church was as she would have wished it; no singing, no flowers save the big bunch of red roses from her Brother Bill's Harvard classmen—Heavens, how proud that would have made her!—and the red roses from the *Gazette* force—in vases at her head and feet. A short prayer, Paul's beautiful essay on "Love" from the Thirteenth Chapter of First Corinthians, some remarks about her democratic spirit by her friend, John H. J. Rice, pastor and police judge, which she would have deprecated if she could, a prayer sent down for her by her friend, Carl Nau, and opening the service the slow, poignant movement from Beethoven's *Moonlight Sonata,* which she loved, and closing the service a cutting from the joyously melancholy first movement of Tschaikovsky's *Pathetic Symphony,* which she liked to hear in certain moods on the phonograph; then the Lord's Prayer by her friends in the High School.

That was all.

For her pall-bearers only her friends were chosen: her Latin teacher, W. L. Holtz; her High School principal, Rice Brown; her doctor, Frank Foncannon; her friend, W. W. Finney; her pal at the *Gazette* office, Walter Hughes; and her brother Bill. It would have made her smile to know that her friend Charley O'Brien, the traffic cop, had been transferred from Sixth and Commercial to the corner near the church to direct her friends who came to bid her good-by.

A rift in the clouds in a gray day threw a shaft of sunlight upon her coffin as her nervous energetic little body sank to its last sleep. But the soul of her, the glowing, gorgeous, fervent soul of her, surely was flaming in eager joy upon some other dawn.

—WILLIAM ALLEN WHITE, 1868-1944

[26] Calvin Coolidge Is Laid to Rest

EARLY in the morning the long special trains came rolling in. The President and his wife, the Vice-President, the Chief Justice, several Cabinet members, and committees of Senators and Congressmen got out of the sleeping cars from Washington and walked through the crowd at the station. Governors of near-by States and other officials arrived in their motors. They went to the Congregational Church and sat in its plain oak pews.

The service was brief. There was no eulogy, no address of any kind. Two hymns were sung, parts of the Bible were read, and the young minister prayed. He rose, and gave the great of the land who stood before him his blessing. They filed slowly out.

The streets emptied as the visitors left. The motors and trains rolled away.

When the town was alone with its own again, six sober-faced policemen lifted the coffin and carried it out to the street. Light rain was falling. Drops glistened on the coffin as it was placed in the hearse. A few motors fell in behind it, and the little procession moved off along the old country roads.

In every village they went through, there were small troops of boy scouts and veterans of the great war, standing at attention in silence as the motors sped by. In the yards of factories, and mills, workmen stood in groups, waiting. Men held their hats or caps to their hearts, women folded their hands. Farms and fields on the road had been tidied up, as a mark of respect, and at a place where carpenters were building a house they had cleared away the lumber and chips.

The rain stopped for a while. The mists that had drifted low over the mountains gave place to blue sky. White, straight birch trunks glistened, and ice began to melt in the sunshine. But as they drove on, deeper into the Green Mountain country, black clouds spread and rain fell again, harder. The red tail lights of the cars gleamed on the road in the wintry and dark afternoon.

When the cars reached the end of the journey, the skies lightened palely a moment. The burying ground was outside the village where the dead man was born. Generations of his ancestors had been laid to rest there, in graves on the hillside. The cars climbed the steep road and stopped. The family and a handful of friends got out and stood waiting.

Across the road, in a rocky field the men and women of the village had gathered. They were not the kind of people to intrude or crowd nearer, and they kept complete silence. The young minister said a few words as the coffin was lowered. A sudden storm of hail pelted down.

The widow, who had tried to smile that morning coming out of the church, could no longer hold back her tears.

The cars left. The bent shouldered sexton signaled to his helpers. They filled in the grave. Four country militiamen took up their positions on guard. Snow fell that night on the hillside and the slopes of Salt Ash Mountain.

The headstone that now marks the quiet spot bears no inscription but the name, Calvin Coolidge, the dates, and the President's seal.

—CLARENCE DAY, 1874-1935

[27] Eulogy for Dr. William MacLure

WHEN the coffin was laid down at the mouth of the grave, the only blackness in the white kirkyard, Tammas Mitchell did the most beautiful thing in all his life. He knelt down and carefully wiped off the snow the wind had blown upon the coffin, and which had covered the name, and when he had done this he disappeared behind the others, so that Drumsheugh could hardly find him to take a cord. For there were the eight that buried Dr. MacLure—Lord Kilspindie at the head as landlord and Drumsheugh at the feet as his friend; the two ministers of the parish came first on the right and left, then Burnbrae and Hillocks of the farmers, and Saunders and Tammas for the ploughmen. So the Glen he loved laid him to rest.

When the bedrel had finished his work and the turf had been spread, Lord Kilspindie spoke:

"Friends of Drumtochty, it would not be right that we should part in silence and no man say what is in every heart. We have buried the remains of one that served this Glen with a devotion that has known no reserve, and a kindliness that never failed, for more than forty years. I have seen many brave men in my day, but no man in the trenches of Sebastopol carried himself more knightly than William MacLure. You will never have heard from his lips what I may tell you today, that my father secured for him a valuable post in his younger days, and he preferred to work among his own people; and I wished to do many things for him when he was old, but he would have nothing for himself. He will never be forgotten while one of us lives, and I pray that all doctors everywhere may share his spirit. If it be your pleasure, I shall erect a cross above his grave, and shall ask my old friend and companion Dr. Davidson, your minister, to choose the text to be inscribed."

"We thank you, Lord Kilspindie," said the doctor, "for your presence with us in our sorrow and your tribute to the memory of William Mac-Lure, and I choose this for his text:

" 'Greater love hath no man than this, that a man lay down his life for his friends.' "

Milton was, at that time, held in the bonds of a bitter theology, and his indignation was stirred by this unqualified eulogium.

"No doubt Dr. MacLure hed mony natural virtues, an' he did his wark weel, but it wes a peety he didna mak mair profession o' releegion."

"When William MacLure appears before the Judge, Milton," said Lachlan Campbell, who that day spoke his last words in public, and they were in defence of charity, "He will not be asking him about his profes-

36

sions, for the doctor's judgment hass been ready long ago; and it iss a good judgment, and you and I will be happy men if we get the like of it.

"It iss written in the Gospel, but it iss William MacLure that will not be expecting it."

"What is't, Lachlan?" asked Jamie Soutar, eagerly.

The old man, now very feeble, stood in the middle of the road, and his face, once so hard, was softened into a winsome tenderness.

" 'Come, ye blessed of My Father . . . I was sick, and ye visited Me.' "

—IAN MACLAREN (JOHN WATSON), 1850-1907

[28] The Miracle of Creation

THIS is a story told by men with microscopes, who can describe the action but who cannot give you the cause. A cell, no bigger than a pin point, meets another cell and absorbes it. The cell divides into two cells. The two cells divide, making four. These divide, and their offspring divide— until by the end of nine months, when the division has repeated itself some 45 times, there are a thousand billion cells, all working together to be a human life. Is that you—a thousand billion cells, all of which began as a single cell? Each of these billion cells carries on a life of its own. Each appears under the microscope as a lump of jelly, which is constantly changing as it absorbs particles from the fluid around it, and digests them. Each chooses some particles by preference. Watch some of these cells when there has been an injury to some portion of the body. They rush to the scene of the injury and there absorb and digest the foreign particles that enter the injury. This scene from the drama of life is a part of the healing process. Carried on by individual cells, each living its own independent life.

In the beginning division, all cells are alike. But some in a few short weeks become as hard as the enamel of your teeth, some specialize to form the lens of the eye. Some become corpuscles carrying iron to trade for oxygen. Each cell specializes into something which is helpful to the whole. From one cell comes a human life. As a dividing mass of cells go to work to form a child, they form a parasite, living on, but not part of, the life of the mother. They are cased in a fluid, in utter darkness. In that darkness, a drama goes on that stupefies the greatest mind. In the dark, where no light is possible or necessary, certain cells form themselves by a wondrous design into an eye that is ready to see. Organs of skin, ear, eye, nose, tongue—all are superfluous in the watery darkness where they are formed. Yet each prepares itself for a daylight, airy world. One set of cells becomes a brain, of no use at the moment, but ready to learn of the world that is to be experienced. How do they know what is to come?

The full story cannot be told in five minutes—nay, in five centuries. But stand in awe before this brief scene of the drama. Before birth the lung is prepared for what it will do. But it does not breathe (except as each individual cell is carrying on its independent life). The lung's blood is sidetracked, in the watery darkness, to an artery. At birth this sidetracking of the lung's blood would mean an end to life. So, in its own time, just at birth, a special muscle closes the channel: and blood flows from the artery into the lung. The lung breathes for all the body! And what of that special muscle, prepared to work just once? It disappears and is never seen again. Exit a hero!

Step by step, as though by some foreknowledge, a single cell has miraculously become a thousand billion cells, each living its own life, but each specialized to work for the whole. This is a human being. This is life! If you stand before a fraction of this process and fail to stand in awe at this greatest drama in the world, the Lord pity you. If you can understand a fraction of the drama within the story, will you join me as we stand before the Maker?

O Lord our Lord, how majestic is Thy name in all the earth. What is man, that Thou art mindful of him? And the son of man that doest care for him? Yet Thou hast made him a little less than God, and dost crown him with glory and honor. O Lord, our Lord, how majestic is Thy name in all the earth!

—ORVAL H. AUSTIN, 1907?-

[29] Modernism Seeks Depth

RELIGIOUS modernism as a general approach has a fairly clear-cut connotation for most of us. We think of it as an attempt to frame lasting verities in a structure of thought and data which will rule out no contemporary note of valid interpretation of reality. Modernism is always seeking to recapture the religious values that count most in the language of the day; it reveres the past, not because of its time element, but rather as a continuing era of struggle which has given the present age a perspective of the perennial values that validate human experience. The centuries refine ideas more carefully than the hours. Consequently a wise modernism is indebted to history for her contribution to the onward progress of truth.

Post-war modernism (World War I), not unlike other periods of history, found many of her interpreters so drunk with estrangement from orthodoxy that with glad abandon (perhaps!) they sought intellectual holidays. The behaviorists "made up their glands that they had no minds." The anti-theological humanists became enamored with the idea of belittling "God" into corporate man, failing to see in perspective how the great minds of Europe in the nineteenth century listened for awhile to Comte and Feuerbach, only to say, "Interesting, but superficial." Many a historian tried to interpret life psychologically rather than to give objectivity to the historical tradition; or, if he retained the objective note he listened more intently to Spengler than to Hegel, crying out, "Progress is an illusion; all will end in decay." To many science became a hybrid of a cosmic Santa Claus and a Baal which would give man the gifts needed to make life significant—maybe!

Modernism did swing far away from a constructive note in these extreme feelings; perhaps they were only growing pains that needed expression, but certainly they were not ends of thought traditions. They were cries of distress that our age needed intellectual panaceas if she were to reach maturity, instead of attaining either sophomoric sophistication or senile debility.

The thesis of pre-war orthodoxy, in which many were reared, and the antithesis of post-war modernity, into which they were shifted, knew so little of one another that the "man-on-the-street" and the student in the classroom found themselves reaching for maturing religious help with little satisfaction. But like all processes of the dialectic, the synthesis for a constructive modernism is beginning to form. It may give to a new generation a religious foundation basic for an intellectually tempered religious revival unparalleled in history!

[30] Knowledge Is Power

I AM frequently asked how I overcame the peculiar conditions under which I worked in college. In the classroom I was of course practically alone. The professor was as remote as if he were speaking through a telephone. The lectures were spelled into my hand as rapidly as possible, and much of the individuality of the lecturer was lost to me in the effort to keep in the race. The words rushed through my hand like hounds in pursuit of a hare which they often missed.

While my days at Radcliffe were still in the future, they were encircled with a halo of romance, which they have lost; but in the transition from the romantic to the actual, I learned many things I should never have known had I not tried the experiment. One of them is the precious science of patience, which teaches us that we should take our education as we would take a walk in the country, leisurely, our minds hospitably open to impressions of every sort. Such knowledge floods the soul unseen with a soundless tidal wave of deepening thought. "Knowledge is power."

Rather, knowledge is happiness, because to have knowledge—broad, deep knowledge—is to know true ends from false, and lofty things from low. To know the thoughts and deeds that have marked man's progress is to feel the great heart-throbs of humanity through the centuries; and if one does not feel in these pulsations a heavenward striving, one must indeed be deaf to the harmonies of life.

—HELEN KELLER, 1880-

[31] An Anthology of Doubt

New York,
July 15, 1931.

Dear_____

Will you interrupt your work for a moment and play the game of philosophy with me?

I am attempting to face a question which our generation, perhaps more than any, seems always to ask and never able to answer—What is the meaning or worth of human life? . . . Astronomers have told us that human affairs constitute but a moment in the trajectory of a star; geologists have told us that civilization is but a precarious interlude between ice ages; biologists have told us that all life is war, a struggle for existence among individuals, groups, nations, alliances, and species; historians have told us that "progress" is a delusion, whose glory ends in decay; psychologists have told us that the will and the self are the helpless instruments of heredity and environment, and that the once incorruptible soul is but a transient incandescence of the brain. The Industrial Revolution has destroyed the home, and the discovery of contraceptives is destroy-

40

ing the family, the old morality, and perhaps (through the sterility of the intelligent) the race. Love is analyzed into a physical congestion, and marriage becomes a temporary physiological convenience slightly superior to promiscuity. Democracy has degenerated into such corruption as only Milo's Rome knew; and our youthful dreams of a socialist Utopia disappear as we see, day after day, the inexhaustible acquisitiveness of men. Every invention strengthens the strong and weakens the weak; every new mechanism displaces men, and multiplies the horrors of war. God, who once was the consolation of our brief life, and our refuge in bereavement and suffering, has apparently vanished from the scene; no telescope, no microscope discovers him. Life has become, in that total perspective which is philosophy, a fitful pullulation of human insects on the earth, a planetary eczema that may soon be cured; nothing is certain in it except defeat and death—a sleep from which, it seems, there is no awakening.

We are driven to conclude that the greatest mistake in human history was the discovery of "truth." It has not made us free, . . . It has not made us happy. . . . As we look on it now we wonder why we hurried so to find it. . . . Spare me a moment to tell me what meaning life has for you, what keeps you going, what help—if any—religion gives you, what are the sources of your inspiration and your energy, what is the goal or motive-force of your toil, where you find your consolations and your happiness, where, in the last resort, your treasure lies. Write briefly if you must; write me at length and at leisure if you possibly can; for every word from you will be precious to me.

Sincerely yours,
—WILL DURANT, 1885-

[32] The "Well-rounded" Man

LET's examine first the model as younger men see him. . . . It goes something like this:

Be loyal to the company and the company will be loyal to you. After all, if you do a good job for the organization, it is only good sense for the organization to be good to you, because that will be best for everybody. There are a bunch of real people around here. Tell them what you think and they will respect you for it. They don't want a man to fret and stew about his work. It won't happen to me. A man who gets ulcers probably shouldn't be in business anyway. . . .

The unity they see between themselves and The Organization has deeper roots, however, than current expediency. Let's take the matter of ambition as further illustration. They do not lack ambition. They seem to, but that is only because the nature of it has changed. It has become a *passive* ambition. Not so many years ago it was permissible for the ambitious young man to talk of setting his cap for a specific goal—like becoming president of a corporation, building a bridge, or making a million dollars. Today it is a very rare young man who will allow himself to talk in such a way, let alone think that way. He can argue, with good grounds, that if it was unrealistic in the past it is even more so today. The life that he looks ahead to will be a life in which he is only one of hundreds of similarly able people and in which they will all be moved hither and yon and subject to so many forces outside their control—not to mention the Bomb—that only a fool would expect to hew to a set course.

But they see nothing wrong with this fluidity. They have an implicit faith that The Organization will be as interested in making use of their best qualities as they are themselves, and thus, with equanimity, they can entrust the resolution of their destiny to The Organization. No specific goal, then, is necessary to give them a sense of continuity. For the short term, perhaps—it would be nice to be head of the electronics branch. But after that, who knows? The young executive does not wish to get stuck in a particular field. The more he is shifted, the more broad-gauge will he become, and the more broad-gauge, the more successful.

But not too successful. Somewhat inconsistently, trainees hope to rise high and hope just as much not to suffer the personal load of doing so. Frequently they talk of finding a sort of plateau—a position well enough up to be interesting but not so far up as to have one's neck outstretched for others to chop at. It figures, the young man can explain. Why knock yourself out when the extra salary won't bring home much more actual pay? You can make a very good living in the middle levels—well, not exactly middle, a little higher than that—and the work, furthermore, can be just as fulfilling. If The Organization is good and big, to put it another way, there will be success without tears.

On the matter of overwork they are particularly stern. They want to work hard, but not too hard; the good, equable life is paramount and they see no conflict between enjoying it and getting ahead. The usual top executive, they believe, works much too hard, and there are few subjects upon which they will discourse more emphatically than the folly of elders who have a single-minded devotion to work. Is it, they ask, really necessary any more? Or, for that matter, moral? . . .

Which brings us to the best part of all. Younger men don't believe there has to be a choice because they believe organizations have been coming around to their own way of thinking. It's just plain good sense for The Organization, they argue, not to have people getting too involved in their jobs. Overwork may have been necessary once, they say, and perhaps you still need a few, very few, dynamic types, but business now sees that the full man is the model. What it needs is not the hard driver but the man who is so rested, so at peace with his environment, so broadened by suburban life, that he is able to handle human relations with poise and understanding.

So they believe, and because they believe this they see the organization life of the future as one in which tensions will be lessening. . . . Out of necessity, then, as well as natural desire, the wise young man is going to enjoy himself—plenty of time with the kids, some good hobbies, and later on he'll certainly go in for more reading and music and stuff like that. He will, in sum, be the apotheosis of the well-rounded man: obtrusive in no particular, excessive in no zeal. He will be the man in the middle.

—WILLIAM H. WHYTE, JR., 1917-

[33] Emerson's Eulogy of Henry David Thoreau

August 1862

HENRY DAVID THOREAU was the last male descendant of a French ancestor who came to this country from the Isle of Guernsey. His character exhibited occasional traits drawn from this blood in singular combination with a very strong Saxon genius. . . .

At this time a strong, healthy youth, fresh from college, while all his companions were choosing their profession or eager to begin some lucrative employment, it was inevitable that his thoughts should be exercised on the same question, and it required rare decision to refuse all the accustomed paths and keep his solitary freedom at the cost of disappointing the natural expectations of his family and friends: all the more difficult that he had a perfect probity, was exact in securing his own independence and in holding every man to the like duty. But Thoreau never faltered. He was born protestant. He declined to give up his large ambition of knowledge and action for any craft or profession, aiming at a much more comprehensive calling, the art of living well. If he slighted and defied the opinions of others, it was only that he was more intent to reconcile his practice with his own belief. Never idle or self-indulgent, he preferred, when he wanted money, earning it by some piece of manual labor

43

agreeable to him—as building a boat or a fence, planting, grafting, surveying, or other short work—to any long engagements. With his hardy habits and few wants, his skill in woodcraft, and his powerful arithmetic, he was very competent to live in any part of the world. It would cost him less time to supply his wants than another. He was therefore secure of his leisure.

A natural skill for mensuration, growing out of his mathematical knowledge, and his habit of ascertaining the measures and distances of objects which interested him—the size of trees, the depth and extent of ponds and rivers, the height of mountains, and the air-line distance of his favorite summits—this, and his intimate knowledge of the territory about Concord, made him drift into the position of land surveyor. It had the advantage for him that it led him continually into new and secluded grounds and helped his studies of nature. His accuracy and skill in this work were readily appreciated, and he found all the employment he wanted.

He could easily solve the problems of the surveyor, but he was daily beset with graver questions, which he manfully confronted. He interrogated every custom and wished to settle all his practice on an ideal foundation. He was a protestant a l'outrance, and few lives contain so many renunciations. He was bred to no profession; he never married; he lived alone; he never went to church; he never voted; he refused to pay a tax to the state; he ate no flesh, he drank no wine, he never knew the use of tobacco; and, though a naturalist, he used neither trap nor gun. He chose, wisely, no doubt, for himself, to be the bachelor of thought and nature. He had no talent for wealth, and knew how to be poor without the least hint of squalor or inelegance. Perhaps he fell into his way of living without forecasting it much, but approved it with later wisdom. "I am often reminded," he wrote in his journal, "that, if I had bestowed on me the wealth of Croesus, my aims must be still the same, and my means essentially the same."

He had no temptations to fight against—no appetites, no passions, no taste for elegant trifles. A fine house, dress, the manners and talk of highly cultivated people were all thrown away on him. He much preferred a good Indian, and considered these refinements as impediments to conversation, wishing to meet his companion on the simplest terms. He declined invitations to dinner parties, because there each was in everyone's way, and he could not meet the individuals to any purpose. "They make their pride," he said, "in making their dinner cost much; I make my pride in making my dinner cost little." When asked at table what dish he preferred, he answered, "The nearest."

—Ralph Waldo Emerson, 1803-1882

[34] Ethel Waters on Opening Night of "Mamba's Daughters"

March 1951

Mamba's Daughters opened at the Empire Theatre, which has the richest theatrical history of any showhouse in America. And the Empire's star dressing room was mine on that opening night. While the carriage trade was arriving outside, I sat at the dressing table where all the great actresses, past and present, had sat as they made up their faces and wondered what the first-night verdict would be—Maude Adams, Ethel Barrymore, Helen Hayes, Katharine Cornell, Lynn Fontanne, and all the others who had brought the glitter of talent and beauty and grace to that old stage.

Yes, there I was, the Ethel who had never been coddled or kissed as a child, the Ethel who was too big to fit, but big enough to be scullion and laundress and bus girl while still a kid. And I could have looked back over my shoulder and blown a kiss to all my yesterdays in show business. I had been pushed on the stage and prodded into becoming Sweet Mama Stringbean and the refined singer of risqué songs in Edmond's Cellar, and on and up to best-selling records, Broadway musicals, and being the best-paid woman in all show business.

That was *the* night of my professional life, sitting there in that old-fashioned dressing room that was a bower of flowers. The night I'd been born for, and God was in the room with me. I talked to God, shivered and cried until the callboy came to say: "Five minutes, Miss Waters."

Five minutes more to get ready to be Hagar and tell the story of my mother in front of the carriage trade. I asked God, "Oh, stay with me! Lord, keep Your hand on my shoulder! Please, God!"

Then I got up and started off on that terrifying last mile a performer has to walk every opening night. Into the wings, a pause there for a moment waiting for the cue—and then on, Ethel Waters, to glory or . . .

I was Hagar that night. Hagar and my mother Momweeze and all of us. Seventeen curtain calls on opening night for me alone. I couldn't stand it. Half collapsing with joy and humility, I pushed through the kissing mouths and the slaps on the back to my dressing room, where Elida Webb, my secretary, was waiting.

"How do you feel now, Miss Waters?" she said. "And what are you thinking?"

"Elida, if I died here and now," I told her, "it would be all right. For this is the pinnacle, and there will never be anything better or higher

45

or bigger for me. I have fulfillment, Elida. At last, I have fulfillment."

And I burst into sobbing as I humbly thanked my God. Because even if no one else knew it, I had been no actress that night. I had only been remembering and all I had done was carry out His orders. . . . Playing in *Mamba's Daughters* enabled me to rid myself of the terrible inward pressure, the flood of tears I'd been storing up ever since my childhood.

—ETHEL WATERS, 1900-

[35] The Anatomy of Courage

OF all types of courage, the one which etymologically and historically leaps first to mind is physical courage. From childhood we have known the lion-hearted man of medieval knighthood. And as we advanced in school we were taught that this brave figure traces his lineage to the Spartan soldier. This is the model whom Plato in *The Republic* glorified as the warrior who obeyed the guardians and shepherded ordinary folk. The warlike courage of this Greek type furnished substance for one of Aristotle's four cardinal virtues. And the pattern which Aristotle discerned was refined by Cicero and even more majestically by the Stoic philosophers.

There are those who believe that in our altered social life, physical surroundings, economy, and technological circumstances we of the West have become too effete to retain our physical courage. Are reckless gallantry and a willingness to subordinate personal physical survival to the ideal of a great cause less compelling motives for men of the West than for men of the East? . . .

The problem of emotional courage is a more subtle issue. The basic nature of emotional courage has long been understood—by none better than Dürer, whose plates of *Melancholia* and of *The Knight, Death and The Devil* reveal the two extreme phases of men's dispositions. Yet new light in our lifetime has been cast by Freud and other psychiatrists and specialists in the sciences of human behavior. Today most men recognize that it takes more than habit, more than training, more than will, to be courageous. Men enter this universe differently equipped; and long before they are consciously educated in any scholastic system, they are conditioned by early experiences.

So it is that some among us, perhaps most, fluctuate in our capacity to summon forth our maximum strength. But some of the greatest contributors to our civilization and welfare have had periods of great emotional instability.

46

Lincoln is a familiar case. Less well known is the example of Charles Evans Hughes. Merlo Pusey was the first to draw the veil to let us see that the great Chief Justice whose majesty impressed us during his life-time in person, as it has since then in marble on the front of the Supreme Court Building, was actually a man in a state of exquisite tension who balanced his years of unbelievable intellectual activity with months when he found it necessary to leave his family and his work and go mountain climbing here and abroad. What we know from the uninhibited Boswell and from Dr. Johnson himself shows that both the Great Cham of Litera-ture and his more volatile biographer each had his alternating moods of elation and despair. . . .

Indeed, have we not learned that candor in revealing one's own limi-tations and acknowledging one's own struggles is the first prescrip-tion for increasing emotional courage? . . . Every man has it in his power deeply to increase his fortitude by facing his weaknesses and taking those elementary precautions of rest and withdrawal which will give him serenity and assurance.

A type of courage much to the front in current discussion is social courage, occasionally called civic courage. . . .

But how, in the circumstances of our time, can each of us develop so that he will be a fully conscious social being contributing to the common weal? Two answers—neither adequate, but both perhaps suggestive—may be given.

The first is that in American society, and indeed in all the Western world, the method by which men grow in social stature is through par-ticipation in voluntary associations—the university, the church, the labor union, and a host of private groups. . . . These voluntary associations in society give man a chance to expand his social nature and to feel his common ties. These associations do for a peaceful society what military association does for a belligerent society. . . .

A second and perhaps more fundamental method of achieving social courage is to recognize how far each one of us bears responsibility for the well-being of our society and the climate of opinion in which we live. We cannot, like the *Hausfrau* who believes herself charged only with duties toward *Kinder, Kuche, Kirche*, turn our backs on the politics of our day.

Can I put my views better than by reminding you of the magnificent illustration of Karl Jaspers re-opening the Medical Faculty at Heidelberg in 1945? You will recall that he said to those assembled that all in the room, himself included, were responsible for the Nazi evil, if for no other reason than the fact that they were still alive: "We who survive have not sought death. . . . We preferred to remain in life for the weak, even

47

if justifiable, reason that our death would not in any way have helped. It is our own fault that we are still alive. . . . It demands that we should take on us the consequences of being alive in such conditions." This, as Sir Walter Moberly said, in his profound study of Responsibility, "is not the language of hysteria but of insight."

And now I come to the fourth division of my topic, spiritual courage. We have been living for centuries upon the spiritual capital bequeathed to us by the men who dwelt in Palestine, in Greece, in India, and in China from 800 B.C. to A.D. 200—the so-called Axial period of our history. The Hebrew prophets, Jesus and his immediate followers, the Greek founders of philosophy, the authors of the Upanishads, the Buddha, gave us a rich store from which we have constantly borrowed. And although our account is not overdrawn, our own contributions to the total fund of faith have been small indeed. . . .

It may be that the spiritual influences of the future will come in shapes quite different from those we and our ancestors have known. But familiarity with the older vessels will make us better prepared for what the future may hold.

—CHARLES E. WYZANSKI, JR., 1906-

[36] Death Plucks My Ears

THE day before his ninetieth birthday he had been to the usual Saturday conference of the Court. The night of his birthday he was to speak on the radio from his library, and there were to be tributes from the Chief Justice, the Dean of the Yale Law School, the President of the American Bar Association. As he wrote to Dean Clark, who was in charge of the program, he expected to say a few words, "mostly short ones." He had never spoken on the air before, Fanny hadn't approved; she probably wouldn't approve now if she were here, but he thought it would be fun. They were putting on a good show. He liked a good show, he thought, chuckling, liked to have the butter spread on thick, and that was all right if you remembered all the time it was butter.

He listened to the others before he spoke. The Chief Justice was speaking, in the rich tones he knew so well. "He has abundantly the zest of life," he heard the Chief say, "and his age crowns that eagerness and unflagging interest with the authority of experience and wisdom. . . . We bring to Mr. Justice Holmes our tribute of admiration and gratitude. We place upon his brow the laurel crown of the highest distinction. But this will not suffice us or him. We honor him, but, what is more, we love him. We give him tonight the homage of our hearts."

The old man was deeply moved as those who listened to him knew. He paused for a moment, then spoke quietly, rather slowly. "In this symposium my part is only to sit in silence," he said. "To express one's feelings as the end draws near is too intimate a task."

He paused.

"But I may mention," he continued, "one thought which comes to me as a listener-in. The riders in a race do not stop short when they reach the goal. There is a little finishing canter before coming to a standstill. There is time to hear the kind voice of friends and to say to one's self: 'The work is done.' But just as one says that, the answer comes: 'The race is over, but the work never is done while the power to work remains.' The canter that brings you to a standstill need not be only coming to rest. It cannot be while you still live. For to live is to function. That is all there is in living." He paused again for a moment, and then—

"And so I end with a line from a Latin poet who uttered the message more than fifteen hundred years ago: 'Death plucks my ears and says, Live—I am coming.'"

—FRANCIS BIDDLE, 1886- , [On Justice Oliver Wendell Holmes]

[37] Lincoln Delivers His Gettysburg Address

FIFTEEN thousand, some said 30,000 or 50,000, people were on Cemetery Hill for the exercises the next day when the procession from Gettysburg arrived afoot and horseback representing the United States Government, the army and navy, governors of States, mayors of cities, a regiment of troops, hospital corps, telegraph-company representatives, Knights Templar, Masonic Fraternity, Odd Fellows, and other benevolent associations, the press, fire departments, citizens of Pennsylvania and other States. They were scheduled to start at ten o'clock and at that hour of the clock Lincoln in a black suit, high silk hat, and white gloves came out of the Wills residence and mounted a horse. A crowd was on hand and he held a reception on horseback. At eleven the parade began to move. The President's horse seemed small for him, as some looked at it. Clark E. Carr, just behind the President, believed he noticed that the President sat erect and looked majestic to begin with and then got to thinking so that his body leaned forward, his arms hung limp, and his head bent far down. . . .

The march was over in fifteen minutes. But Mr. Everett, the orator of the day, had not arrived. Bands played till noon. Mr. Everett arrived. On the platform sat Governors Curtin of Pennsylvania, Bradford of Maryland, Morton of Indiana, Seymour of New York, Parker of New Jersey, Dennison of Ohio, with ex-Governor Tod and Governor-elect Brough of Ohio, Edward Everett and his daughter, Major Generals Schenck, Stahel, Doubleday, and Couch, Brigadier General Gibbon and Provost Marshall General Fry, foreign Ministers, members of Congress, Colonel Ward Hill Lamon, Secretary Usher, and the President of the United States with Secretary Seward and Postmaster General Blair immediately at his left.

The United States House chaplain, the Reverend Thomas H. Stockton, offered a prayer while the thousands stood with uncovered heads. . . .

Benjamin B. French, officer in charge of buildings in Washington, introduced the Honorable Edward Everett, orator of the day, who rose, bowed low to Lincoln, saying, "Mr. President." Lincoln responded, "Mr. Everett."

The orator of the day then stood in silence before a crowd that stretched to limits that would test his voice. Beyond and around were the wheat fields, the meadows, the peach orchards, long slopes of land, and five and seven miles farther the contemplative blue ridge of a low mountain range. His eyes could sweep them as he faced the audience. He had taken note of it in his prepared and rehearsed address. "Overlooking these broad fields now reposing from the labors of the waning year, the mighty Alleghenies dimly towering before us, the graves of our brethren beneath our feet, it is with hesitation that I raise my poor voice to break the eloquent silence of God and Nature. But the duty to which you have called me must be performed; grant me, I pray you, your indulgence and your sympathy." Everett proceeded, "It was appointed by law in Athens," and gave an extended sketch of the manner in which the Greeks cared for their dead who fell in battle. He spoke of the citizens assembled to consecrate the day. "As my eye ranges over the fields whose sods were so lately moistened by the blood of gallant and loyal men, I feel, as never before, how truly it was said of old that it is sweet and becoming to die for one's country. . . ."

He had spoken for an hour and fifty-seven minutes, some said a trifle over two hours, repeating almost word for word an address that occupied nearly two newspaper pages, as he had written it and as it had gone in advance sheets to many newspapers. Everett came to his closing sentence without a faltering voice: "Down to the latest period of recorded time, in the glorious annals of our common country there will be no brighter page than that which relates *The Battles of Gettysburg.*"

It was the effort of his life and embodied the perfection of the school of oratory in which he had spent his career. His erect form and sturdy shoulders, his white hair and flung-back head at dramatic points, his voice, his poise, and chiefly some quality of inside goodheartedness, held most of his audience to him, though the people in the front rows had taken their seats three hours before his oration closed. . . .

Having read Everett's address, Lincoln knew when the moment drew near for him to speak. He took out his own manuscript from a coat pocket, put on his steel-bowed glasses, stirred in his chair, looked over the manuscript, and put it back in his pocket. The Baltimore Glee Club finished. The specially chosen Ward Hill Lamon rose and spoke the words "The President of the United States," who rose, and holding in one hand the two sheets of paper at which he occasionally glanced, de-livered the address in his high-pitched and clear-carrying voice. The *Cincinnati Commercial* reporter wrote, "The President rises slowly, draws from his pocket a paper, and when commotion subsides, in a sharp, unmusical treble voice, reads the brief and pithy remarks." Hay wrote in his diary, "The President, in a firm free way, with more grace than is his wont, said his half dozen words of consecration." Charles Hale of the *Boston Advertiser,* also officially representing Governor Andrew of Massachusetts, had notebook and pencil in hand, took down the slow-spoken words of the President, as follows:

"Fourscore and seven years ago, our fathers brought forth upon this continent a new nation, conceived in Liberty and dedicated to the propo-sition that all men are created equal.

"Now we are engaged in a great civil war, testing whether that nation —or any nation, so conceived and so dedicated—can long endure.

"We are met on a great battle-field of that war. We are met to dedicate a portion of it as the final resting place of those who have given their lives that that nation might live.

"It is altogether fitting and proper that we should do this.

"But, in a larger sense, we cannot dedicate, we cannot consecrate, we cannot hallow, this ground. The brave men, living and dead, who struggled here, have consecrated it, far above our power to add or to detract.

"The world will very little note nor long remember what we say here; but it can never forget what they did here.

"It is for us, the living, rather, to be dedicated, here, to the unfinished work that they have thus far so nobly carried on. It is rather for us to be here dedicated to the great task remaining before us; that from these honored dead we take increased devotion to that cause for which they here gave the last full measure of devotion; that we here highly resolve that these dead shall not have died in vain; that the nation shall, under God, have a new birth of freedom, and that government of the people, by the people, for the people, shall not perish from the earth."

—CARL SANDBURG, 1878-

[38] The Humility of Einstein

WHEN he [Einstein] arrived one day at Brussels on a visit to the Belgian queen, the thought that there might be a welcoming party awaiting him at the station had not entered his head, and so he failed to notice the shining limousine and the group of smartly uniformed dignitaries waiting for him. Lugging a suitcase in one hand and his violin in the other, he proceeded to walk to the castle of his hostess. The welcoming party fumed and fretted as no sign of the distinguished scientist could be found. Then they returned to the castle and informed the Queen that Einstein must have changed his mind about coming. Just then the frowning Queen noticed a dusty figure ambling up the road, whistling cheerfully. In her mood of intense displeasure, a tramp was the last thing she wanted to see and she turned to give peremptory orders to whisk him from the estate.

But, wait! The figure of the "tramp" had come closer now, and her Majesty's frown turned to consternation, then pleased surprise, as, calling up all her reserves of self-command she managed to stammer:

"Why, Herr Doktor Einstein! How do you do! I am so happy to see you, but why didn't you use the car I sent for you? Why did you walk all that distance?"

"Why, your Majesty, I didn't think about a car being sent for me," replied the visitor with a naïve smile. "When I got off the train, I just came out. And it was a very pleasant walk!"

Only one thing Einstein wanted from the world, and this, apparently, money could not buy—privacy and seclusion for a life of quiet contemplation. Probably no man was so plagued by offers of gold for newspaper articles, for public appearances, for testimonials of every imaginable article from toothpaste and shaving soap to pimple eradicators and cigars. He considered all such overtures as "corruption," and rejected them with cold disdain. To Einstein money had no lure—it was simply something to give away. At one time he was supporting 150 families in Berlin. A German journal proposed to him to reprint one of his important lectures, offering him 1000 marks for the privilege. The scientist refused. The editor persisted. It was Einstein's duty to science to permit

52

publication, he was told, and he finally capitulated. But his consent was given on one condition. He could not, he said, accept 1000 marks for the paper. That was far beyond the true worth of the address. He would permit its publication only if the editor agreed to reduce his price to 600 marks!

—H. GORDON GARDEDIAN, 1905-

[39] The Day Had Come

LOU GEHRIG PLAYS HIS LAST GAME

THE season opened [1939]. The Yankees played eight games. They were winning, but Lou was lagging. He made only four hits for an average of .143, and he was so slow covering first base that the other players had to wait for him before making a throw. Little was said about him in the newspapers but his teammates were looking at him anxiously and the baseball writers talked about him among themselves. Nobody said anything to him about his poor playing, naturally. For one thing, he obviously was in a very bad mental state as he tried to pull himself together.

"How long can McCarthy keep him in there?" one writer asked another.

"I have an idea that when the Yankees go West, Joe will take him out. I think he just doesn't want to take him out while they are at home."

"And when he goes out . . . do you think it will be for good?"

"Maybe. Maybe if he just rests for a while, he will be all right."

The Yankees left for Detroit on the night of April 30. The next day was an off day. That day Lou spent alone, wrestling with the problem of his decline as a player, reaching a decision. McCarthy had spent the day at his home in Buffalo. When he reached Detroit on the morning of May 2, Lou was waiting for him in the lobby and went up to his room with him.

"Yes, Lou?" McCarthy said as the door of his room closed behind the boy who had carried his bags.

"I'm benching myself, Joe," Lou said.

McCarthy looked at him for a moment.

"Why?" he asked.

"For the good of the team," Lou said. "I can't tell you how grateful I am to you for the kindness you have shown me and for your patience. I've tried hard, Joe. You know that. But I just can't seem to get going, and nobody has to tell me how bad I've been and how much of a draw-

53

back I've been to the team. I've been thinking, ever since the season opened—when I saw that I couldn't start as I'd hope I would—that the time had come for me to quit."

"Quit?" Joe said. "You don't have to quit. Take a rest for a week or so, and maybe you'll feel all right again."

Lou shook his head.

"I don't know," he said. "I don't know what's the matter with me. But I know I can't go on the way I am . . . Johnny Murphy told me so."

McCarthy frowned angrily.

"Murphy told you! I'll—"

"No, Joe," Lou said. "I didn't mean it that way. All the boys have been so swell to me and nobody has said a word that would hurt my feelings. But Johnny Murphy said something the other day that made me know it was time for me to get out of the line-up. And all he meant to to was to be encouraging."

"How was that?"

"Do you remember the last play in the game—the last game at the Stadium?"

"Yes."

"A ball was hit between the box and first base—"

"And Johnny fielded it?"

"And I got back in time to take the throw—just in time?"

"Yes."

"I had a hard time getting back there, Joe," Lou said. "I should have been there in plenty of time. And then, as I made the putout and started for the clubhouse, Johnny waited for me near the box and said:

" 'Nice play, Lou.' "

McCarthy was silent.

"I knew then that it was time to quit," Lou said. "When the boys were feeling sorry for me—"

"All right, Lou," Joe said. "Take a rest. I'll put Dahlgren on first base, but I want you to know that that's your position—and whenever you want it back, all you have to do is to walk out there and take it."

The day had come. The day when he was to fulfill a promise he had made a year before. On an August day in 1938, he had come back to the dugout after taking a swing in batting practice and hadn't gone up again when it was his turn.

"What's the matter?" a reporter had asked.

"I have a bad thumb," he said. "I think maybe the darned thing is broken."

"Are you going to stay out of the line-up?"

"I should say not! It isn't as bad as that. I can grip a bat and handle

54

the ball all right, and there is no reason why I shouldn't play."

"You aren't thinking too much about your record, are you?" the reporter asked.

"No," he said. "I'm all right. I can play. And I'll promise you this: When the day comes that I don't think I can help the ball club, I won't be in there, record or no record."

The day had come. The record had been set at 2,130 games.

—FRANK GRAHAM, 1893-

[40] The Dogma Is the Drama

JUDGING by what my young friends tell me, and also by what is said on the subject in anti-Christian literature written by people who ought to have taken a little trouble to find out what they are attacking before attacking it, I have come to the conclusion that a short examination paper on the Christian religion might be very generally answered as follows:

Q. What does the Church think of God the Father?

A. He is omnipotent and holy. He created the world and imposed on man conditions impossible of fulfilment; He is very angry if these are not carried out. He sometimes interferes by means of arbitrary judgments and miracles, distributed with a good deal of favouritism. He likes to be truckled to and is always ready to pounce on anybody who trips up over a difficulty in the Law, or is having a bit of fun. He is rather like a dictator, only larger and more arbitrary.

Q. What does the Church think of God the Son?

A. He is in some way to be identified with Jesus of Nazareth. It was not His fault that the world was made like this, and, unlike God the Father, He is friendly to man and did His best to reconcile man to God (see *Atonement*). He has a good deal of influence with God, and if you want anything done, it is best to apply to Him.

Q. What does the Church think of God the Holy Ghost?

A. I don't know exactly. He was never seen or heard of till Whit-Sunday. There is a sin against Him which damns you for ever, but nobody knows what it is.

Q. What is the doctrine of the Trinity?

A. "The Father incomprehensible, the Son incomprehensible, and the whole thing incomprehensible." Something put in by theologians to make it more difficult—nothing to do with daily life or ethics.

Q. What was Jesus Christ like in real life?

55

A. He was a good man—so good as to be called the Son of God. He is to be identified in some way with God the Son (q.v.). He was meek and mild and preached a simple religion of love and pacifism. He had no sense of humour. Anything in the Bible that suggests another side to His character must be an interpolation, or a paradox invented by G. K. Chesterton. If we try to live like Him, God the Father will let us off being damned hereafter and only have us tortured in this life instead.

Q. What is meant by the Atonement?

A. God wanted to damn everybody, but His vindictive sadism was sated by the crucifixion of His own Son, who was quite innocent, and, therefore, a particularly attractive victim. He now only damns people who don't follow Christ or who never heard of Him.

Q. What does the Church think of sex?

A. God made it necessary to the machinery of the world, and tolerates it, provided the parties (a) are married, and (b) get no pleasure out of it.

Q. What does the Church call sin?

A. Sex (otherwise than as excepted above); getting drunk; saying "damn"; murder, and cruelty to dumb animals; not going to church; most kinds of amusement. "Original sin" means that anything we enjoy doing is wrong.

Q. What is faith?

A. Resolutely shutting your eyes to scientific fact.

Q. What is the human intellect?

A. A barrier to faith.

Q. What are the seven Christian virtues?

A. Respectability; childishness; mental timidity; dullness; sentimentality; censoriousness; and depression of spirits.

Q. Wilt thou be baptized in this faith?

A. No fear!

I cannot help feeling that as a statement of Christian orthodoxy, these replies are inadequate, if not misleading. But I also cannot help feeling that they do fairly accurately represent what many people take Christian orthodoxy to be, and for this state of affairs I am inclined to blame the orthodox.

—Dorothy L. Sayers, 1893-1957

[41] A Tribute to "Bill" Stidger

It seems strange to be referring to the friendly man who always signed his wonderful letters "Bill" as the Reverend Dr. William L. Stidger. It's stranger still to try to realize that his friendship, his inspiration, his keen interest in people and things, patterns and pictures that included all living, even the sports kind of living, are ended.

Dr. Stidger was truly a distinguished clergyman. A Methodist, nationally known through his coast-to-coast broadcasts, his books, his lectures, his extensive travels, his basic affiliation was with the faculty of the Boston University School of Theology. That's what the formal obituaries say, and they go on to list his honors, his degrees, his accomplishments and emoluments.

What they can't list, however, is the lift he gave all who knew him, the stronger belief in some finer way, the breadth of vision, the respect for decent things, belief in God and all that a clergyman should represent and be, but, above all, perhaps, on the layman's level, the living example that a man can be a Christian, not only a clergyman, but a teacher of clergymen, without sacrificing contacts, interest, humor, nor happiness in the workaday world as the rest know it. Proof of that is the name by which most of us knew him, Bill Stidger. I never knew a name that fit a man so exactly.

Dr. Stidger was interested in a great many things. He would have made a great reporter. In fact he was a great reporter. That is proved by his writings, and likewise by his sermons and lectures. But all his reporting wasn't confined to the formal products. Some of it was in letters that came to this office. Keenly interested in people, all kinds of people, he sometimes encountered athletes of major or minor import in his travels.

Interested in how they lived, what they thought, why they did it, he generally managed to draw them out. His interest was so sincere, his approach so sympathetic, albeit so masculine, that they generally confided far more to him than they ever would to a sports writer. So far as I know, he never violated real confidences, but he occasionally did pass on some of his observations and conclusions in letters to this office. . . .

Those who read this column, however, will probably remember best of the references made to him here through the years, the summation of a radio talk he once made. It was entitled "Rest Where You Are." That was likewise his philosophy and practical prescription.

There was nothing religious in this particular message. Spirituality wasn't even involved. It was nothing but a small dose of common sense— a practical suggestion in the business of living. The gist of it was that we could all save energy in this hard-driving world if we'd only learn completely to relax in the many opportunities all of us have in even the busiest routines. Instead of staying tense all the day, and all the way, the saving trick is to relax every muscle, and every nerve. Completely as the opportunity offers. . . .

It would be hard to tell how many millions have benefited, and are still benefiting, from that simple suggestion. During the grinding years of the war, without even asking his permission, I revived "Rest Where You Are" here, giving him full credit, of course. From here, it literally went 'round the world. Other papers and publications reprinted it. The Armed Forces immediately appropriated it. Soldiers and sailors mailed it back from where their theatre, post or unit publications had featured it in all parts of the globe. They even had a name for it—"Stidgerizing."

Bill Stidger was interested in photography. He was interested in sports. He knew his baseball, and he knew it from away back. . . .

There's not much you can say when the Lord calls His own, but here's one case, certainly, where death is not the end of living. Today they will bury the mortal remains of the fine friend, the great preacher and the teacher we knew. But as long as those who were privileged to share his friendship themselves continue to live, all that was warm and human and inspirational and Christian in Bill Stidger will live. Men such as that don't die; they merely pass on.

"Rest, sweet rest, where you are."

—BILL CUNNINGHAM, 1896-1960

[42] Eight Steps to Courage and Serenity

LEARNING "how to take heart" requires an inclusive program of intelligent living. Toward that end, I have devised and adopted an eight-point plan. It seems simple enough, and indeed it is. Yet I am sure it will work for you if you want to take heart, and live your life with more serenity, cheer, and confidence.

The first point is:

1. *Look Outward.* William Burnham says it is the task of a child to be selfish until he is seven or eight, in order to identify himself as a personality in the eyes of others; but after that, he must learn to graduate from egocentricity.

Every great religion tells its devotees to get away from self-attention: Confucius advised his followers to love themselves in their families; Hinduism tells its members to become absorbed in their caste or the world spirit; Gautama taught his devotees that they must discipline their selfish desires by the Four Noble Truths in order to find Nirvana; Jesus said to his disciples, "Whosoever shall lose his life . . . shall save it."

People with such an attitude of selflessness have mastered the first great art of taking heart.

2. *Know Your Fears*. Angelo Patri is right in saying, "Education consists in being afraid at the right time." There are logical fears which consist of those things about which we should be frightened: We ought to be afraid of atomic warfare and do everything possible to curb its development, we ought to fear jumping from a ten-story building; we ought not swim in turbulent water. Sometimes we may even need to practice fear!

But the fears that encompass most of us are not logical fears; they are illogical fears, the result of tired, sick imaginations which create illusory monsters. We may fear criticism, adventure, sickness, old age, poverty —anything that pops into our minds.

Those who are tortured by such fears would do well to emulate the woman who realized that worry was her chief means of coloring the universe into a state of unfriendliness, and so made for herself a "worry table." In tabulating her worries she discovered that only ten per cent of her worries were about things that might happen, and that many of these could be vanquished by intelligent action. She also rememberd that such experiences, when they did happen, made her a stronger and more sympathetic person.

Make up your own worry table. It will help you "take heart" more effectively than you may think.

3. *Get a Physical Checkup*. Recently, I read of a man victimized by fear because he was enervated by poison pouring into his blood stream from an abscessed tooth. Another person with infected tonsils found a new lease on life after a simple operation.

We must realize that the mind-body relation is extremely sensitive, and often a sick body is the main contribution to a disturbed mental state.

4. *Exercise Prudently*. Harry J. Johnson, M.D., director of the Life Extension Examiners, recently stated, "There's no better way to get in shape than by walking. Try to walk an hour a day—to the railroad station, to your lunch—then walk part of the way home at night. . . . Vigorous sports like handball, boxing, volleyball and tennis should be limited, as a rule, to those under 45 years of age."

Overexercise frequently leads to extreme enervation, which in turn may produce a state of apprehension. But exercise, properly balanced, increases circulation of the blood; this develops physical buoyance; and physical vigor has a healthy reaction on mental attitudes.

5. *Get Enough Rest*. The tired mind is most susceptible to every kind of negative suggestion. One psychiatrist has plainly named fatigue as the great beginning of fears and neuroses. Therefore, to take heart, take rest—but do not make sleep itself a worry to you. Retire at reasonably

early hours. If you find yourself unable to sleep, do not be disturbed. Be content to lie quietly and rest. It may be a good opportunity to change your mood with strong, positive thoughts. Read the Bible, or other literature which you find puts you in an optimistic, easy frame of mind. Such reading will either relax you and court sleep—or take the place of it.

6. *Vary Your Interests.* A writer friend of mine who spent too much time in his study was victimized by illogical fears and went to a psychiatrist. He was told that he was focusing his attention upon one project too narrowly, that he needed to balance his living with numerous interests. Now he alternates between his writing and a variety of experiences. He has a hobby shop with wood and tools; he listens to music; he reads and learns poetry; he goes to the theater. No longer is he afraid. Like Cyrano de Bergerac, he has found a number of interesting things to "get him off the earth," and like Cyrano, I am sure, he will wear his white plume of courage to the end.

7. *Practice Humility.* Humility is a virtue; it is a positive way of living; it is the quality of a great personality who sees his achievements as worthy, yet small in relationship to greater accomplishments. Self-confidence is a companion of humility. Katherine Mansfield had humility, when shortly before her premature death she said of her writing, "Not one of these dare I show to God." Jesus had humility: "Why callest thou me good?" said Jesus. "None is good save one, that is, God." Men of humility do not worry about themselves; their lives are centered in purposes greater than themselves; their worlds can never break in two.

8. *Develop Faith.* Faith is perhaps the most vital factor in taking heart. William James once said that people with no abiding religious philosophy terminate in sadness and possess sick souls. Mme. Chiang Kai-shek tells of passing from fear to courage as her religious philosophy developed.

[43] You

IF timid folk could only realize the potentiality that is implanted in each one of us—singly! These folk have aspirations, the urge to do. But, invariably, they are deprecatory, even disparaging of self. They fall back upon the plaint: "I am just one man" or "one woman." "What can I do?"

What was Florence Nightingale but one woman? Yet her work led straight to the Red Cross! How far would be the humane processes of healing the wounded and sorrowful all over the world today had this English nurse . . . bemoaned the fact that she was "just one woman"?

Where would the marvelous work done by radium be today if Madame Curie had folded her arms when her husband passed away and minimized herself by saying: "I am just one woman"?

Yes, but exceptional women, you say. Quite to the contrary. "I had faith: that was all," said Florence Nightingale. "I had confidence, little else," said Madame Curie, and to their work each applied her fullest aspiration and trust.

Was that mother "exceptional" whose six-year-old boy came home from school one day with a note from his teacher suggesting that he be taken from school as he was "too stupid to learn"? "My boy is not stupid," said the mother. "I will teach him myself." She did, and Thomas A. Edison was the result.

How often a woman says, "I am just a home body, busy with the daily task." . . . Abraham Lincoln's stepmother was "just a home body." But she taught and inspired the son of her husband—not even of her own blood—and held a torch before him which he carried to emancipate a people. "The greatest book I ever read, you ask me?" said Lincoln in a letter. "My mother." So was Dwight L. Moody's wife "just a home body," but she taught her husband how to write, put the love of God and of his fellow men into his heart, and sent him forth as the greatest evangelical force of his century. . . .

We do not seem to get it into our heads that the great works of the world always begin with one person. Emerson put a sermon in a dozen words: "A great institution is but the lengthened shadow of a single man." A man disgusted with committees thus expressed a large truth: "The ideal committee consists of three, with two of the members ill." Every institution that has contributed to American progress has been built upon the initiative and enthusiasm of an individual.

—Edward W. Bok, 1863-1930

[44] Are You Alive?

My notes show a classification of eleven states of being in which I feel I am alive, and five states in which I feel I only exist. These are major states needless to say. In addition, I find scores of sub-states which are too obscure for me to analyze. The eleven "plus" reactions are these:

I seem to live when I am creating something—writing this article, for instance; making a sketch, working on an economic theory, building a bookshelf, making a speech.

Art certainly vitalizes me. A good novel, some poems, some pictures, operas, many beautiful buildings and particularly bridges affect me as though I took the artist's blood into my own veins. There are times, however, when a curtain falls over my perceptions which no artist can penetrate.

The mountains and the sea and stars—all the old subjects of a thousand poets—renew life in me. As in the case of art, the process is not automatic—I hate the sea sometimes—but by and large, I feel the line of existence below me when I see these things.

Love is life, vital and intense. Very real to me also is the love one bears one's friends.

I live when I am stimulated by good conversation, good argument. There is a sort of vitality in just dealing in ideas that to me at least is very real.

I live when I am in the pressure of danger—rock-climbing, for example.

I feel very much alive in the presence of a genuine sorrow.

I live when I play—preferably out-of-doors at such things as diving, swimming, skating, skiing, dancing, sometimes driving a motor, sometimes walking.

One lives when one takes food after genuine hunger, or when burying one's lips in a cool mountain spring after a long climb.

One lives when one sleeps. A sound healthy sleep after a day spent out-of-doors gives one the feeling of a silent, whirring dynamo. In vivid dreams I am convinced one lives.

I live when I laugh—spontaneously and heartily.

—STUART CHASE, 1888-

[45] Creative You

A STIRRING, a yearning, a force moves within us, urging us, impelling us this way and that.

What boundless energy is this whose drive we must not ignore? It is our greatness, an omnipresent power—the essential part of living, growing, enduring things.

Size is not greatness. A giant tree, a blade of grass, the fragile petals of a rose all have greatness. It is that part of living which makes all life immortal. All are born great, few realize it.

With a song in our hearts and the creative tools of our choice in hand, let us allow our greatness to carry us forward. . . .

A slip of ivy clings to the studio wall and is green in both summer and winter. It had grown but a few inches when it sought a wall on which to climb, seeking support before it started upward. Have more patience with your ascending creativeness. Seek joys in which you believe, for happiness is the strong, supporting wall on which you climb.

There is time enough to reach your goal—the top of your wall. Be patient. . . .

From the tiniest buckwheat seed to the loftiest mountain, nature is perfectly balanced. As we knowingly become part of this balance our creative natures mature and living has significance. . . .

Painting is sharing. A sharing of what? A sharing of the glory of the day with Him who made it. . . .

Knowledge received that does not lead to joy is not yet knowledge. It is only information. . . .

To know is little. To know the Knower is all. . . .

Our watch gives us our time, our now. We figure in terms of days, years, centuries—measure those behind and those ahead. Still, our time is now. Our now is always with us.

Time moves through all things, changing appearances as it goes. We cannot destroy time, nor will it destroy us. Time is, and we are an indestructible part of it.

Our lives, lengthy though they seem to us, are but a tick in time.

Within the measured majesty of creation's cadence, our hearts must beat, our brushes swing.

Within the rhythmic movement of the whole, we find our place—we find ourselves. We learn of our importance and our unimportance. . . .

The art of painting is a craft. The art of living is still a greater craft. Love is life itself. . . .

If we would walk with God, let us put on our seven league boots and be unafraid. . . .

Tomorrow's art, I feel, will develop and mature as man rids himself of his own material sense limitations and becomes aware of universal spiritual relationships.

—GERRY PEIRCE, 1900-

[46] Dickens Reports Little Dora's Death

"*. . . read this letter very slowly . . .*"

Devonshire-terrace
Tuesday morning, 15th April, 1851

My dearest Kate,—Now observe, you must read this letter very slowly and carefully. If you have hurried on thus far without quite understanding (apprehending some bad news) I rely on your turning back and reading again.

Little Dora, without being in the least pain, is suddenly stricken ill. There is nothing in her appearance but perfect rest—you would suppose her quietly asleep, but I am sure she is very ill, and I cannot encourage myself with much hope of her recovery. I do not (and why should I say I do to you, my dear?) I do not think her recovery at all likely.

I do not like to leave home, I can do no good here, but I think it right to stay. You will not like to be away, I know, and I cannot reconcile it to myself to keep you away. Forster, with his usual affection for us, comes down to bring you this letter and to bring you home, but I cannot close it without putting the strongest entreaty and injunction upon you to come with perfect composure—

> to remember what I have often told you, that we never can expect to be exempt, as to our many children, from the afflictions of other parents, and that if—if when you come I should even have to say to you, "Our little baby is dead," you are to do your duty to the rest, and to show yourself worthy of the great trust you hold in them.

If you will only read this steadily I have a perfect confidence in your doing what is right.

Ever affectionately,
—CHARLES DICKENS, 1812-1870

[47] The Four Heroic Chaplains

No more glorious story has come out of World War II than the one related of the four chaplains who served on the "Dorchester," a United States transport ship sunk off the coast of Greenland by a submarine in June, 1943. The chaplains gave their life preservers to four of the combatant men on the boat who were without preservers, since as chaplains they had promised to care for their men in every need. Last reports of these four chaplains—George Fox and Clark Poling, Protestant ministers; Alexander Goode, a Jewish rabbi; and John Washington, a Roman Catholic priest—portrayed them on the sinking ship, arms about one another, singing, "Nearer, my God, to thee!" If in the last few moments before a rendezvous with death men can have such an intensified, courageous rendezvous with life, ought it not be possible that the whole span of life be lived with a similar intensity? The thought of death does intensify the urge to live if death is seen in its proper perspective.

[48] Darkness Changed to Light

SOMEONE has suggested that the figure in Rodin's "The Thinker" was contemplating the question, Is the universe friendly? After World War I J. Middleton Murry, finding himself in a state of morbidity—depressed, lonely, afraid—pondered this problem. Listen to his words: "I had come to the end of my tether. I had reached a point of total dereliction and despair. It was 'irrecoverably dark, total eclipse.'"

Many of his friends had been killed in France; others had been maimed and gassed; most were having a difficult time in making postwar adjustments. His life was so torn within that he contemplated suicide in Trafalgar Square. And then his famous wife, the writer, Katherine Mansfield, died. This sent Middleton Murry into seclusion, with the hope that he might see the problem of his life in better perspective. This is what happened in his solitude:

A moment came when the darkness of that ocean changed to light, the cold to warmth; when it swept in one great wave over the shores and the frontier of myself, when it bathed me and I was renewed; when the room was filled with a Presence, and I knew that I was not alone, that I never could be alone any more; that the universe beyond held no menace, for I was a part of it; that in some way for which I had sought in vain so many years, I belonged; and because I belonged I was no longer I, but something different, which could never be afraid in the old ways or cowardly with the old cowardice.

[49] The Church Alone Has Courage

BEING a lover of freedom, when the revolution came in Germany, I looked to the universities to defend it, knowing that they had always boasted of their devotion to the cause of truth; but, no, the universities immediately were silenced. Then I looked to the great editors of the newspapers whose flaming editorials in days gone by had proclaimed their love of freedom; but they, like the universities, were silenced in a few short weeks. . . . Only the Church stood squarely across the path of Hitler's campaign for suppressing truth. I never had any special interest in the Church before, but now I feel a great affection and admiration because the Church alone has had the courage and persistence to stand for intellectual truth and moral freedom. I am forced thus to confess that what I once despised I now praise unreservedly.

—ALBERT EINSTEIN, 1879-1957

[50] Push and Pull

SEVERAL years ago James R. Angell, then president of Yale University, gave the baccalaureate address at Columbia University. While walking with the Columbia University faculty into the chapel where the exercises were to be held, he noticed on the outside of the chapel door the word "Push." He saw a sermon in that word and decided to weave it into his morning talk as the key of his advice to the Columbia graduates. In introducing his address he said,

I am taking my text this morning, not from a philosopher, a literateur, or a biblical writer. Rather I have taken it from the one word engraved on the door of this great chapel, and offer it to you as the one thing each of you needs most when you leave the corridors of this university for the amphitheater of the world.

Whereupon several of the seniors, sitting near the back of the chapel, turned around and saw inscribed—on the *inside* of the chapel door—"Pull."

As we turn this homily from the facile to the serious, man's life, if it be complete, *is* highly sensitized by his response to both the push and the pull of life: the *push* is the inner drive or motivation man has for being religious, while the *pull* is that outside of man (often revered as God) which encourages or supports man in his good endeavors.

[51] Basic Rules for Daily Living

1. Take twenty minutes by yourself at the beginning of each day.

2. Live above small troubles by losing yourself in big, worth-while interests.

3. Grow every day; life is a game; keep your eye on the ball, rather than on the scoreboard.

4. Have power to see things through; keep remembering that most accomplishments are three-fourths drudgery, and one-fourth joy.

5. Alternate your interests. It is better to be busy than bored. Balance your life with work, play, love, and worship.

6. Be gracious to others; do kind deeds beyond the call of duty; remember that every person is fighting a battle.

7. Talk over your problems with others—with confiding friends, your doctor of medicine, your minister, your God.

8. Work and co-operate with God, praying that God will do something *through* you rather than *for* you.

[52] Let Your Soul Catch Up

A FRIEND of mine, a distinguished explorer who spent a couple of years among the savages of the upper Amazon, once attempted a forced march through the jungle. The party made extraordinary speed for the first two days, but on the third morning, when it was time to start, my friend found all the natives sitting on their haunches, looking very solemn and making no preparation to leave.

"They are waiting," the chief explained to my friend. "They cannot move farther until their souls have caught up with their bodies."

I can think of no better illustration of our own plight today. Is there no way of letting our souls, so to say, catch up with our bodies? If one thinks over the sort of life led in innumerable homes a generation ago, our immense speeding up in the process of living today is clear. People then, as we say, "had time." Now, no one "has time."

—JAMES TRUSLOW ADAMS, 1878-1949

[53] As I Grow Older I Grow Calm

As I grow older I grow calm. If I feel what are perhaps an old man's apprehensions, I do not lose my hopes. I do not pin my dreams for the future to my country or even to my race. I think it probable that civilization somehow will last as long as I care to look ahead—perhaps with smaller numbers, but perhaps also bred to greatness and splendor by science. I think it is not improbable that man, like the grub that prepares a chamber for the winged thing it has never seen but is to be—that man may have cosmic destinies that he does not understand. And so beyond the vision of battling races and an impoverished earth I catch a dreaming glimpse of peace.

The other day my dream was pictured to my mind. It was evening. I was walking homeward on Pennsylvania Avenue near the Treasury, and as I looked to the west the city was aflame with scarlet and crimson

67

from the setting sun. But like the note of downfall in Wagner's opera, below the skyline there came from little globes the pallid discord of the electric lights. And I thought to myself the Götterdämmerung will end, and from those globes clustered like evil eggs will come new masters of the sky. It is like the times in which we live. But then I remembered the faith that I partly have expressed, faith in a universe not measured by our fears, a universe that has thought and more than thought inside it, and as I gazed, after the sunset and above the electric lights there shone the stars.

—OLIVER WENDELL HOLMES, JR., 1841-1935

[54] The Meaning of "America"

AMERICA means far more than a continent bounded by two oceans. It is more than pride of military power, glory in war or in victory. It means more than vast expanse of farms, or great factories or mines, magnificent cities or millions of automobiles and radios. It is more even than the traditions of the great tide westward from Europe which pioneered the conquest of a continent. It is more than our literature, our music, our poetry. Other nations have these things also.

What we have in addition, the intangible we cannot describe, lies in the personal experience and the living of each of us rather than in phrases, however inspiring. . . .

I have seen America in contrast with many nations and races. My profession took me into many foreign lands with their great spiritual leaders and their great statemen. I have worked in governments of free men, of tyrannies, of Socialists and of Communists. I have met with princes, kings, despots, and desperados.

I have seen the squalor of Asia, the frozen class barriers of Europe. . . . And outstanding everywhere to these great masses of people there was a hallowed word—America. To them it was the hope of the world.

Every homecoming was for me a reaffirmation of the glory of America. Each time my soul was washed by the relief from the grinding poverty of other nations, by the greater kindliness and frankness which comes from acceptance of equality and wide-open opportunity to all who want a chance. It is more than that. It is a land of self-respect born alone of free men. . . .

I have had every honor to which any man could aspire. There is no

68

place on the whole earth except here in America where all the sons of a man could have this chance in life.

The meaning of our word America flows from one pure source. Within the soul of America is the freedom of mind and spirit in man. Here alone are the open windows through which pours the sunlight of the human spirit. Here alone human dignity is not a dream but a major accomplishment.

—HERBERT HOOVER, 1874-

[55] Higher and Lower Criticism

THERE is a great difference between making honest evaluations of people and being censorious; the former is positive and constructive, the latter is negative and destructive. As we speak of "higher criticism" and "lower criticism" in biblical studies, so the two expressions can be used regarding the judgments we make of others.

In higher criticism we make careful evaluations of others for an honest end. A president of a college in seeking recommendations of a candidate for a teaching position expects correct testimonies. An athletic director must make evaluations of his players in order to judge which are better than others.

Lower criticism, however, is something very different: here criticisms are made mainly for the purpose of diminishing the stature of another person. Such derogatory criticisms are usually made by inferior persons who cannot raise themselves to the statures of others, so in self-defense they tear down others to their levels of living. It is these people whom Jesus has in mind when he says, "Judge not, that you be not judged." He is aware that such cruel judgments of others are usually criticisms those people are making of themselves in their insecurity. Censorious persons usually worry about others' criticisms of them. They resemble Napoleon, who after each battle would inquire, "What is Paris saying?"

[56] Most People Worry

MOST people seem to worry. A group of 104 psychologists through a study of their cases determined a timetable for anxieties: At eighteen we

69

worry about ideals and personal appearance; at twenty, about appearance; at twenty-three, about morals; at twenty-six, about making a good impression; at thirty, about salary and the cost of living; at thirty-one, about business success; at thirty-three, about job security; at thirty-eight, about health; at forty-one, about politics; at forty-two, about marital problems; at forty-five, about the loss of ambition; over forty-five, about health.

As one looks over this chart of anxieties, one needs to hear the words of an older, mature person, "If I could live my life over again, there is one thing I would not do—I would not worry. I have suffered too much from worry, and now realize that it never got me anywhere. It is just plain foolish!" In similar words Jesus said, "Do not be anxious about your life. . . . Which of you be being anxious can add one cubit to his span of life?"

[57] The Folly of Worry

EDUCATION and religion ought to teach people to be anxious about the right things. It is estimated that nine tenths of our worries are about events that will not occur. We worry over others' criticisms of us, about our health, about decisions we have made, although in our sane moments we know that worry will not better any of these situations but will only make us worse individuals. A study of 176 business executives, who average forty-four years of age, shows that one third suffer from one of three ailments due to anxiety and hypertension: heart disease; digestive tract ulcers; high blood pressure. About such high-pressure living Winfred Rhoades writes: "Emotional dissipation is no less an intemperance than alcoholic dissipation. The effect upon a man's life may be equally bad though not in the same way." Regarding man's race for success Fritz Kunkel speaks: "All egocentric tension can easily be traced to our striving for superiority and fear of inferiority. We survey a task, and the more we are afraid of failure, the more we over-estimate the energy which is needed." To these same people Jesus' words ring an alarm: "Do not be anxious about tomorrow, for tomorrow will be anxious for itself. Let the day's own trouble be sufficient for the day."

[58] Just for Today

JUST for today I will try to live this day only, and not tackle my whole life problem at once. . . . Just for today I will be happy. . . . Just for today I will strengthen my mind. I will study. I will learn something useful. . . . Just for today I will adjust myself to what is, and not try to adjust everything to my own desires. . . . Just for today I will exercise my soul in three ways: I will do somebody a good turn, and not get found out. I will do at least two things I don't want to do—just for exercise. I will not show anyone that my feelings are hurt; they may be hurt, but today I will not show it. Just for today I will be agreeable. I will look as well as I can, dress becomingly, talk low, act courteously, criticize not one bit, not find fault with anybody and not try to improve or regulate anybody except myself. Just for today I will have a program. . . . Just for today I will have a quiet half hour all by myself, and relax. . . . Just for today I will be unafraid. Especially I will not be afraid to enjoy what is beautiful, and to believe that as I give to the world, so the world will give to me.

—KENNETH HOLMES, 1917-

[59] Seven Ways to Be Happy Though Married

AMOS ALONZO STAGG, famous football coach, on his thirty-seventh wedding anniversary gave out "seven ways to be happy though married": (1) Play the fifty-fifty game. Help the wife with the dishes, and she will help you with your charts and the signals. (2) Apply the rules of good sportsmanship to your married life. And that means follow the Golden Rule. (3) Be mutually unselfish. (4) Have mutual confidence. Keep no secrets from one another, and let no jealousy creep in. (5) Never complain. Be cheerful. (6) Have children. A family without children is not normal, and the views of one or both of the couples are apt to become warped without children. (7) Work together. Find your happiness at home and in your play together. The couple that spends all their lives looking for pleasure won't find it.

[60] It Is Not Marriage that Fails

"IT is not marriage that fails; it is people that fail"; and figures show that those who turn to the teachings of Jesus fail less in their marriage relations. Wherein one out of 4.3 marriages ends in divorce in the United States, only one marriage in fifty fails where couples have casual church relations, and but one in 113 marriages ends in divorce where husband and wife are members of the same church. A recent Gallup Poll shows ten reasons for marital difficulties: money, rearing children, liquor, infidelity, in-laws and relatives, late hours, leisure time, trivial things, selfishness, lack of religious faith.

[61] The American Canon for Freedom

THE American commonwealth is formed on the basis that men are free. Alfred North Whitehead has said that during the first three centuries, under Christian influence, freedom began her march; that freedom through the centuries has been retarded, but never stopped. Jesus' teachings about the high cost of spiritual freedom in his Sermon on the Mount have given to his followers the high discipline which free men must accept.

In *The American Canon,* Daniel L. Marsh shows how our great articles of freedom compose for us a "Bible": (1) The Genesis of American democracy is the Mayflower Pact; (2) Our Exodus into our new country is the Declaration of Independence; (3) The Constitution of the United States composes the Law; (4) Prophecies are seen in writings like Washington's Farewell Address; (5) Psalms are contained in songs like "The Star-Spangled Banner"; (6) The Gospel of true Americanism is found in Lincoln's Second Inaugural Address; (7) Epistles are observed in articles like the last one written by Woodrow Wilson, "The Road Away from Revolution," in which he said:

The sum of our whole matter is this, that our civilization cannot survive materially unless it is redeemed spiritually. It can be saved only by becoming permeated with the spirit of Christ, and being made free and happy by the practices which spring out of that spirit.

72

[62] Can Religion Bring Us Happiness?

In the summer of 1949 a group of eighteen esteemed citizens met at Westchester Country Club at Rye, New York, for the express purpose of answering the question, "Can religion bring us happiness and joy?" Among their valuable conclusions they said:

Happiness is possible as one is able to relate oneself to the world in love and thought. . . . Religious faith has more to do with happiness for the individual than anything else. . . . Self-sacrifice is necessary for happiness. . . . Suffering is not good in itself, but it shifts our expectations for happiness from without to within.

Such statements echo Jesus' teachings about joy as a deep religious quality. Napoleon and Helen Keller in their contrasting types of lives vividly illustrate the views of Jesus and the findings of the Westchester Country Club conference. Said Napoleon amidst his power, position, and glory, "I have never known six happy days in my life." Helen Keller exclaimed from her state of being blind, deaf, and dumb, "I have found life so beautiful!" Joy is an inner state which is a reward for our religious loyalties.

[63] Seneca Dies Nobly

SENECA and Jesus were born in the same year (4 B.C.). Like Jesus, Seneca was a great religious teacher. Banished to Corsica in A.D. 41 by the emperor Claudius, he was recalled in 49 to become the tutor of Domitius, who later became the emperor Nero. He acted as one of Nero's advisors, and held great influence during the earlier years of Nero's reign, only to have Nero turn against him in 65, when Nero ordered Seneca to commit suicide. Tacitus describes the closing moments of Seneca's life:

He turned to his friends and said that he would leave to them the one thing, and yet the best thing, that he had to leave—the pattern of his life. . . . At the same time he reminded his weeping friends of their duty to be strong, now by his conversation, now by sterner rebuke, asking them what had become of the precepts of wisdom, of the philosophy which through so many years they had studied in face of impending evils. . . . Then he embraced his wife, and, with a tenderness somewhat in contrast to his fortitude, entreated her to moderate her grief and not to nurse it for ever, but in the contemplation of a well-spent life to find honourable consolation for the loss of her husband.

73

[64] Relax and Live

MOST of us need to "relax and live"! A book by this title summarizes six major principles for our incarnation, if we are to become peace-makers. Its author, Joseph A. Kennedy, has helped many people find poise for living. His six suggestions are: (1) Learn to relax passively— don't live actively all the time. (2) Learn to practice rhythm between work and play. (3) Obtain a philosophy of life; take difficulties in their stride. (4) Quit speeding up; take your time; live one day at a time. (5) Eradi-cate attitudes of fear, futility, tension, and doubt, which defeat you. Act as if you are going to succeed. (6) Remember that relaxation can cure tension; but that there are times you ought to see your doctor.

[65] How to Attain an Ideal

BEFORE man can attain spiritual stature, he must have a desire to be a spiritual giant. Man needs yearning and perseverance in religion as in other walks of life. Paderewski did not become a concert pianist except by a hunger to be a great concert artist. "Anyone who takes up piano-playing," he said, "with a view to becoming a professional pianist has taken on himself an awful burden. But it is better than the drudgery of giving pianoforte lessons. The one is purgatory, but the other is hell!"

For five years Paderewski suffered torments of starved aspiration and thwarted ambition; he taught when he should have been studying. He married, only to lose his wife by death within a year. Finally in despair, the pedagogue turned pupil; he studied for two years under the great Lechetizky in Vienna, practicing eighteen hours a day. If Paderewski had not hungered and thirsted for the ideal of becoming a great artist, he would not have attained his goal. The same is true in the realm of re-ligion; spiritual satisfaction comes only to those who want it and are willing to strive for it.

[66] We Are All Islands in a Common Sea

How wonderful are islands! Islands in space, like this one I have come to, ringed about by miles of water, linked by no bridges, no cables, no

74

telephones. An island from the world and the world's life. Islands in time, like this short vacation of mine. The past and the future are cut off; only the present remains. Existence in the present gives island living an extreme vividness and purity. One lives like a child or a saint in the immediacy of here and now. Every day, every act, is an island, washed by time and space, and has an island's completion. People, too, became like islands in such an atmosphere, self-contained, whole and serene; respecting other people's solitude, not intruding on their shores, standing back in reverence before the miracle of another individual. "No man is an island," said John Donne. I feel we are all islands—in a common sea.

We are all, in the last analysis, alone. And this basic state of solitude is not something we have any choice about. It is, as the poet Rilke says, "not something that one can take or leave." We *are* solitary. We may delude ourselves and act as though this were not so. That is all. But how much better it is to realize that we are so, yes, even to begin by assuming it.

—ANNE MORROW LINDBERGH, 1907-

[67] On Old and New Books

My venerated Columbia professor, Raymond Weaver, whose knowledge and personality are alike classical, is credited with an apposite legend. At a dinner party one evening a bright young thing queried, in her most buffed and polished finishing-school voice, "Mr. Weaver, have you read So-and-so's book?" (naming a modish best seller of the moment).

Mr. Weaver confessed he had not.

"Oh, you'd better hurry up—it's been out over three months!"

Mr. Weaver, an impressive gentleman with a voice like a Greek herald, turned to her, and said, "My dear young lady, have you read Dante's *Divine Comedy?*"

"No."

"Then you'd better hurry up—it's been out over six hundred years. . . ."

Books are not rolls, to be devoured only when they are hot and fresh. A good book retains its interior heat and will warm a generation yet unborn. He who confines himself only to today's books is more narrowly circumscribed by time than he who reads only yesteryear's. You can be inexorably old-fashioned or perennially up to the minute. In either case you are dated.

75

We are driven, then, to the dull, sane conclusion that the proper diet is a mixed one. No special magic virtue inheres in either old or new books.

—CLIFTON FADIMAN, 1904-

[68] The Value of Books

OF this recall value William Hazlitt says: "In reading a book which is an old favorite with me (say the first novel I ever read) I not only have the pleasure of imagination and of a critical relish of the work, but the pleasures of memory added to it. It recalls the same feelings and associations which I had in first reading it, and which I can never have again in any other way. Standard productions of this kind are links in the chain of our conscious being. They bind together the different scattered divisions of our personal identity. They are landmarks and guides in our journey through life. They are pegs and loops on which we can hang up, or from which we can take down, at pleasure, the wardrobe of a moral imagination, the relics of our best affections, the tokens and records of our happiest hours. They are 'for thoughts and for remembrance!' They are like Fortunatus's Wishing Cap—they give us the best riches—those of Fancy; and transport us, not over half the globe, but (which is better) over half our lives, at a word's notice!"

—CLIFTON FADIMAN, 1904-

[69] Oberlin's Love of a Jew

OBERLIN became instinctively the protector of ill-treated people of Jewish faith. A Jew who was crossing the mountain heights above the Valley of Stone was robbed and murdered. For some years after this event Oberlin passed on to the widow, each year, the sum of 50 francs. The woman, astonished at receiving such a rich gift from the pastor of so poor a parish, asked what had drawn him into the affair. Oberlin replied that since the murder had been committed in his parish, he felt that not only the villagers but himself as well, were blood-guilty, and that so far as he had the power he wished to atone for the crime and help to avert the curse resting upon the place where innocent blood had been shed. . . .

One morning, as Oberlin was at work in his study, he heard a great noise in the village. Rushing out, he saw a foreigner in the midst of a howling, threatening mob. Oberlin dashed into the crowd. On all sides the cry was raised, "A Jew! A Jew!" With the greatest difficulty, the pastor at last commanded silence. When he could make himself heard he exclaimed: "Those who treat so cruelly one who is not a Christian, are themselves unworthy of that name." Then, lifting the peddler's pack upon his own shoulders, he took the man by the hand, led him to the manse, and sheltered him from the mob's blind fury.

That evening, the peddler sat down at the dinner-table with the Oberlin family, the little curtsying maids, and the pensionnaires. In answer to the reluctant stranger's protest, Oberlin had said: "The pot will not know the difference, since there are already so many mouths to share the feast." As the two men were sitting together talking, when the dishes had been cleared away, a neighboring Catholic priest who had found the Waldsbach manse a cozy place to visit, joined them, and they drew their chairs together before the fire.

The priest was in a mellow mood. He beamed upon the Jewish peddler. Then laying his hand on Oberlin's shoulder, he said: "How I wish, my good friend, that you and I were of the same religion."

The Waldsbach minister was silent a moment before he spoke. He looked first at the priest, then at the Jew. Putting one arm upon the priest's shoulder, while the other circled the man he had rescued from the mob, he said: "Love is the religion of Jesus Christ. The Savior is love personified."

The eyes of the Jew were moist with tears. Bowing his head, he murmured: "What doth the Lord require of thee, but to do justly, to love mercy, and to walk humbly with thy God?"

The priest said, softly: "He who loves his fellow-man, whom he has seen, loves God whom he has not seen."

—MARSHALL DAWSON, 1880-

[70] My People Like Me, but They Don't Love God

ONE of the most spacious souls it was ever my privilege to know was S. Parkes Cadman. . . . The first time I met him was when he gave a lecture in a small city in the hinterlands where I was preaching. It was my privilege to present him to the audience, and when I asked him if there was anything in particular I should say, he replied, "Just say I happen

77

to be the minister of the largest Congregational Church in the country."
It was. It was a huge amphitheater, corrugated sheet iron inside and outside, and old back-breaking pews. It seated eighteen hundred people, and
ushers in morning dress showed people to their pews. Standing room
was at a premium. The best pews were auctioned off to the highest
bidder.

When I first went to Brooklyn his church was beginning to run down
at the heels. The crowds were no longer there. The preacher was still
vigorous in mind and body, but the organization was showing signs of
wear and tear. Financial deficits were reported annually. . . .

Then one night three months before he died, I took S. Parkes Cadman
home in my car after a meeting of the Clerical Union. One would have
thought that with the vigor of mind and body he possessed when he was
past seventy, he would live forever. He left a lonesome place against
the sky when he suddenly died. But that little ride to his home, and what
he said, opened a window through which I have seen the condition of
the church ever since. With a choking voice he said, "Fred, my church
is slipping, and my men won't do anything about it. Do you know what
is wrong with my church? My people like me, but they don't love God."
Thirty-five years a minister at one church, and at the end the verdict
ran, "They don't love God!"

—FREDERICK KELLER STAMM, 1883-

[71] Emerson Answers a Critic

ONE way to prevent the past from becoming a tyrant in your life is to
deal with unpleasant situations as they come up. Don't let them sink
into the memory, but instead get rid of them as soon as possible. If you
shed an unpleasant memory before it has the opportunity to become a
memory, then it can hardly do you harm later.

Ralph Waldo Emerson once lectured to the students at Middlebury
College. After his address, a minister who was invited to pray said, "O
Lord, may we never hear again in Middlebury College such transcen-
dental nonsense as we have just listened to tonight." After the meeting,
the president of the college hurried over to Emerson, full of apologies
for the incident. Emerson listened for a few moments, then stopped him.

"Why, my dear friend," he said, "I think the minister was very sincere
and honest."

—PRESTON BRADLEY, 1888-

78

[72] Heroism, the Mystery of Happiness

HEROISM is a concept which has been defined in many ways. In the Fascist ideology it comes close to being a pretty name for the crude masculine urge to violence. But we shall define heroism as the happy spiritual defensive force that arises when we fight against tremendous odds or inescapable powers. Heroism seems to be the mystery of happiness, and it cannot be explained if we understand by happiness only bodily wellbeing and the pleasures and joys of the mind, or the combination of both. Heroism is the spiritual power that not only is vouchsafed to us but is demanded when we meet pain and suffering, even the agony of death by torture, and fear and doubt in the mind—everything that is dark and hard to bear—in order to follow our ideal.

The paradox of the mystery is that in heroism the stream of happiness runs entirely contrary to our instinctual energy. . . .

The Swiss philosopher Henri Frederic Amiel, whose life was quite "unheroic" from the Fascist point of view, has written the most beautiful words I have found about heroism in his posthumously published *Journal intime:* "Heroism is the triumphant victory of the soul over the flesh, that is to say, over fear: fear of poverty, suffering, slander, sickness, loneliness, and death. There is no true piety without heroism. Heroism is the glorious and shining concentration of courage."

Yes, heroism is the triumph of the soul, because in it the forces of the body and the mind oppose the soul. In the true heroic struggle it is the soul, our religious "I," that takes the lead and wages the battle to the end. Heroism's only reward is the happiness that comes not from the body or the mind but from the sources of the soul. Without heroism the history of mankind would not have risen noticeably above that of the animals; the happiness of heroism is man's alone. It is the highest happiness, the sublime happiness, even when it does not rise to the heaven of ecstasy but manifests itself in the tough, patient battle of drab, everyday life. The everyday manifestation of heroism we ordinarily call courage, and courage is a good enough source of happiness in our battle through life's troubles; it gives us powers of resistance which are comforting and good to have.

How much happiness it gives to be a little brave in pain and suffering! How happy those are who have learned the knack, we might call it, of taking their fate calmly and composedly. If we could compute statistically the things in our life that have made us most unhappy, I believe that for most of us they would be the painful anticipation of the evil that may befall us or the way in which our imagination exaggerates the extent of our misfortunes. The way we react to the small fortunes and misfortunes

79

of daily life is, to be sure, a matter of temperament, but to take things calmly and to try to make the best of matters is a quality of character which we acquire with practice. This is actually how we can use our happiness-potential, put it to work as a counterforce when something unpleasant happens or we are exposed to pain. A happy person, one who has acquired happiness as a quality of character, can easily learn to use his reserve of happiness when misfortune comes. . . .

Shintoism, fascism, and nazism have tried to debase the ideal of heroism with their vulgar teaching of happiness in sacrificing life and blood for world domination. And the most despicable thing about the disease they have brought upon the world is their attempt to use even the powers of the soul in their struggle for world supremacy, through their religious proclamation of "blood and soil," and their idolatry of the warrior, the soldier. Heroism in the Nazi sense of the word has led millions of soldiers into death for an inhuman system, a psychopath's dream of becoming God. "Let us be cruel; let us learn to be cruel with a good conscience." That is heroism in fiendish distortion.

We Norwegians, through our historic evolution, had become a peaceful and "unheroic" people, deeply imbued with humanistic ideals of Christianity, but who nevertheless had to struggle with genuine heroism to keep alive in a hard country. It took us time to realize what the "heroism" proclaimed in Italy and Nazi Germany really meant. Even after two months of hopeless struggle against the Nazi invaders on the battlefield, many Norwegians could not realize that the occupation was anything but a brutal move in a ruthless war between two great powers. But when the Germans made it clear that this was no ordinary military occupation in keeping with international law but an attempt to force us to practice their form of heroism, we realized what was up. From that day the martyrdom of the Norwegian people began. And from that day we began to experience what real heroism meant.

Through my little window I can look out over an East Norwegian landscape. Forests stretch as far as the eye can see. There is a glimpse of the river here and there, of red barns and white dwelling houses on the big and little farms in the valley and in the clearings along the hillsides. I know that in this peaceful and beautiful country people are living in fear and suffering because of the "heroic" power that has conquered us. I know the details. I know where this one, and this one, and this one live, who do not know anything about the fate of father or brother in the claws of the Gestapo. And I know that the sufferings of these country people are mild in comparison with the things the people in the towns must endure, day in and day out.

But I also know that fear and unhappiness and disgrace are not the

80

only things that have forced their way into this peaceful countryside and into the entire country. Happiness also has come in, a strange and unknown happiness which very few can express but which all those feel who have kept their souls free from the poison of treason: the joy of battle, the happiness of suffering, the bliss of martyrdom, *the happiness of heroism arising from the depths of the soul.*

—GEORG BROCHMANN, 1894-

[73] Accepting the Universe

I SEE the Nature Providence going its impartial way. I see drought and flood, heat and cold, war and pestilence, defeat and death, besetting man at all times, in all lands. I see hostile germs in the air he breathes, in the water he drinks, in the soil he tills. I see the elemental forces as indifferent toward him as toward ants and fleas. I see pain and disease and defeat and failure dogging his footsteps. I see the righteous defeated and the ungodly triumphant—this and much more I see; and yet I behold through the immense biological vista behind us the race of man slowly, oh, so slowly! emerging from its brute or semi-human ancestry into the full estate of man, from blind instinct and savage passion into the light of reason and moral consciousness. I behold the great scheme of evolution unfolding despite all the delays and waste and failures, and the higher forms appearing upon the scene. I see on an immense scale, and as clearly as in a demonstration in a laboratory, that good comes out of evil; that the impartiality of the Nature Providence is best; that we are made strong by what we overcome; that man is man because he is as free to do evil as to do good; that life is as free to develop hostile forms as to develop friendly; that power waits upon him who earns it; that disease, wars, the unloosened, devastating elemental forces have each and all played their part in developing and hardening man and giving him the heroic fiber.

—JOHN BURROUGHS, 1837-1921

[74] Twelve Rules for Poise

First: Do the unpleasant task first. Constant use of this rule will strengthen our personalities, and make each difficult task we have to face easier. . . .

81

Second: Stick to the job you are doing until it is done. . . . There is the great reward of a feeling of satisfaction in having completed a task, and this satisfaction tends to strengthen the personality. It increases self-confidence, a very necessary attribute of living.

Third: Keep well rested and get adequate sleep. . . . The person who is not rested is easily aggravated, and small problems have a way of being magnified for him. All of us should give some attention to our sleep habits, and see that we are adequately preparing our bodies for the day ahead with sufficient rest.

Fourth: Be friendly with others. Go out of your way to be friendly. . . .

Fifth: Talk over your real troubles with someone in whom you have confidence. The purpose of this is mainly to help you get the proper perspective of these troubles. And the second purpose of such a conference is to keep you from bottling up the acid of worry and trouble inside yourself—for it is mightily corrosive, and an ulcer of the stomach is its mildest form of harm to you. It can warp and twist your whole outlook on life, and change your very way of living. . . .

Sixth: Do not go around looking for sympathy. The man who looks for sympathy is a negative personality, already full to overflowing of self-pity. And self-pity is a type of conceit, wherein the bearer believes himself more put upon than any other human being who ever existed. Personally, I like to remember the old Arabian proverb: "I felt sorry for myself because I had no shoes until I met the man who had no feet." . . .

Seventh: Forget your small troubles. In the fifth rule we spoke of talking over your real troubles with a trusted person. We here emphasize the word *real*. All other troubles should be forgotten. Usually a little reasoning will distinguish between a large and a small trouble, and then a direct act of the will can banish the small ones. . . .

Eighth: Look for the cheerful side of things. Keep a sense of humor. God has given us a great many things to enjoy in this world, and they all help us to get through life's rougher moments. . . .

Ninth: Think about something other than your own aches and pains. Pain is a strange thing. The more you think about it the more acute it gets. The more you think about other things, the less you feel the pain. . . .

Tenth: Try carrying your burdens on your own shoulders. . . .

Eleventh: Relax from time to time during the day. . . . To remain poised, you must be able to control the flow of energy. You must not dissipate energy when it isn't necessary, and you must be able to call on your body for extra energy when the occasion demands. . . .

Twelfth: Believe in yourself and in your life's work. . . . You have tremendous capabilities, but unless you believe in them, you will never

82

be able to use them. Don't lose your faith in yourself, for that faith has a creative power to transform your life into a career of such contribution that you will partake of the dignity of God.

—Preston Bradley, 1888-

[75] A Letter of Consolation

". . . we are soon to follow . . ."

Philadelphia, February 23, 1756.

I condole with you. We have lost a most dear and valuable relation. But it is the will of God and nature, that these mortal bodies be laid aside, when the soul is to enter into real life. This is rather an embryo state, a preparation for living.

A man is not completely born until he is dead. Why then should we grieve, that a new child is born among the immortals, a new member added to their happy society? We are spirits. That bodies should be lent us, while they can afford us pleasure, assist us in acquiring knowledge, or in doing good to our fellow creatures, is a kind and benevolent act of God. When they become unfit for these purposes, and afford us pain instead of pleasure, instead of an aid become an encumbrance, and answer none of the intentions for which they were given, it is equally kind and benevolent, that a way is provided by which we may get rid of them. Death is that way. We ourselves, in some cases, prudently choose a partial death. A mangled painful limb, which cannot be restored, we willingly cut off. He who plucks out a tooth, parts with it freely, since the pain goes with it; and he, who quits the whole body, parts at once with all pains and possibilities of pains and diseases which it was liable to, or capable of making him suffer.

Our friend and we were invited abroad on a party of pleasure, which is to last forever. His chair was ready first, and he is gone before us. We could not all conveniently start together; and why should you and I be grieved at this, since we are soon to follow, and know where to find him?

Adieu,

Benjamin Franklin, 1706-1790

[76] Let the Church Adventure

WHATEVER else may be the character of the redemptive society which the crisis of our time demands, it is at least clear that the society must make the habit of adventure central to its life. If this were done, vast changes might come quickly. Just as Wesley's class meetings were markedly different from what has been seen before in the religious life of England, so we may need to produce fellowships markedly different from what has been seen before in the religious life of America. It may be that the church of tomorrow will be as different from the church of today as a modern transport plane is different from the little machine the Wright brothers flew at Kitty Hawk. It should not be forgotten that the Christian religion began as such an adventure in fellowship, the members often meeting in synagogues, but introducing real novelty into the association as their needs became clear. One important innovation was the regular communal meal, with the use of ordinary food. It would not be false to say that their central room was a dining room. It is conceivable that ours should be the same. In any case, those who break bread together have a basis of genuine fellowship and the sad fact is that this is what so many organizations now lack. . . .

We must rid our minds of most current conceptions about what a church should be in order to try to see what the real needs of men are. Perhaps there ought not to be any distinction at all between clergy and laity; perhaps the life of the church should function better without the ownership of buildings or any property. Many of the early Christian groups met in homes and several met in caves, while some of the seventeenth-century Quaker meetings were held in prison. Perhaps real membership should be rigorously restricted to the deeply convinced; perhaps the normal unit should be the small cell rather than the large gathering. Many churches would be ten times as influential if their membership were half as great.

—ELTON TRUEBLOOD, 1900-

[77] All Is Darkness

"All is darkness."

3rd Aug. 98

My dear Garnett
    I am not dead tho' only half alive. Very soon I shall send you some

84

Ms. I am writing hopelessly—but still I am writing. How I feel I cannot express. Pages accumulate and the story stands still.

I feel suicidal.

Drop me a line and tell me when and how you are. If you could come down it would be an act of real friendship and also of charity.

My kind regards and Jessie's love to your wife: Jess is knocked up with the boy's teething performances. He has (and she has also) a rough time of it.

I am afraid there's something wrong with my thinking apparatus. I am utterly out of touch with my work—and I can't get in touch. All is darkness.

Ever yours
JOSEPH CONRAD, 1857-1924

[78] Meditations from Walden

1. PUT FOUNDATIONS UNDER CASTLES

I LEARNED this, at least, by my experiment: that if one advances confidently in the direction of his dreams, and endeavors to live the life which he has imagined, he will meet with a success unexpected in common hours. . . . In proportion as he simplifies his life, the laws of the universe will appear less complex, and solitude will not be solitude, nor poverty poverty, nor weakness weakness. If you have built castles in the air, your work need not be lost; that is where they should be. Now put foundations under them.

2. WHY FEEL LONELY?

Men frequently say to me, "I should think you would feel lonesome down there, and want to be nearer to folks, rainy and snowy days and nights especially." I am tempted to reply to such,—This whole earth which we inhabit is but a point in space. How far apart, think you, dwell the two most distant inhabitants of yonder star, the breadth of whose disk cannot be appreciated by our instruments? Why should I feel lonely? is not our planet in the Milky Way? This which you put seems to me not to be the most important question. What sort of space is that which separates a man from his fellows and makes him solitary? I have found that no exertion of the legs can bring two minds much nearer to one another. What do we want most to dwell near to? Not to many men surely, the depot, the post-office, the bar-room, the meeting-house, the school-house, the grocery, Beacon Hill, or the Five Points, where men most congregate, but to the perennial source of our life, whence in all our experience we have found that to issue, as the willow stands near the water and sends out its roots in that direction. This will vary with different natures, but this is the place where a wise man will dig his cellar.

—HENRY DAVID THOREAU, 1817-1862

[79] A Letter to His Students

". . . the pride of my life and delight of my existence."

Cambridge, Apr. 6, 1896.

Dear Young Ladies,—I am deeply touched by your remembrance. It is the first time anyone ever treated me so kindly, so you may well believe that the impression on the heart of the lonely sufferer will be even more durable than the impression on your minds of all the teachings of Philosophy 2A. I now perceive one immense omission in my Psychology— the deepest principle of Human Nature is the craving to be appreciated, and I left it out altogether from the book, because I had never had it gratified till now. I fear you have let loose a demon in me, and that all my actions will now be for the sake of such rewards. However, I will try to be faithful to this one unique and beautiful azalea tree, the pride of my life and delight of my existence. Winter and summer will I tend and water it—even with my tears. Mrs. James shall never go near it or touch it. If it dies, I will die too; and if I die, it shall be planted on my grave.

Don't take all this too jocosely, but believe in the extreme pleasure you have caused me, and in the affectionate feelings with which I am and shall always be faithfully your friend,

—WILLIAM JAMES, 1842-1910

[80] Real Peace Comes from Struggle

I AM finding that life here [at the South Pole] has become largely a life of the mind. Unhurried reflection is a sort of companion. Yes, solitude is greater than I anticipated. My sense of values is changing, and many things which before were in solution in my mind now seem to be crystallizing. I am better able to tell what in the world is wheat for me and what is chaff. In fact, my definition of success itself is changing. Just lately my views about man and his place in the cosmic scheme have begun to run something like this:

The human race, my intuition tells me, is not outside the cosmic process and is not an accident. It is as much a part of the universe as the trees, the mountains, the aurora, and the stars. My reason approves this; and the findings of science, as I see them, point in the same direction. And, since man is a part of the cosmos and subject to its laws, I see no reason to doubt that these same natural laws operate in the psychological as well as in the physical sphere and that their operation is manifest in the working of the consciousness. . . .

Therefore, the things that mankind has tested and found right make for harmony and progress—or peace; and the things it has found wrong hinder progress and make for discord. . . . But the peace I describe is not passive. It must be won. Real peace comes from struggle that involves such things as effort, discipline, enthusiasm. This is also the way to strength. An inactive peace may lead to sensuality and flabbiness, which are discordant. It is often necessary to fight to lessen discord. This is the paradox.

When a man achieves a fair measure of harmony within himself and his family circle, he achieves peace; and a nation made up of such individuals and groups is a happy nation. As the harmony of a star in its course is expressed by rhythm and grace, so the harmony of a man's life-course is expressed by happiness; this, I believe, is the prime desire of mankind.

—RICHARD E. BYRD, 1888-1957

[81] Faith or Despair? Yours to Choose

THE way a person nourishes himself as a religious creature makes a tremendous difference regarding his feeling of a total life purpose. Not many months ago I received a letter from a person who had lost the verve of religion. The note contained these tragic words: "I would rather be dead than live as I am. I feel like ending it all—and this is the way I have felt for a year."

The same day I was visited by a rabbi friend who had started in an American city a new congregation with twenty-five families. He had left one of America's richest and finest synagogues to start this new venture. The first services were held in an abandoned night club. Seven hundred invitations were sent to prospective families in the neighborhood of the night club; an excellent cantor was paid $1,500 for the holidays, and $5,000 was underwritten for other music. At the third service those who shared the venture with this rabbi pledged $14,000. The first year $32,000 was received and spent for the religious program; today this rabbi is building a beautiful temple for the congregation. He said to me as he told me about his experience, "This to me was a great venture of faith, in which I expected great things from God and those consecrated to his purpose."

It seems as though God does have an uncanny way to help persons who take themselves seriously as religious creatures.

[82] Retain the Mystery in Christianity

CHRISTIANITY is a religion which one should hold with awe and mystery. Shirley Jackson Case speaks about the mystery of Jesus: "Jesus is the enigma of the centuries. What to make of him has been a puzzle [or a mystery] to both saints and skeptics." In similar language the writer of Ephesians says of his letter: "When you read this you can perceive . . . the mystery of Christ." In like fashion the Gospel of Mark speaks about the mystery of the kingdom of God which can be understood only by those who experience it (Mark 4:11); Paul speaks about the mystery of the salvation of the whole world through the Christian faith (Rom. 11:25); I Timothy indicates that deacons "must hold the mystery of faith with a clear conscience" (I Tim. 3:9). Paul also looks upon evil as the result of "the mystery of lawlessness . . . at work" (II Thess. 2:7). It is only the proud man who feels that human reason can corral all of religion in little man-made creeds; the humble person with his continuous note of wonder feels the mystery of the atom, the star, God, Jesus Christ.

[83] Seven Wonders of the World

As magnificent as the ancient seven wonders of the world were, how imperfect they seem when compared with seven modern wonders of the world created by God: (1) the Jungfrau, towering 13,669 feet, near

Interlaken, Switzerland; (2) the Grand Canyon of the Colorado, 200 miles in length, with a depth of 2,000 to 6,000 feet; (3) the atom with its tremendous possibilities to re-create (or destroy) the story of mankind; (4) the Milky Way, or Galaxy, appearing as a wreath of hazy light in its many light-years from this planet, yet a system of stars of which our earth is one; (5) a sunset viewed on a fall day when autumn leaves shed myriad colors; (6) the surging ocean on a starlit night, as one contemplates its mysterious depth and energy; (7) the tender flower in the crannied wall, about which Tennyson pondered:

> Little flower—but if I could understand
> What you are, root and all, and all in all,
> I should know what God and man is.

[84] The Idea of the Holy

To speak of God as "holy" means that he is perfectly good. But it means more than this. It signifies that God is so infinite and eternal, so powerful and wonderful, that man can never by reason capture God's infinite greatness as the life of the universe in a creed, formula, or definition. He can understand God's holiness only as he in his creature-like humility "feels" by contrast God's greatness and goodness. A person who took an imaginary astronomical trip into the universe began to understand God's holiness. After he had traveled 35,000,000 miles, he came to Mars; at 750,000,000 miles from the earth he arrived at Saturn; when he had gone 2,500,000,000 miles, he arrived at Neptune; and at 25,000,000,000 miles he reached Alpha Centauri. There he was told that if he traveled back to the earth at 2,200 feet per second, it would take him one and one-half million years to arrive home. He was further informed that, although Alpha Centauri is but 4.4 light-years away from this planet, the universe can be measured in terms of two billion light years! Seeing God as the Life of this immense universe, he then began to understand what God's holiness really means!

[85] How Is Your Mental Health?

SOME of us need to be alone in order to give ourselves a test in mental health. The Illinois Society for Mental Health prepared a series of questions entitled "How Is Your Mental Health?": (1) Does worry interfere with all you do, or do you let little things pass without being anxious about them? (2) Do you run away from hard tasks, or do you like to tackle difficult responsibilities? (3) Do you make excuses for yourself, or are you willing to admit your mistakes and to laugh at them? (4) Do you feel that you are always right and cannot see others' viewpoints, or are you tolerant with other people? (5) Do you lack faith in yourself, or do you have a quiet confidence in what you do? (6) Do you fly into fits of temper and go around with chips on your shoulder, or do you control your emotions? (7) Do you avoid people, or do you enjoy meeting people and helping them? (8) Do you have no aim in life, or do you feel that you are trying to achieve some goal? After pondering these questions in solitariness, a person should ask of himself, "How do I rate?"

[86] Religion Is Solitariness

RELIGION is what the individual does with his own solitariness. It runs through three stages, if it evolves to its final satisfaction. It is the transition from God the void to God the enemy, and from God the enemy to God the companion. Thus religion is solitariness; and if you are never solitary, you are never religious. Collective enthusiasms, revivals, institutions, churches, rituals, bibles, codes of behaviour, are the trappings of religion, are its passing forms. They may be useful, or harmful; they may be authoritatively ordained, or merely temporal expedients. But the end of religion is beyond all this. Accordingly, what should emerge from religion is individual worth of character.

—ALFRED NORTH WHITEHEAD, 1861-1947

[87] Living—Without Being Alive

I WAS tired in the head and in the spirit. Now I think it came partly from never being alone, because in the world in which I lived nobody ever seemed to want to be alone. They seemed to have a terror of it. They all wanted to lunch together, or play golf together, or go to the country club or women's clubs together, or meet in the hotel bar or in the corner drugstore to kill time over the pinball machines. On their tombstone will

90

be written, "He lived without ever being alive. Nothing ever happened to him." [Mr. Smith]

—LOUIS BROMFIELD, 1896-1957

[88] Our Elder Brother in Suffering

AT first the whole world was shaken beneath my feet. Then slowly a few simplicities came steadily before me. God's existence never wavered in my thought. His nature of Fatherhood stood steadfast. I could not cry out against him for I realized I thought him powerless without us. I seemed to sense his tears as real as my own, and to hear his cry as poignantly as that of the boy's mother. A God who works under law and plays no favorites became the center of the universe. My philosophy of history never faltered. . . . One comes to feel that God is above and in all things, working with his universe and his people toward the final goal. History lightens up with the glow from spirits who are immortal and into whose company Bray [his son] now has entered. Deep peace comes with the thought of the struggling millions whose lives are lifted a little by the tragedy of war. Moral vigor enters to defeat the continuing selfishness and to urge us to continue in our work. Christ seems in honest truth to be the Elder Brother of our suffering.

—EDWIN P. BOOTH, 1898-

[89] The Great Event at the Goethe Bicentennial

SOME time ago when my mind went out to Aspen, Colorado, in that little town, a group were celebrating the Goethe Bicentennial. They were celebrating it because Goethe was one of the great universalists who sought reality in the farthest reaches of his imagination. He was the great man to be remembered, and so they asked great men to come and help us to remember him. There were great philosophers and great educators, great poets and great novelists. But something strange happened. The great men they brought there, and even Goethe who was to be remembered, sank into the background. The great thing which happened at Aspen was Albert Schweitzer! The cynical Goethe would have smiled at that. Here was a medical missionary from Equatorial Africa. The

91

gentlemen of the press called him the greatest missionary who ever lived. They spoke of him as a lion who laughs. They referred to him as the thirteenth disciple. They made much of the fact that he is the only man who ever earned a doctorate in medicine and music and philosophy and theology. The reporters assigned to Aspen vied with one another in finding words which would describe the greatness of this man. So much so that they finally lost their sense of proportion and spoke of him as monolith. Now, I am not convinced that Albert Schweitzer is the greatest missionary who ever lived; he is probably the most versatile. But that is immaterial. Why was he so great at Aspen? Because he stands for the only things that really have value in life: a dedication, a surrender of self, a forgetting of one's personal well-being, a trying to lift the lowest to the highest level possible, healing somebody's wounds, pushing someone's horizon of hope farther out. And so the missionary who lost himself in the jungle becomes the greatest thing in our modern day.

—ARNOLD HILMAR LOWE, 1888-

[90] If I Read a Book

". . . no fire can ever warm me . . ."

August 1870

TRUTH is such a rare thing, it is delightful to tell it.

I find ecstasy in living; the mere sense of living is joy enough.

How do most people live without any thoughts? There are many people in the world,—you must have noticed them in the street,—how do they live? How do they get strength to put on their clothes in the morning?

If I read a book and it makes my whole body so cold no fire can ever warm me, I know that is poetry. If I feel physically as if the top of my head were taken off, I know that is poetry. These are the only ways I know it. Is there any other way?

—EMILY DICKINSON, 1830-1886

[91] These People Are the Christians

THE scene is a garden in Carthage, North Africa. It is the middle of the third century of the Christian Era and a middle-aged man, Cyprian by name, is writing to his friend Donatus. This is what he says:

This seems a cheerful world, Donatus, when I view it from this fair garden under the shadow of these vines. But if I climbed some great mountain and looked out over the wide lands you know very well what I would see. Brigands on the high roads, pirates on the seas, in the amphitheatres men murdered to please applauding crowds, under all roofs misery and selfishness. It is really a bad world, Donatus, an incredibly bad world. Yet in the midst of it I have found a quiet and holy people. They have discovered a joy which is a thousand times better than any pleasure of this sinful life. They are despised and persecuted but they care not. They have overcome the world. These people, Donatus, are the Christians—and I am one of them.

[92] Dreams of an Astronomer

A FEW years ago I read *Dreams of an Astronomer* by Camille Flammarion, in which he tells of going to Mars (35,000,000 miles away), and then to Neptune (2,500,000,000 miles away), then to the nearest light-star, Alpha Centauri (25,000,000,000 miles away), and then out into infinite space, on and on and on, where he finally learned that our little second-rate planet, related to a second-rate sun, is but a tiny room in a solar mansion. Then as I thought of God's Spirit as related to every area in this infinite universe, the littleness of myself overwhelmed me. I felt my humility.

[93] These I Love

TIME was, in my youth, when a man would add up the things he had to be thankful for, and ask for more. The year was 1914 and the man I am thinking of, Rupert Brooke—a poet much quoted after his death, but now in eclipse. Brooke was the most glamorous of the Georgian poets, and his self-aware, self-examining mind had the gift of embellishing things. His poem, "The Great Lover," identified for others the beauties of an unbelligerent world, and the most evocative lines in it begin with

93

> These I have loved:
>   White plates and cups, clean-gleaming,
> Ringed with blue lines; and feathery, faëry dust;
> Wet roofs, beneath the lamp-light; the strong crust
> Of friendly bread; and manytasting food;
> Rainbows; and the blue bitter smoke of wood.

His catalogue of delight ends with these lines:

> Sleep; and high places; footprints in the dew;
> And oaks; and brown horse-chestnuts, glossy-new;
> And new-peeled sticks; and shining pools on grass;—
> And these have been my loves. And these shall pass.

I love big family gatherings, and the banter, the candor, and the woman's sympathy (whether the mother's, the aunt's, or the older sister's) which bring children to self-confidence.

I love American distance: the wild untapped areas you look down upon from the Smokies or the Shenandoahs, from the plane spanning Maine, or Utah, the Texas plains, or the conifer forests of the Northwest. As you look, you feel the immensity of a growing country.

I love water, not only "the benison of hot water," as Rupert Brooke wrote; I mean water in brooks and salmon rivers, in the cresting surf of Barnegat, Monomoy, or Plum Island.

Of trees I love the beech, the elm, and the oak—the beech for its leafy umbrageous shadow, the elm for grace, the oak for strength; in spring the dogwood, in October the swamp maple and sumac whose blaze lights up New England.

I love the American humor of John Mason Brown, of Fred Allen, E. B. White, and James Thurber.

I love dogs—the mad circles of infatuation a young dog will cut around you on a morning walk, and the paw and muzzle on knee at day's end.

I love the Brahms Fourth, the Schubert "Unfinished," Tchaikovsky's Fifth, the César Franck—and if I had one long-playing record between me and final silence, the last movement of Beethoven's Ninth.

I love quiet—so quiet that you do not look up from your book until the log in the open fire falls apart. So I love the Sabbath, as a time to clear the mind of worries and collect one's thoughts. Sunday is the great restorer; we need such respite, and the best of the year is ahead in those twelve days from Christmas to Twelfth Night.

—EDWARD WEEKS, 1898-

[94] Queen Once More

DARK years came. Years of failure, of sheer disaster, when everything went wrong. Like all the Barrymores, she had no sense of any kind about money, which should grow on trees. Her plays failed. There were suits for bills, bitter humiliations in ridiculous stories in the newspapers, the tragedy of Jack's marriages, and Lionel's ill health—and her own.

She went into exile, like many a queen before her. And came back. Came back to greater triumph than she had ever known, as the old lady in *Whiteoaks*, as the schoolteacher in *The Corn Is Green*, until now she sits once more firmly upon her throne. . . .

I asked her if she could give me the reason for it all, the simplest rule of her own philosophy worked out through such a life.

"I'm not much good at that," Ethel Barrymore said, almost shyly. "But I'll try. You must learn above all not to waste your soul and energy and brain and strength upon all the little things. It takes a long time to learn that, because gnats are annoying. . . . You must learn day by day, year by year, to broaden your horizon. The more things you love, the more you are interested in, the more you enjoy, the more you are indignant about—the more you have left when anything happens."

She was silent a moment and I knew she had forgotten me altogether.

"I suppose the greatest thing in the world is loving people and—and wanting to destroy the sin but not the sinner. And not to forget that when life knocks you to your knees, which it always does and always will— well, that's the best position in which to pray, isn't it? On your knees. That's where I learned."

Then, being Ethel Barrymore, she twinkled suddenly and said, "You grow up the day you have the first real laugh—at yourself. Sometimes it takes a while, but you have to keep trying."

—ADELA ROGERS ST. JOHN, Twentieth Century

[95] What Is an Aristocrat?

ITS first and most salient character is interior security, and the chief visible evidence of that security is the freedom that goes with it—not only freedom to act . . . but also and more importantly freedom in thought, in liberty to try and err, the right to be his own man. It is the instinct of a true aristocracy, not to punish eccentricity by expulsion, but to throw the mantle of protection about it. . . . An aristocracy is the custodian of the qualities that make for change and experiment; it is the class that organizes danger to the service of the race; it pays for its high prerogatives by standing in the forefront of the fray.

—HENRY L. MENCKEN, 1880-1957

[96] Aids in Rufus Jones' Maturing

IN my senior year, in connection with my course in philosophy, Professor Pliny Chase suggested to me that I should read all of Emerson's essays. When I came upon the essay on "The Over-Soul" it was an epoch moment in my life. It sent me at once to Cooke's *Life and Thought of Emerson* to discover the sources of Emerson's thought, and here I came upon Plotinus and Proclus, Jacob Boehme, and George Fox—freshly interpreted— and the mystical contribution of the Orient. It threw open the windows of my soul. My beloved professor helped me to appraise what I had discovered. He suggested that I should make a study of mysticism, and write my thesis in that field. That sent me to *Vaughan's Hours with the Mystics*. With that inadequate guide I came into friendly relations with the great mystics of the ages, and a whole new world opened overhead. . . . I knew now that "bond unknown to me was given," that henceforth I was to be an interpreter of this religion of the inward way.

As soon as I could arrange for it—a year after graduation—I went abroad to master French and German, which would be essential for my work of research, and I visited some of the leading authorities on the history of mysticism. The most significant of my contacts were those with Paul Sabatier, the biographer of St. Francis of Assisi, and with Carl Schmidt of Strasbourg, who was then the leading interpreter of the Friends of God of the fourteenth century. I started at once to get the philosophical and psychological preparation for an adequate treatment of the approach to mystical experience. Eventually I worked with some of the most stimulating thinkers in the University of Heidelberg, Oxford University, and Harvard, and I got into correspondence or personal relations with students of mysticism wherever I heard of any.

I had had, during my first period abroad, my own experience to guide me. Alone on a solitary walk, near Dieu-le-fit, in the foothills of the Alps, I had felt the walls grow thin between the visible and the invisible and there came a sudden flash of eternity, breaking in on me. I kneeled down then and there in that forest glade, in sight of the mountains, and dedicated myself in the hush and silence, but in the presence of an invading Life, to the work of interpreting the deeper nature of the soul and its direct mystical relation to God.

A new epoch opened to me in 1897. I was on a walking tour that summer in Switzerland with Dr. Rendel Harris. At Murren I met John Wilhelm Rowntree of York, England, a highly gifted young Quaker of unique leadership, who had himself had an extraordinary mystical experience. We climbed the Schilthorn and we formed that day a spiritual partnership of great significance. He was planning an extensive history of the Society of Friends, and I was to write the history of the mystical movements which in some sense formed the background of the Quaker movement.

For the next eight years we met frequently and were in constant correspondence about our projects. In 1905, he died and left us bereft of his remarkable leadership. His father, Joseph Rowntree, urged me to undertake the editorial direction of the Quaker history as well as the history of mysticism. He put at my disposal a fund for the purchase of books on mysticism, and for travel, and during the next sixteen years William Charles Braithwaite and I produced the seven volumes of the Rowntree Histories, of which I wrote five, including *Studies in Mystical Religion,* and *Spiritual Reformers in the Sixteenth and Seventeenth Centuries,* and introductions to all the volumes.

I have, during these fifty creative years, been interpreting in volume after volume the nature and the significance of the mystical approach to religion, and what is hardly less important, I have been interpreting during this period what seems to me to be a religion of reality and power to vast numbers of students in American universities and colleges and to universities in most other countries of the world. Meanwhile my major business in the world has been teaching psychology, philosophy, and ethics, and the principles of life to the succession of students in Haverford College.

But I have always known what William James called "a religion of veracity rooted in spiritual inwardness" is only a half-religion. It is like a concave, without the convex, side of a curve. An authentic religion must express itself in constructive outwardness as well as being rooted in spiritual inwardness. That has always been implied in my dynamic faith. But that faith did not emerge in adequate action until 1917, when I became one of the creators and the chairman of the American Friends Service Committee, which now for thirty years has undertaken the burden of the world's suffering in stricken areas around the globe.

—RUFUS M. JONES, 1863-1948

97

[97] The Human Side of Gandhi

MANY years ago I had been deeply impressed by the insight of the great writer Romain Rolland, who had described Mahatma Gandhi as the "St. Paul of our own days." This seemed to me to contain an important truth; for Gandhi, like Paul, comes clearly under the category of the twice-born among men of religion. He experienced at a special moment in his life that tremendous convulsion of the human spirit, which we call "conversion." In his early days he had followed a career at the Bar as a lawyer with great ardor. Success had been a main ambition—success in his profession; success in life as a man; and deeper down in his heart, success as a national leader.

He had gone out to South Africa on a business visit to act as a lawyer in an important trial, wherein two Indian merchants were engaged in litigation. Hitherto, he had only a distant knowledge of the color bar and had never considered what it might mean to himself if he was personally attacked and insulted. But as he journeyed from Durban and reached Maritzburg this dreadful experience came to him suddenly in all its cruel nakedness. He was thrown out of his compartment by the railway official, though he carried a first-class ticket; and the mail train went on without him. It was late at night and he was in an utterly strange railway station, knowing no one. There, all night long, as he sat shivering with cold, after enduring this insult, he wrestled within himself, whether to take the next steamer back to India, or to go through to the bitter end, suffering what his own people had to suffer. Before the morning the light came to his soul. He determined by God's grace to play the man. More humiliations were soon to be heaped upon him of the same character and in South Africa he was never without them. But he had put his hand to the plough and he would never turn back.

I heard him tell the story of that night to Dr. Mott last November. He made clear, as he told it, that this was the turning point from which his own new life began.

—CHARLES F. ANDREWS, 1871-1940

[98] An Initial Impression of Gandhi

I HAVE often been asked to describe my initial impression of Gandhi. I do not find this question hard to answer. It centered, first of all, in my somewhat amusing recognition of the fact that he looked exactly like the photographs and cartoons that I have seen of him in recent years. In one way, this was inevitable, so distinctive were the characteristics of his personality. In another way, this was remarkable, so difficult was it to get Gandhi before a camera or drawing board. I suppose I have seen hundreds of his pictures, but I find it hard to remember one for which the Mahatma had made a deliberate pose. My second and strangely simultaneous impression was of the infinite grace and charm of Gandhi, who, in his physical appearance, was so awkward. Thus, everybody who entered this little room in which we stood, was in one way or another, under strain, and thus uneasy. The officials present were anxious that there should be no error or mischance in the proceedings of the occasion. Journalists were eager to get their stories, photographers their pictures, each one his own and thus original. Friends were embarrassed by the difficulties of getting at their beloved Mahatma, and paying him the attention and protection which a tired man would welcome. Some few persons, like myself, were frankly frightened—this stupendous personal experience was too much for our equanimity and courage! But all these varied reactions speedily vanished, like the morning mist, before Gandhi's easy grace.

—JOHN HAYNES HOLMES, 1879-

[99] Secrets for Spiritual Growth

I HAVE lived seventy-one years. I do not recall my birth by incident, but I do believe that providential blessing was bestowed upon me when I came to be the fifteenth child of my devoted parents. Before I came into the world, I was given an unusual advantage. My mother was a consecrated, clear-thinking, careful woman, and my father was a principled man with more than average devotion to his family and to the best that he knew. I was loved before I came into being, and I have treasured this heritage of love and have made it the foundation of my life. It seems to me that from the very beginning I have practiced the affirmation of my devotion to love of humanity, and I have precious contentment in my realization of God as my spiritual Father. . . .

Early in my childhood, my mother taught me to hold the little New Testament, which the minister brought around, and to sit quietly in communion with it and God, even before I could read. My tongue was ready to recite the 23rd Psalm and other precious passages from the written page, when once my intellect was prepared to meet the yearnings of my heart—to read the Scriptures. The *word* had been hidden in my heart by that knowing which is not literacy, but which is so basic to literacy. As we sing the beautiful spirituals and remember that they flowed from unlearned hearts, we can appreciate more deeply how their social significance is interwoven with their spiritual understandings. Our forefathers had been freed from the yoke of bondage about twelve years when I was born. My early heritage was the spirit of fight and determination which had helped my parents and others to fight for freedom, and which was during my childhood helping them to build security for their children. My dear old grandmother told me the stories because she thought I would understand, and hold the idea until I was mature enough to do something about it. When our fathers sang—

Nobody knows the trouble I see

they did not stop on a note of complaint. They burst forth immediately with "Glory Hallelujah." That is definitely a part of my spirit. To be sure I have seen trouble, I have had difficulty, the way has not been easy . . . but I have thanked God and said, "Glory Hallelujah!"

—MARY McLEOD BETHUNE, 1875-

[100] Faith Stimulated by a Praying Mother

I CAN remember when I longed to know the inner voice and searched my mind for an answer to its meaning. It came about in the late hours of those nights when I listened to my mother. She held her lonely vigils when she thought everyone in the house was asleep. There she was in the dark, on her knees. I knew the form, sometimes silhouetted by the moonlight which poured in upon her kneeling there—sometimes beside her bed, sometimes beside a chair. She would ask God for faith, for strength, for love, for forgiveness, for knowledge, for food and clothing—not for herself but for her children, and for all the poor people. I gained faith in her way, when I saw these things she prayed for coming to pass. Many a poor man left our home happy because Mother and Father had given some simple thing that met his need. Many were the times that our little family was happy when a gift of something we needed came almost miraculously. And my mother's "Thank you, Father," made me realize—early in life—that all things must come from God. I began to see that the full life must be mine only as I learned to live close to God and to trust Him always. I thank my mother and my heavenly Father for imparting to me this strength and vitality which has

100

led me from that picture in the closed hours of those nights to the light of this full new day, when I am enjoying the fruits of that first seed-sowing. The desire for spiritual start in living grew on me, and I know today that effectual fervent desire does not go unrewarded.

—MARY MCLEOD BETHUNE, 1875-

[101] Expect the Best

MY spiritual philosophy provides a full life for me. I give my best at all times and accept without complaint the results. I expect the best. Life is full and joyous and after three-score years and ten, I know the secret of peaceful living. I am not waiting for peace and happiness to come to me in another world. I am enjoying it here day by day. Because of this growing, giving, learning experience, I believe that I shall have greater capacity for receiving when I shall see Him Who is the foundation of for my life. We hear much about "readiness" today in the field of education; readiness to read, readiness to act; readiness to learn. I am in a state of spiritual readiness at all times. I am ready to read the signs of the times and interpret them for my people, for the world. I am ready to act with faith and love and wisdom for justice and progress and peace. I am ready to keep an open mind—to follow the guides toward upward trends and forward progress which will make our world the *one great world*—a world where all men are brothers.

—MARY MCLEOD BETHUNE, 1875-

[102] On the Uses of Philosophy

THERE is a pleasure in philosophy, and a lure even in the mirages of metaphysics, which every student feels until the coarse necessities of physical existence drag him from the heights of thought into the mart of economic strife and gain. Most of us have known some golden days in the June of life when philosophy was in fact what Plato calls it, "that dear delight"; when the love of a modestly elusive Truth seemed more glorious, incomparably, than the lust for the ways of the flesh and the dross of the world. And there is always some wistful remnant in us of that early wooing of wisdom. "Life has meaning," we feel with Browning —"to find its meaning is my meat and drink." So much of our lives is meaningless, a self-cancelling vacillation and futility; we strive with the chaos about us and within; but we would believe all the while that there is something vital and significant in us, could we but decipher our souls. We want to understand; "life means for us constantly to transform into light and flame all that we are or meet with" [Nietzsche]; we are like Mitya in *The Brothers Karamazov*—"one of those who don't want millions, but an answer to their questions"; we want to seize the value and perspective of passing things, and so to pull ourselves up out of the maelstrom of daily circumstance. We want to know that the little things are little, and the big things big, before it is too late; we want to see things now as they will seem forever—"in the light of eternity." We want to learn to laugh in the face of the inevitable, to smile even at the looming of death. We want to be whole, to coordinate our energies by criticising and harmonizing our desires; for coordinated energy is the last word in ethics and politics, and perhaps in logic and metaphysics. "To be a philosopher," said Thoreau, "is not merely to have subtle thoughts, nor even to found a school, but so to love wisdom as to live, according to its dictates, a life of simplicity, independence, magnanimity, and trust." We may be sure that if we can but find wisdom, all things else will be added unto us. "Seek ye first the good things of the mind," Bacon admonishes us, "and the rest will either be supplied or its loss will not be felt." Truth will not make us rich, but it will make us free.

—WILL DURANT, 1885-

[103] Lincoln Writes to Mrs. Bixby

". . . how weak and fruitless must be any word of mine . . ."

Executive Mansion
Washington, Nov. 21, 1864

To Mrs. Bixby, Boston, Mass.

DEAR MADAM,

I have been shown in the files of the War Department a statement of the Adjutant General of Massachusetts that you are the mother of five sons who have died gloriously on the field of battle. I feel how weak and fruitless must be any word of mine which should attempt to beguile you from the grief of a loss so overwhelming. But I cannot refrain from ten-

dering you the consolation that may be found in the thanks of the republic they died to save. I pray that our Heavenly Father may assuage the
anguish of your bereavement, and leave you only the cherished memory
of the loved and lost, and the solemn pride that must be yours to have
laid so costly a sacrifice upon the altar of freedom.

Yours very sincerely and respectfully,
—A. LINCOLN, 1809-1865

[104] Lindbergh Lands at Le Bourget, May 21, 1927

IN spite of my speed, the *Spirit of St. Louis* seems about to stall. My lack
of feel alarms me. I've never tried to land a plane without feel before.
I want to open the throttle wider, to glide faster, to tauten the controls
still more. But—I glance at the dial—the needle points to eighty miles an
hour. The *Spirit of St. Louis* is lightly loaded, with most of its fuel gone.
Even at this speed I'll overshoot the lighted area before my tail skid
strikes the ground. No, I'll have to pull the nose higher instead of pushing it down. I'll have to depend on the needle, on judgment more than
instinct. I kick rudder and push the stick to one side, just to be sure—
yes, controls are taut, there's plenty of speed. And feeling is not completely gone. I still have a little left. I can feel the skid and slip. But the
edge of perception is dull, very dull. It's better to come in fast, even if I
roll into that black area after I land. And it's better to come in high—
there may be poles or chimneys at the field's edge—Never depend on
obstruction lights—especially when you don't see any.

It's only a hundred yards to the hangars now—solid forms emerging
from the night. I'm too high—too fast. Drop wing—left rudder—sideslip
—Careful—mustn't get anywhere near the stall. I've never landed the
Spirit of St. Louis at night before. It would be better to come in straight.
But if I don't sideslip, I'll be too high over the boundary to touch my
wheels in the area of light. That would mean circling again—Still too
high. I push the stick over to a steeper slip, leaving the nose well down—
Below the hangar roofs now—straighten out—A short burst of the
engine—Over the lighted area—Sod coming up to meet me—Deceptive
high lights and shadows—Careful—easy to bounce when you're tired—
Still too fast—Tail too high—Hold off—Hold off—But the lights are far
behind—The surface dims—Texture of sod is gone—Ahead, there's nothing but night—Give her the gun and climb for another try?—The wheels
touch gently—off again—No, I'll keep contact—Ease the stick forward—

Back on the ground—Off—Back—the tail skid too—Not a bad landing, but I'm beyond the light—can't see anything ahead—Like flying in fog —Ground loop?—No, still rolling too fast—might blow a tire—the field *must* be clear—Uncomfortable though, jolting into blackness—Wish I had a wing light—but too heavy on the take-off—Slower, now—slow enough to ground loop safely—left rudder—reverse it—stick over the other way—The *Spirit of St. Louis* swings around and stops rolling, resting on the solidness of earth, in the center of *Le Bourget*.

I start to taxi back toward the floodlights and hangars—But the entire field ahead is covered with running figures!

—Charles A. Lindbergh, 1902-

[105] Use Your Eyes

I who am blind can give one hint to those who see—one admonition to those who would make full use of the gift of sight: Use your eyes as if tomorrow you would be stricken blind. And the same method can be applied to the other senses. Hear the music of voices, the song of a bird, the mighty strains of an orchestra, as if you would be stricken deaf tomorrow. Touch each object you want to touch as if tomorrow your tactile sense would fail. Smell the perfume of flowers, taste with relish each morsel, as if tomorrow you could never smell and taste again. Make the most of every sense; glory in all the facets of pleasure and beauty which the world reveals to you through the several means of contact which Nature provides. But of all the senses, sight must be the delightful.

—Helen Keller, 1880-

[106] Death Be Not Proud

The next morning the boys assembled early for the quarter-mile walk to the white-frame Deerfield church, arranging themselves four abreast in order of their height. I did not think Johnny could manage such a march. He shook us off and disappeared. The procedure is that the boys, reaching the church, line up behind the pews, and then walk one by one down the center aisle, as each name is called. Mr. Flynt, the president of the board of trustees, then shakes hands with each boy, giving him his diploma in the left hand. We explained that Johnny might not be able to grasp the smooth roll of diploma with his left fingers, and asked Mr. Flynt to try to slip it into his right hand instead. The boys began to march in slowly, and though Johnny should have been conspicuous with his white bandage, we did not see him and I was in an agony fearing that he had fallen out. Mr. Boyden, sweeping the assembly with his all-embracing sharp affectionate glance, caught Frances's eye and nodded to her reassuringly. One by one the names were called out, and each boy disassociated himself from the solid group and marched forward alone. The call was alphabetical, and by the time the G's were reached we were limp with suspense, since we did not know for sure that Johnny had even got into the church. As each boy passed down the aisle, there was applause, perfunctory for some, pronounced for others. Gaines, Gillespie, Goodwin, Griffin, Gunther. Slowly, very slowly, Johnny stepped out of the mass of his fellows and trod by us, carefully keeping in the exact center of the long aisle, looking neither to the left nor to the right, but straight ahead, fixedly, with the white bandage flashing in the light through the high windows, his chin up, carefully, not faltering, steady, but slowly, so very slowly. The applause began and then rose and the applause became a storm, as every single person in that old church became whipped up, tight and tense, to see if he would make it. The applause became a thunder, it rose and soared and banged, when Johnny finally reached the pulpit. Mr. Flynt carefully tried to put the diploma in his right hand, as planned. Firmly Johnny took it from right hand to left, as was proper, and while the whole audience rocked now with release from tension, and was still wildly, thunderously applauding, he passed around to the side and, not seeing us, reached his place among his friends.

[*Death Be Not Proud,* the story of his son who became ill of a brain tumor at age sixteen, and who died of it a month after graduation. His last words were to ask whether Harvard had admitted him.]

—JOHN GUNTHER, 1901-

[107] Joy of Youth in Old Age

NEVER have I enjoyed youth so thoroughly as I have in my old age. In writing *Dialogues in Limbo, The Last Puritan,* and now all these descriptions of the friends of my youth and the young friends of my middle age, I have drunk the pleasure of life more pure, more joyful, than it ever was when mingled with all the hidden anxieties and little annoyances of actual living. Nothing is inherently and invincibly young except spirit. And spirit can enter a human being perhaps better in the quiet of old age and dwell there more undisturbed than in the turmoil of adventure. But it must be in solitude. I do not need or desire to hobnob artificially with other old men in order to revisit them in their salad days, and to renew my own. In Rome, in the eternal city, I feel nearer to my own past, and to the whole past and future of the world, than I should in any cemetery or in any museum of relics. Old places and old persons in their turn, when spirit dwells in them, have an intrinsic vitality of which youth is incapable; precisely the balance and wisdom that comes from long perspectives and broad foundations. Everything shines then for the spirit by its own light in its own place and time; but not as it shone in its own restless eyes. For in its own eyes each person and each place was the centre of a universe full of threatening and tempting things; but old age, having less intensity at the centre has more clearness at the circumference, and knows that just because spirit, at each point, is a private centre for all things, no one point, no one phase of spirit is materially a public centre for all the rest.

—GEORGE SANTAYANA, 1863-1952

[108] The Zero Hour

IN Clifford Dowdey's book on the War Between the States, entitled *Experiment in Rebellion,* he has a strange passage which tells that during the Peninsular Campaign, when the Union Army under General McClellan was about twenty miles from Richmond and it looked as though the city would be captured, Jefferson Davis, President of the Confederate States, was baptized in his home by the rector of a neighboring church and received into the fellowship of the church.

Think of putting that off until the zero hour had arrived! All through his sixty years he had refused to line himself up with the Church of Christ. But when the Union Army was twenty miles away, he ran for cover!

Do not a great many people put off any real attention to religion until some time of crisis?

This last moment taking up of religion is too late. It is never too late for God to forgive sins, but it is too late for the Christian religion to have its effects in life which it might have. If we wait until some time

106

of crisis, *we are too late to have religion as a guiding force during the whole of life.*

If we wait until some crisis comes upon us, *it is too late for faith, guiding us through the years, to build support for the crisis itself. . . .* When wo como to Christianity only in a crisis, *it is too late to have one of its greatest joys—that of rendering a life of service.*

—HALFORD E. LUCCOCK, 1885-

[109] Regarding Albert Einstein

*"The future will give more and more proofs
of the merits of Herr Einstein . . ."*

(1911)

HERR EINSTEIN is one of the most original minds that we have ever met. In spite of his youth he already occupies a very honorable position among the foremost savants of his time. What we marvel at him, above all, is the ease with which he adjusts himself to new conceptions and draws all possible deductions from them. He does not cling to classical principles, but sees all conceivable possibilities when he is confronted with a physical problem. In his mind this becomes transformed into an anticipation of new phenomena that may some day be verified in actual experience. . . . The future will give more and more proofs of the merits of Herr Einstein, and the University that succeeds in attaching him to itself may be certain that it will derive honor from its connection with the young master.

—HENRI POINCARÉ, 1854-1912
—MARIE CURIE, 1867-1934

[110] A Worry Table

MANY people are inwardly unhappy and in their unhappiness imagine an unfriendly universe. The solution of their problem is to lose themselves in something bigger than themselves. They suffer from psychological (imaginary), not logical, fears. Those who are distorted by a state of psychological fear need to realize how basic worry is in creating such a state of mind. They would do well to emulate the woman who realized that worry was her chief means of coloring the universe into a state of unfriendliness and so made for herself a "worry table." In tabulating her worries she discovered that 40 per cent of them probably would never happen, her anxiety being the result of a tired mind; that 30 per cent of them were over old decisions which she could not alter, try as she might; that 12 per cent of them were about others' criticisms of her, most of them untrue and made by people who felt inferior to her; that 10 per cent of them concerned her health, which she knew would become worse the more she worried; that only 8 per cent of her worries were "legitimate"—and these "legitimate" worries were the types of experiences which when faced with her own resources, the help of friends, and the help of God, not only *taught* her something but *made* her something as well. Hence through her alleviation of worry she found one approach to a friendly universe.

[111] The Luminous Trail

ALL too soon this boy, "by the vision splendid on his way attended," came to an end here on earth where I could see him. He had diphtheria in the spring of 1903. He was given antitoxin and recovered, as far as we could see, completely. In July I went to England to lecture in the Quaker Summer School, which was to be the opening of the Woodbrooke Settlement at Selly Oak, near Birmingham. Lowell was to stay at his grandmother's home in Ardonia, New York, with a very efficient Friend who was to be caretaker and companion. He was always happy at Ardonia, with aunts and cousins, and we left feeling very comfortable about him. But the night before landing in Liverpool I awoke in my berth with a strange sense of trouble and sadness. As I lay wondering what it meant, I felt myself invaded by a Presence and held by Everlasting Arms. It was the most extraordinary experience I had ever had. But I had no intimation that anything was happening to Lowell. When we landed in Liverpool a cable informed me that he was desperately ill, and a second cable, in answer to one from me, brought the dreadful news that he was gone. When the news reached my friend John Wilhelm Rowntree, he experienced a profound sense of Divine Presence enfolding him and me, and his comfort and love were an immense help to me in my trial. Philip Wicksteed, the great Dante and Wordsworth scholar, gave me unique help in that early darkness, and he became one of my guides to St. Francis of Assisi, and to the triumph of love.

There had mysteriously come to Lowell an attack of paralysis which affected his speech and his breathing. He seems to have fully realized that he could not live long, and he wrote on a slip of paper: "Give some of my books to Philip and Norris"—two of his dearest friends at Haverford. His little friends and playmates later joined together and raised a memorial fund and finished and furnished "The Lowell Jones Reading Room" in the Boys' School at Ramallah, Palestine. Lowell's picture hangs in this attractive room, and Arabic boys have carried on a happy memory of him. . . .

I know now, as I look back across the years, that nothing has carried me up into the life of God or done more to open out the infinite meaning of love than the fact that love can span this break of separation, can pass beyond the visible and hold right on across the chasm. The mystic union has not broken and knows no end. Lowell had here only eleven years of happy, joyous life. The victory that comes through the long years of struggle in a world full of hard choices could not be his. He was not to have the chance, "with toil of heart and knees and hands, through the long gorge to the far light," to form his character and to do his lifework; but who knows what chances there are for transplanted human worth to bloom, to profit in God's other garden? As certainly as God lives there is more to follow after this brief span of preparation ends. Those who are only potential saints here—"probable" saints—may very well become full-fledged shining ones, when God has brought the beginning to its complete fulfillment. When my sorrow was at its most acute stage, I was walking along a great city highway, when suddenly I saw a little child come out of a great gate, which swung to and fastened behind her. She wanted to go to her home behind the gate, but it would not open. She pounded in vain with her little fist. She rattled the gate. Then she wailed as though her heart would break. The cry brought the mother. She caught the child in her arms and kissed away the tears. "Didn't you know I would come? It is all right now." All of a sudden I saw with my spirit that there was love behind my shut gate.

Yes, "where there is so much love, *there must be more*."

—RUFUS JONES, 1863-1948

[112] The "Second Conversion" of Charles Wesley

1. 21ST MAY 1738

CHARLES WESLEY, distressed in body and mind, was lodging in London with John Bray, a brazier by trade. It would seem that he had taken this lodging so that he might be in touch with a man who had found "rest to his soul" through simple, sure trust in Christ. For that open secret Charles Wesley had sought for years in England and America.

The brazier's home was a port of call for others who, like Charles Wesley, were seekers for spiritual assurance and peace. Thither on 17th May came William Holland from the meeting of a religious society in Fetter Lane. He brought Luther's *Commentary on the Epistle to the Galatians*. We have two accounts of what happened. Holland's diary says—

"After my return [from America], in speaking with one of our society on the doctrine of Christ, as preached by him, and reading the eighth chapter of the Epistle to the Romans, I was conscious that I was not in the state there described. I became very uneasy, made a diligent search for books treating of faith in Christ, and was providentially directed to Martin Luther's *Commentary on the Epistle to the Galatians*. I carried it round to Mr. Charles Wesley, who was sick at Mr. Bray's, as a very precious treasure that I had found, and we three sat down together, Mr. Charles Wesley reading the Preface aloud. At the words, 'What, have we then nothing to do? No, nothing! but only accept of Him who of God is made unto us wisdom and righteousness and sanctification and redemption', there came such a power over me as I cannot well describe; my great burden fell off in an instant; my heart was so filled with peace and love that I burst into tears. I almost thought I saw our Saviour! My companions, perceiving me so affected, fell on their knees and prayed. When I afterwards went into the street, I could scarcely feel the ground I trod upon."

The diary kept by Charles Wesley records: "Today I first saw Luther on the Galatians, which Mr. Holland had accidentally lit upon. We began, and found him nobly full of faith." Later the same day he wrote: "I spent some hours this evening in private with Martin Luther, who was greatly blessed to me, especially his conclusion of the second chapter. I laboured, waited and prayed to feel 'who loved *me,* and gave himself for *me.'* " Luther had described in the *Commentary on the Epistle to the Galatians* his own childhood, when he was taught to fear Christ as a stern law-giver and judge. It was the revelation, the new-found certainty, that God in Christ was love, that Christ loved him, Martin Luther, and had given Himself for him, that set him free from fear, irresolution, and the bondage of self-despair. So, on the twentieth verse of the second chapter of the Galatian Epistle—where Paul says of himself: "I live by the faith of the Son of God, who loved me, and gave himself for me"—Luther had written:

"Who is this 'me'? Even I, wretched and damnable sinner, so dearly beloved of the Son of God, that he gave himself for me. If I, then, through works or merits could have loved the Son of God, and so come unto him, what needed he to deliver himself for me? . . .

"But because there was no other price either in heaven or on earth, but Christ the Son of God, therefore it was most necessary that he should be delivered for me. Moreover, this he did of inestimable love: for Paul saith, 'which loved me.' For he delivered neither sheep, ox, gold, nor silver, but even God himself entirely and wholly, 'for me', even for 'me', I say, a miserable and wretched sinner. . . .

Read therefore with great vehemency these words, *me* and *for me*, and so inwardly practise with thyself, that thou, with a sure faith, mayst conceive and print this *me* in thy heart, and apply it unto thyself, not doubting but thou art of the number of those to whom this *me* belongeth."

It was four days later, on Whitsunday, that Charles Wesley entered into the same experience. He tells of the hymn to the Holy Spirit that John sang with him that morning; of his own urgent prayer, "Thou art God who canst not lie; I wholly rely upon Thy most true promise; accomplish it in Thy time and manner"; of the voice of a friend that reached him in the sick-room, "In the name of Jesus of Nazareth, arise, and believe, and thou shalt be healed of all thy infirmities"; of the Scriptures which spoke to his condition, especially the first verse of Isaiah 40; and then of the acceptance of the free gift which he had sought so ardently: "I now found myself at peace with God, and rejoiced in hope of loving Christ."

—HENRY CARTER, 1874-1951

[113] John Wesley's "Second Conversion": The Aldersgate Experience

2. 24TH MAY 1738

WHEN on 21st May John heard of Charles's new experience he wrote: "I received the surprising news that my brother had found rest to his soul. His bodily strength returned also from that hour. 'Who is so great a God as our God?' " But for himself, in a letter to a friend written at the same time, he could but say: "All my works, my righteousness, my prayers, need an atonement for themselves. So that my mouth is stopped. I have nothing to plead. God is holy, I am unholy. . . . Yet I hear a voice (and is it not the voice of God?) saying, 'Believe, and thou shalt be saved.' " . . .

This brings him to Wednesday 24th May 1738, the day of revelation and rediscovery. His sensitive mind recalls and recounts each completing step in the long quest:

"I think it was about five this morning that I opened my Testament on those words, 'There are given unto us exceeding great and precious promises, even that ye should be partakers of the divine nature' (2 Peter 1).

"Just as I went out, I opened it again on those words: 'Thou art not far from the kingdom of God.'

"In the afternoon I was asked to go to St. Paul's. The anthem was, 'Out of the deep have I called unto Thee, O Lord: Lord, hear my voice. O let Thine ears consider well the voice of my complaint. If Thou, Lord, wilt be extreme to mark what is done amiss, O Lord, who may abide it? For there is mercy with Thee; therefore shalt Thou be feared. O Israel, trust in the Lord: for with the Lord there is mercy, and with Him is plenteous redemption. And He shall redeem Israel from all his sins.' "

The oft-quoted description of the change which he experienced that evening follows:

"In the evening I went very unwillingly to a society in Aldersgate Street, where one was reading Luther's preface to the *Epistle to the Romans*. About a quarter before nine, while he was describing the change which God works in the heart through faith in Christ, I felt my heart strangely warmed. I felt I did trust in Christ, Christ alone for salvation; and an assurance was given me that He had taken away *my* sins, even *mine*, and saved *me* from the law of sin and death."

The two succeeding paragraphs in the *Journal* are not so often cited, though they are charged with significance:

"I began to pray with all my might for those who had in a more especial manner despitefully used me and persecuted me. I then testified openly to all there what I now first felt in my heart. But it was not long before the enemy suggested, 'This cannot be faith; for where is thy joy?' Then was I taught that peace and victory over sin are essential to faith in the Captain of our salvation; but that, as to the transports of joy that usually attend the beginning of it, especially in those who have mourned deeply, God sometimes giveth, sometimes withholdeth them, according to the counsels of His own will.

"After my return home, I was much buffeted with temptations; but cried out, and they fled away. They returned again and again. I as often lifted up my eyes, and He 'sent me help from His holy place'. And herein I found the difference between this and my former state chiefly consisted. I was striving, yea, fighting with all my might under the law, as well as under grace. But then I was sometimes, if not often, conquered; now, I was always conqueror."

—HENRY CARTER, 1874-1951

[114] What Is Religion?

RELIGION in the life of man is a momentary glance from time into eternity.

It is Augustine visioning his *Civitas Dei* when the City of Man is about to crumble.

It is Pythagoras discerning eternal truths in the framework of a right triangle.

It is Plato grasping Beauty, Truth, and Goodness as eternal verities through human reason.

It is Edna St. Vincent Millay writing "Renascence" and crying out,
>The soul can split the sky in two,
>And let the face of God shine through.

It is Socrates saying, "Knowledge is virtue."

It is Newton at twenty-four discovering the binomial theorem and the law of gravitation.

It is Händel with a paralyzed limb, destitute of money, facing imprisonment, gathering new courage and writing his greatest oratorio, *The Messiah.*

It is Paul hearing the voice of his Lord on the Damascus Road.

It is Jesus in terrible agony crying, "Father, into thy hands I commit my spirit."

It is an ordinary man dedicating every fiber of himself to the betterment of the world.

It is Albrecht Dürer painting his "Praying Hands."

It is Washington praying alone at Valley Forge.

It is Isaiah changing his purple garments of a prince for the tattered cloth of a prophet to save a nation from chaos.

It is Augustine forsaking a lustful heart and fleeing into the arms of God, and later becoming the Bishop of Hippo.

It is a priest jotting down the last words of a dying Marine at Guadalcanal and composing a letter of comfort to a widowed mother in St. Louis.

It is Jesus saying to his disciples, "Take up your cross and follow me."

It is a teacher refusing a gainful salary elsewhere that he may instruct youth in the wisdom of the ages.

It is Mary weeping at the foot of the cross.

It is Clement of Alexandria interpreting the divine Logos as the inspiration for all truth.

It is a father sacrificing a suit of clothes that his son may stay in college.

It is a widow in a tenement taking in washing to support three orphaned children of a former neighbor across the hall.

It is Luther standing firm at Worms saying, "I cannot and will not recant anything, since it is unsafe and dangerous to do anything against the conscience."

It is Francis of Assisi preaching to the birds and the flowers.

It is a man centering his focus on God and not himself, and finding his life changed from a state of worry to a state of wonder.

It is Edith Cavell before a firing squad in Brussels saying, "Patriotism is not enough."

It is a man saying, "My soul is so absorbed in the bigger issues of life that I cannot afford to be jealous and suspicious of any person."

It is the sacrifice of a meal by an American family in order that starvation in China may be averted.

It is Bernard at a monastery in Clairvaux in love with Christ and married to the church.

It is Servetus burning at the stake in Geneva for the sake of truth.

It is Amos forsaking his flock at Tekoa to preach against hypocrisy at Bethel.

It is Schleiermacher discerning religion as man's feeling of absolute dependence upon God.

It is Katherine Mansfield saying about her literary creations shortly before her death, "Not one of these writings dare I show to God."

It is Thomas Aquinas wedding reason and faith.

It is my feeling of humility when I contemplate God as the Life of a universe extending a million light years into space.

It is Deutero-Isaiah discerning the nations as specks of sand when compared to God's majesty and infinity.

It is my little self on a second-rate planet eradicating fear, self-centeredness, resentment, and guilt in order that it may become an instrument of God's energetic redemptive love.

It is the writer of the Gospel of John reporting, "Let not your hearts be troubled; believe in God."

Yes, these are all religion. For religion is as big as life and as normal an experience as breathing, eating, and sleeping.

[115] A Letter by Phillips Brooks to a Grieving Husband Who Lost His Wife

233 Clarendon Street,
Boston, Nov. 19th, 1891

My dear Friend,

I have thought much about our meeting last Sunday, and the few words we had together. May I try to tell you again where your comfort lies? It is not in forgetting the happy past. People bring us well-meant but miserable consolation when they tell us what time will do to our grief. We do not want to lose our grief, because our grief is bound up with our love and we could not cease to mourn without being robbed of our affection. But if you know—as you do know—that the great and awful change, which has come into your life and brought you such distress, has brought your dear wife the joy of heaven, can you not, in the midst of all your suffering, rejoice for her? And if knowing she is with God, you can be with God, too, and every day claim His protection and try to do His will, may you not still in spirit be very near to her?

She is not dead, but living, and if you are sure what care is holding her, and educating her, you can be very contendedly with her in spirit, and look forward confidently to the day when you shall also go to God and be with her. I know that this does not take away your pain—no one can do that—you do not want any one to do that—not even God, but it can help you to bear it, to be brave and cheerful, to do your duty, and to live the Pure, Earnest, Spiritual life which she, in heaven, wishes you to live. . . . My dear friend, she is yours forever. God never takes away what He has once given. May He make you worthy of her! May He comfort you, and make you strong!

PHILLIPS BROOKS, 1835-1893
Your friend, sincerely,

115

[116] John Woolman Censors Friends Who Hold Slaves

In this Yearly Meeting [Philadelphia, 1758] several weighty matters were considered, and towards the last that in relation to dealing with persons who purchase slaves. During the several sittings of the said meeting my mind was frequently covered with inward prayer, and I could say with David, that "tears were my meat day and night." The case of slave-keeping lay heavy upon me, nor did I find any engagement to speak directly to any other matter before the meeting. Now when this case was opened several faithful Friends spake weightily thereto, with which I was comforted; and feeling a concern to cast in my mite, I said in substance as follows:

"In the difficulties attending us in this life nothing is more precious than the mind of truth inwardly manifested; and it is my earnest desire that in this weighty matter we may be so truly humbled as to be favored with a clear understanding of the mind of truth, and follow it; this would be of more advantage to the Society than any medium not in the clearness of Divine wisdom. The case is difficult to some who have slaves, but if such set aside all self-interest and come to be weaned from the desire of getting estates or even from holding them together, when truth requires the contrary, I believe a way will so open that they will know how to steer through these difficulties." . . .

Finding an engagement to speak, I said, "My mind is often led to consider the purity of the Divine Being and the justice of His judgments; and herein my soul is covered with awfulness. I cannot omit to hint of some cases where people have not been treated with the purity of justice, and the event hath been lamentable. Many slaves on this continent are oppressed, and their cries have reached the ears of the Most High. Such are the purity and certainty of His judgments that He cannot be partial in our favor. In infinite love and goodness He hath opened our understanding from one time to another concerning our duty towards this people, and it is not a time for delay. Should we now be sensible of what He requires of us, and through a respect to the private interest of some persons, or through a regard to some friendships which do not stand on an immutable foundation, neglect to do our duty in firmness and constancy, still waiting for some extraordinary means to bring about their deliverance, God may by terrible things in righteousness answer us in this matter."

Many faithful brethren labored with great firmness, and the love of truth in a good degree prevailed. Several who had Negroes expressed their desire that a rule might be made to deal with such Friends as offenders who bought slaves in future. To this it was answered that the root of this evil would never be effectually struck at until a thorough search was made in the circumstances of such Friends as kept Negroes, with respect to the righteousness of their motives in keeping them, that impartial justice might be administered throughout. Several Friends expressed their desire that a visit might be made to such Friends as kept slaves, and many others said that they believed liberty was the Negro's right; to which, at length, no opposition was publicly made. A minute was made more full on that subject than any heretofore, and the names of several Friends entered who were free to join in a visit such as kept slaves.

—JOHN WOOLMAN, 1720-1772

[117] Caspar Rene Gregory: Saint and Scholar

LET me refer to another "voice in the wilderness," a man who in an original and inimitable way tried to express in his personal life that connection between the Church and the working classes which had been lost during the nineteenth century. Caspar René Gregory, Professor of Theology at Leipzig, American by birth, German by fate, born in 1846 at Philadelphia, killed in 1916 as an officer in the German army, was professionally a great scholar in textual criticism of the New Testament. His life was devoted to the aid and assistance of people on every possible occasion, especially of the working classes. He wanted to make them feel the spirit of Christian love—we may say: the spirit of the Sermon on the Mount.

Innumerable stories of such acts of assistance were told by the students of Leipzig University at the beginning of this century. There was the street-car switchman (they had no automatic switches in those days at Leipzig) who one evening stood at his post in the rain, cold and wet. Professor Gregory gave him some money and said "Go over to that coffee-shop and drink a hot cup of coffee." Then the professor took his place and carried on the work of a street-car switchman as long as the other was absent. Once he ran after a street-car to give an American stamp to the conductor because he knew that the man was a passionate stamp collector. . . .

And it was solely as the result of this point of view that he, aged sixty-eight, became a soldier in 1914. At that time he wrote in a letter: "My friends, the workmen, were compelled to join the army. It was intolerable for me, that they should say: 'Our friend, the Professor, has an

117

easy life; goes to the University and we have to carry on war for him.' I wanted to stay with them in the rank and file and to share their pain of military life." The military service of Professor Gregory and his death by a shell hitting his quarters in France was indeed an illustration of the word: "Greater love has no man than this, that a man lay down his life for his friends." It was neither youthful enthusiasm which led him nor national hate; he wanted to be faithful unto death.

—MARTIN DIBELIUS, 1883-1947

PRAYERS

 OF YESTERDAY AND TODAY

[118] God Changest Not

O God, who remainest the same though all else fades, who changest not with our changing moods, who leavest us not when we leave Thee; we thank Thee that when we lose faith in Thee, soon or late we come to faith in something that leads us back again with firmer trust and more security. Even if we wander into the far country we take ourselves with us; ourselves who are set towards Thee as rivers to the sea. If we turn to foolishness, our hearts grow faint and weary, our path is set with thorns, the night overtakes us, and we find we have strayed from light and life.

Grant to us clearer vision of the light which knows no shade of turning, that we stray not in folly away; incline our hearts to love the truth alone, so that we miss Thee not at last; give us to realise of what spirit we are, so that we cleave ever to Thee, who alone can give us rest and joy. Amen.

—W. E. Orchard, 1877-1955

[119] The Helper of the Helpless

WE beseech Thee, O Lord, remember all for good; have mercy upon all, O God. Remember every soul who, being in any affliction, trouble, or agony, stands in need of Thy mercy and help; all who are in necessity or distress; all who love, or hate us.

Thou, O Lord, art the Helper of the helpless; the Hope of the hopeless; the Saviour of them who are tossed with tempests; the Haven of them who sail; be Thou All to all. The glorious majesty of the Lord our God be upon us; prosper Thou the work of our hands upon us; Oh, prosper Thou our handywork. Lord, be Thou within me, to strengthen me; without me, to keep me; above me to protect me; beneath me, to uphold me; before me, to direct me; behind me, to keep me from straying; round about me, to defend me. Blessed be Thou, O Lord, our Father, for ever and ever. Amen.

—LANCELOT ANDREWES, 1555-1626

[120] Make My Heart Thy Holy Temple

O GOD, our true Life, in whom and by whom all things live, Thou commandest us to seek Thee, and art ready to be found; Thou biddest us knock, and openest when we do so. To know Thee is life, to serve Thee is freedom, to enjoy Thee is a kingdom, to praise Thee is the joy and happiness of the soul. I praise, and bless, and adore Thee, I worship Thee, I glorify Thee, I give thanks to Thee for Thy great glory. I humbly beseech Thee to abide with me, to reign in me, to make this heart of mine a holy temple, a fit habitation for Thy Divine majesty. O Thou Maker and Preserver of all things, visible and invisible! keep, I beseech Thee, the work of Thine own hands, who trusts in Thy mercy alone for safety and protection. Guard me with the power of Thy grace, here and in all places, now and at all times, forevermore. Amen.

—AUGUSTINE, 354-430

[121] A Prayer of Renewal

O GOD, speak to our hearts when men faint for fear, and the love of many grows cold, and there is distress of the nations upon earth. Keep us resolute and steadfast in the things that cannot be shaken, abounding in hope and knowing that our labour is not in vain in thee. Restore our faith in the omnipotence of good; renew the love which never faileth; and make us to lift up our eyes and behold, beyond the things which are seen and temporal, the things which are unseen and eternal. Amen.

—BOOK OF COMMON PRAYER

[122] To Make Life an Adventure

MAKE us ready for the great adventure of living. We do not pray for immunity from risks; we pray for courage to face risks. We do not ask to be saved out of the world; we ask for strength to ally ourselves with the saviours of the world. Among the immediate and incidental problems of personal life, give us courage to face the facts which confront us without evasions or self-deception; to atone for our blunders, not by repentance only, but by braver determination and decision. Among the perplexities of daily life give us equanimity and self-control, that we be not the slaves of circumstances but their masters, with the exhilaration of conflict and the joy of victory. Finally, we pray that the adventure of living may be guarded and sustained by an undefeated patience, willing to wait for new light and to re-enforce duty by loyalty. We do not know what a day may bring forth. Arm us for the campaign of life with an unperturbed faith and an unconquered hope, that when the end of our adventure arrives, and we face the mystery that lies beyond, we may have the same tranquil courage to meet the things which eye hath not seen, nor ear heard, nor have entered into the heart of man, but which thou hast prepared for them that love thee.

—FRANCIS G. PEABODY, 1847-1936

[123] To Realize My Talents

WONDERFUL Lord of all creation, thy universe is ever full of surprises— gorgeous sunsets of myriad colors, starlit heavens touching eternity, scientists in laboratories uncovering hidden wonders, heroic men and women of Christlike devotion making their environments like thy kingdom. I know that my life has latent possibilities, to be gloriously real-

123

ized as I harmonize my will with thine. May I spend my experience in thrilling, abundant living, rather than feel that I must live out my years with drudgery. May I welcome this day with a feeling of great adventure with thee. May my spirit be mastered by thy Spirit, thus to know the meaning of thy kingdom within me. Strengthen me to be thy emissary to help others find the joy and strength of thy Spirit. Amen.

[124] Surety of God's Companionship

GREAT God of majestic power, I pray that I may have strength and courage to live with righteous heroic adventure. If I have minimized thy power as my continuous help, do forgive me for such lack of faith. May I never forget that thou art the great God upon whom the creation and the sustenance of the universe depend. In my feeling of deep humility, as I contrast my tiny self with thy infinite majesty, I realize how greatly thy gracious power can relate itself to me and flow through my spirit. Thou art out among the galaxies; but thou art as near as the breath I breathe. With a surety of thy spiritual companionship, may I become empowered to help reclaim all this earthly setting as "the temple of God." Amen.

[125] Invitations to Seek Thy Help

ETERNAL God, the utterance of thy name hushes me with humility. The thought of thy creation tempers me with awe. The contemplation of thy forgiveness makes me marvel at thy eternal mercy. Life is filled with so many mysteries. Because we are men there is so much we do not understand; but *because* we are men, we adore thee as God and Creator. Frequently we have doubts, despair, and perplexity. Sometimes our problems seem too great. We are tormented by fear, jealousy, suspicion, anger, and anxiety. We wonder if life is worth the effort. Yet, as we turn to thee in such moments, thou art nearer than breathing; life's problems become invitations to seek thy help to mature into heroic Christians. May the life of Jesus Christ, arising triumphant above the opposition of his enemies, encourage us to continue laboring for a Christian world. Amen.

124

[126] May My Soul Be a Temple

O ETERNAL God, make my body and soul to be a holy temple, purified for the habitation of Thy Holy Spirit. Cast out of it, O Lord, all worldly affections, all covetous desires; let it be a place of prayer and holy meditation; of pure intentions, and zealous desires of pleasing Thee; so that, loving Thee above all the world, and worshipping Thee continually in humblest adoration, I may be prepared to glorify Thee to all eternity in heaven; through Jesus Christ our Lord. Amen.

—JEREMY TAYLOR, 1613-1667

[127] Today Is the Great Adventure

Father,
No glimpse of light can we see
On our future path;
But our hands are in Thy strong hand;
And Thou canst see.

Therefore, fearless and unafraid,
We will march through the darkness,
Upheld and guarded and led by Thy love,
Well knowing that every step of the way
Shall prove Thee more faithful and tender,
More wholly enough for all that we need.

O Father,
Our hearts and our lives, with deep and secret delight,
We render to Thee;
And forward we press, on our great adventure
On this day Thou hast given,
To discover still wider and fairer realms
Of Thy great love,
And to labor for Thee.

—JOHN S. HOYLAND, 1887-1957

[128] For a Pure Will

MOST great and glorious God, who hast appointed the rivers to hasten with a rapid motion to the sea, be graciously pleased, I most humbly beseech Thee, to make the stream of my will perpetually to flow a cheerful and impetuous course, bearing down pleasure, interest, afflictions, death, and all other obstacles and impediments whatsoever before it, till it plunge itself joyfully into the unfathomable ocean of Thy divine will, for the sake of Thy beloved Son, my Saviour, Jesus Christ. Amen.

—CHARLES HOWE, 1661-1745

[129] Preserve Us from Despondency

O GOD, animate us to cheerfulness. May we have a joyful sense of our blessings, learn to look on the bright circumstances of our lot, and maintain a perpetual contentedness under Thy allotments. Fortify our minds against disappointment and calamity. Preserve us from despondency, from yielding to dejection. Teach us that no evil is intolerable but a guilty conscience; and that nothing can hurt us, if, with true loyalty of affection, we keep Thy commandments, and take refuge in Thee. Amen.

—WILLIAM ELLERY CHANNING, 1780-1842

[130] Content to Do God's Will

O GOD, too near to be found, too simple to be conceived, too good to be believed; help us to trust, not in our knowledge of Thee, but in Thy knowledge of us; to be certain of Thee, not because we feel our thoughts of Thee are true, but because we know how far Thou dost transcend them. May we not be anxious to discern Thy will, but content only with desire to do it; may we not strain our minds to understand Thy nature, but yield ourselves and live our lives only to express Thee.

Shew us how foolish it is to doubt Thee, since Thou Thyself dost set the questions which disturb us; reveal our unbelief to be faith fretting at its outworn form. Be gracious when we are tempted to cease from moral strife: reveal what it is that struggles in us. Before we tire of mental search enable us to see that it was not ourselves but Thy call which stirred our souls.

126

Turn us back from our voyages of thought to that which sent us forth. Teach us to trust not to cleverness or learning, but to that inward faith which can never be denied. Lead us out of confusion to simplicity. Call us back from wandering without to find Thee at home within. Amen.

—W. E. ORCHARD, 1877-1955

[131] Last Prayer

ALMIGHTY and most merciful Father, I am now, as to human eyes it seems, about to commemorate, for the last time, the death of thy Son Jesus Christ our Saviour and Redeemer. Grant, O Lord, that my whole hope and confidence may be in his merits, and his mercy; enforce and accept my imperfect repentance; make this commemoration available to the confirmation of my faith, the establishment of my hope, and the enlargement of my charity; and make the death of thy Son Jesus Christ effectual to my redemption. Have mercy upon me, and pardon the multitude of my offences. Bless my friends; have mercy upon all men. Support me, by the grace of thy Holy Spirit, in the days of weakness, and at the hour of death; and receive me, at my death, to everlasting happiness, for the sake of Jesus Christ. Amen.

—SAMUEL JOHNSON, 1709-1784

[132] A Prayer for Guidance

FATHER of Spirits: we bless thee for every gracious and holy soul that hath led us nearer to thee; and especially for him who to us hath chiefly been the way, the truth, and the life. We bless thee that, in every darker passage of our pilgrimage, in the strife of temptation, in the hour of danger, in solitude of spirit, in the weakness of anguish, and the paths of death, we may fix our eye on him as the leader of faithful souls, who hath divinely borne our woes and passed to the glorious rest. Give us wisdom to walk as he walked; and by keeping ever close to thee may we too have strength to overcome the world. May no pleading of indolence and fear, no levity or vainglory, no coldness of faith and love, withhold us from strenuously doing thy will and finishing thy work.

—JAMES MARTINEAU, 1805-1900

[133] Redeeming the Time

O GOD, our everlasting hope, who holdest us in life, and orderest our lot; we ask not for any prosperity that would tempt us to forget thee. As disciples of One who had not where to lay his head, may we freely welcome the toils and sufferings of our humanity, and seek only strength to glorify the cross thou layest on us. Every work of our hand may we do unto thee; in every trouble, trace some lights of thine; and let no blessing fall on dry and thoughtless hearts. Redeeming the time, may we fill every waking hour with faithful duty and well-ordered affections, as the sacrifice which thou hast provided. Strip us, O Lord, of every proud thought; fill us with patient tenderness for others, seeing that we also are in the same case before thee; and make us ready to help, and quick to forgive. And then, fix every grace, compose every fear, by a steady trust in thine eternal realities, behind the changes of time and delusions of men. Thou art our Rock: we rest on thee. Amen.

—JAMES MARTINEAU, 1805-1900

[134] Keep Life Steadfast

ALMIGHTY Father, who with untiring love dost watch over thy children from one generation to another, amid all the changes of our earthly life thou abidest. Graciously help us to abide in thee, that evermore we may be steadfast and strong. For the light that never failed and the grace that never left us in the days gone by; for the visions that dispelled our doubt and the hopes that chastened our sorrow, we lift up our hearts to thee in praise and joy. May the coming days be filled with a high sense of the sacredness of life and the value of time. With the dawning of each new day, shine on us with thy face. Uplift our hearts by the thought of the glory of our calling in Christ and of the joy that is set before us in his service. May the numberless memories of thy patient love deliver us from every crooked way, from every evil thought and imagination, that when all our days on earth are done we may be set before the presence of thy glory without blemish in exceeding joy; through Jesus Christ, our Lord. Amen.

—ALBERT PARKER FITCH, 1877-1944

[135] Patience in the Time of Sorrow

O FATHER of infinite Compassion, God of all Comfort, reveal thyself to those who have been brought into the darkness of sorrow as the Light of Life. Strengthen the hearts that faint under the heavy burden, and support them in the arms of thine infinite love. May they know that in all their distress thou dost care for them with unfailing tenderness. May they remember him who, a man of sorrows and acquainted with grief, was able to say in sorest trial, Father, not my will but thine be done. Help them to bear with patience their affliction, and bring them at last to that heavenly home where God shall wipe away all tears from their eyes; through Jesus Christ our Lord. Amen.

—BOOK OF CHURCH SERVICES

[136] Compassion for All Men

CREATOR and Ruler of mankind, we pray thee this day for our country, that her life may be established and built up in thyself, that all hatred and malice, all indifference to the sufferings of others, all narrow exclusiveness and selfish greed, may be swept away by the breath of the Spirit, and that public spirit, honour and justice, co-operation in service, self-sacrifice for the good of the whole people, may flourish abundantly amongst us. Purify us from all baseness, fill us with thy divine passion to uplift the weak, to sweep away oppression and wrong, to give to every man the opportunity of a full life that may be lived to thy glory and to the service of mankind; through Jesus Christ our Lord. Amen.

—AUTHOR UNKNOWN

[137] A Prayer of Consecration

ETERNAL God, who committest to us the swift and solemn trust of life; since we know not what a day may bring forth, but only that the hour for serving thee is always present, may we wake to the instant claims of thy holy will; not waiting for tomorrow, but yielding today. Lay to rest, by the persuasion of our spirit, the resistance of our passion, indolence, or fear. Consecrate with thy presence the way our feet may go; and the humblest work will shine, and the roughest place be made plain. Lift us above unrighteous anger and mistrust, into faith, and hope, and charity, by a simple and steadfast reliance on thy sure will: and so may we be modest in our time of wealth, patient under disappointment, ready for danger, serene in death. In all things draw us to the mind of Christ, that thy lost image may be traced again, and thou mayest own us as at one with him and thee. Amen.

—JAMES MARTINEAU, 1805-1900

[138] Repentance

O MERCIFUL God, full of compassion, long-suffering, and of great pity, who sparest when we deserve punishment, and in thy wrath thinkest upon mercy; make me earnestly to repent, and heartily to be sorry for all my misdoings; make the remembrance so burdensome and painful, that I may flee to Thee with a troubled spirit and a contrite heart; and, O merciful Lord, visit, comfort and relieve me; cast me not out from thy presence, and take not thy Holy Spirit from me, but excite in me true repentance; give me in this world knowledge of thy truth, and confidence in thy mercy, and in the world to come life everlasting, for the sake of our Lord and Saviour, thy Son Jesus Christ. Amen.

—SAMUEL JOHNSON, 1709-1784

[139] God, the Food for Eternity

THOU, O my God, art ever new, though Thou art the most ancient. Thou alone art the food for eternity. I am to live forever; not for a time—and I have no power over my being; I must live on, with intellect and consciousness for ever, in spite of myself. Without Thee eternity would be another name for eternal misery. In Thee alone have I that which can stay me up for ever; Thou alone art the food of my soul. Thou alone art inexhaustible, and ever offerest to me something new to know, something new to love. And so on for eternity I shall ever be a little child beginning to be taught the rudiments of Thy infinite Divine nature. For Thou art Thyself the seat and centre of all good, and the only substance in this universe of shadows, and the heaven in which blessed spirits live and rejoice. Amen.

—JOHN HENRY NEWMAN, 1801-1890

[140] Guide Me Today

WARM my cold heart, Lord, I beseech Thee. Take away all that hinders me from giving myself to Thee. Mould me according to Thine own image. Give me grace to obey Thee in all things, and ever to follow Thy gracious leading. Make me this day to be kind to my fellow-men, to be gentle and unselfish, careful to hurt no one by word or deed, but anxious to do good to all, and to make others happy. O Lord, forgive the sins of my temper. Pardon all my hasty words and unchristian thoughts. Make me watchful, that I offend not with my tongue. Give me a meek and loving spirit, which is in Thy sight of great price. I would not live unto myself, but unto Thee. Keep me from sin this day, and all that may offend Thee; for Jesus Christ's sake. Amen.

—ASHTON OXENDEN, 1808-1892

[141] In My Misery, Thou Art Omnipotent

O LORD, my God! the amazing horrors of darkness were gathered round me, and covered me all over, and I saw no way to go forth; I felt the depth and extent of the misery of my fellow-creatures separated from the Divine harmony, and it was heavier than I could bear, and I was crushed down under it; I lifted up my hand, I stretched out my arm, but there was none to help me; I looked round about, and was amazed. In the depths of misery, O Lord, I remembered that Thou art omnipotent; that I had called Thee Father; and I felt that I loved Thee, and I was made quiet in my will, and I waited for deliverance from Thee. Thou hadst pity upon me, when no man could help me; I saw that meekness under suffering was showed to us in the most affecting example of Thy Son, and Thou taughtest me to follow Him, and I said, "Thy will, O Father, be done!"

—JOHN WOOLMAN, 1720-1772

[142] Strong then Our Souls

LET Thy love so warm our souls, O Lord, that we may gladly surrender ourselves with all we are and have unto Thee. Let Thy love fall as fire from heaven upon the altar of our hearts; teach us to guard it heedfully by continual devotion and quietness of mind, and to cherish with anxious care every spark of its holy flame with which Thy good Spirit would quicken us, so that neither height, nor depth, things present nor things to come, may ever separate us therefrom. Strengthen Thou our souls; awaken us from the deathly sleep which holds us captive; animate our cold hearts with Thy warmth and tenderness, that we may no more live as in a dream, but walk before Thee as pilgrims in earnest to reach their home. And grant us at last to meet with Thy holy saints before Thy throne, and there rejoice in Thy love for ever and ever. Amen.

—GERHARD TERSTEEGEN, 1697-1769

[143] Safe in Thy Arms

O MY Lord, in Thine arms I am safe; keep me, and I have nothing to fear; give me up, and I have nothing to hope for. I know nothing about the future, but I rely upon Thee. I pray Thee to give me what is good for me. I leave it all to Thee, because Thou knowest and I do not. If Thou bringest pain or sorrow on me, give me grace to bear it well; keep me from fretfulness and selfishness. If Thou givest me health and strength and success in this world, keep me ever on my guard lest these great gifts carry me away from Thee. Give me to know Thee, to believe on Thee, to love Thee, to serve Thee, to live to and for Thee. Give me to die just at that time and in that way which is most for Thy glory. Amen.

—JOHN HENRY NEWMAN, 1801-1890

[144] Thou Didst Find Me

LATE have I loved Thee, O Thou Eternal Truth and Goodness: late have I sought Thee, my Father! But Thou didst seek me, and, when Thou shinedst forth upon me, then I knew Thee and learnt to love Thee. I thank Thee, O my Light, that Thou didst thus shine upon me; that Thou didst teach my soul what Thou wouldst be to me, and didst incline Thy face in pity unto me. Thou, Lord, hast become my Hope, my Comfort, my Strength, my All! In Thee doth my soul rejoice. The darkness vanished from before mine eyes, and I beheld Thee, the Sun of Righteousness. When

132

I loved darkness, I knew Thee not, but wandered on from night to night. But Thou didst lead me out of that blindness; Thou didst take me by the hand and call me to Thee, and now I can thank Thee, and Thy mighty voice which hath penetrated to my inmost heart. Amen.

—AUGUSTINE, 354-430

[145] Protect All Persons

O LORD, we praise Thee for our sister, the Night, who folds all the tired folk of the earth in her comfortable robe of darkness and gives them sleep. Release now the strained limbs of toil and smooth the brow of care. Grant us the refreshing draught of forgetfulness, that we may rise in the morning with a smile on our face. Comfort and ease those who toss wakeful on a bed of pain, or whose aching nerves crave sleep and find it not. Save them from evil or despondent thoughts in the long darkness, and teach them so to lean on Thy all-pervading life and love, that their souls may grow tranquil and their bodies, too, may rest. And now, through Thee we send Good Night to all our brothers and sisters near and far, and pray for peace upon all the earth. Amen.

—WALTER RAUSCHENBUSCH, 1861-1918

[146] Make Me Like unto Jesus

O ALMIGHTY God, give to Thy servant a meek and gentle spirit, that I may be slow to anger, and easy to mercy and forgiveness. Give me a wise and constant heart, that I may never be moved to an intemperate anger for any injury that is done or offered. Lord, let me ever be courteous, and easy to be entreated; let me never fall into a peevish or contentious spirit, but follow peace with all men; offering forgiveness, inviting them by courtesies, ready to confess my own errors, apt to make amends, and desirous to be reconciled. Let no sickness or cross accident, no employment or weariness, make me angry or ungentle and discontented, or unthankful, or uneasy to them that minister to me; but in all things make me like unto the holy Jesus. Amen.

—JEREMY TAYLOR, 1613-1667

133

[147] Rule Our Whole Inner Self

O LORD, we acknowledge Thy dominion over us; our life, our death, our soul and body, all belong to Thee. Oh, grant that we may willingly consecrate them all to Thee, and use them in Thy service. Let us walk before Thee in childlike simplicity, steadfast in prayer; looking ever unto Thee, that whatsoever we do or abstain from we may in all things follow the least indications of Thy will. Become Lord of our hearts and spirits; that the whole inner man may be brought under Thy rule, and that Thy life of love and righteousness may pervade all our thoughts and energies and the very ground of our souls; that we may be wholly filled with it. Come, O Lord and King, enter into our hearts, and live and reign there for ever and ever. O faithful Lord, teach us to trust Thee for life and death, and to take Thee for our All in All. Amen.

—GERHARD TERSTEEGEN, 1697-1769

[148] May We Add Strength to Our Faith

MOST gracious God, who hast been infinitely merciful to us, not only in the year past, but through all the years of our life, be pleased to accept our most unfeigned thanks for Thine innumerable blessings to us; graciously pardoning the manifold sins and infirmities of our life past, and bountifully bestowing upon us all those graces and virtues which may render us acceptable to Thee. And, every year which Thou shalt be pleased to add to our lives, add also, we humbly implore Thee, more strength to our faith, more ardor to our love, and a greater perfection to our obedience; and grant that, in a humble sincerity and constant perseverance, we may serve Thee most faithfully the remainder of our lives, for Jesus Christ's sake. Amen.

—CHARLES HOWE, 1661-1745

[149] Prayer and Thanksgiving When One Rises

I THANK Thee, O God my Heavenly Father, through Jesus Christ, Thy Son, our Lord and Saviour, for all blessings, for Thy gracious protection and defense, that Thou hast held Thy Hand over me, and shielded me this night from the Devil's cunning and deceit and from all evil. And now I commit into Thy Hands my body and soul (and all that which Thou hast given me and [all that] in which Thou hast placed me as Thy steward), as well as all my senses, thoughts and desires. Rule Thou me this day, and all time, with Thy holy Spirit, and lead me along the right ways. Give me Thy Word into my heart, and teach me Thy Truth, that I may neither speak, think, nor do anything except that which is right and true. Protect me from falsehood and from all who live in falsehood and deceit so that I do not follow them but lead Thy Truth into my heart so that I go the right way. Clothe my heart and soul with the cloak of Salvation and with the coat of Righteousness and purity. . . . Grant me pure and prudent eyes so that no false passions may awaken within me. And guard me from wrath and profanity that I do not take Thy Name in vain. But [so that I] go thus as is pleasing to Thee, through Jesus Christ, Thy dear Son, our Lord and Saviour. Amen.

—JAKOB BOEHME, 1575-1624

[150] At Eventime There Is a Light

Now that the daily task is laid aside and we are gathered in the house of God, the hush of solemnity comes over us, and we feel a refreshing rest in the holy quiet of the sanctuary. Softer than the twilight calm is the peace that comes to us here with healing on its wings. It restores our soul and we are refreshed out of the abundance of God's grace.

When the shades of night veil from our eyes the beauties of the earth, a world of holier splendor opens before the mind. At eventide, behold, there is light. The brightness of the fireside shines forth to tell that a divine spirit of love holds sway. How solemn does life, with its joys and its trials, appear in view of the duties and affections of home; how greatly all blessings are enriched, all cares and sorrows softened. At this hour, O God, Thy messenger of peace descends from on high to turn the hearts of the parents to the children and the hearts of the children to the parents, strengthening the bonds of devotion in the home and making it a sanctuary worthy of Thy presence.

—THE UNION PRAYERBOOK FOR JEWISH WORSHIP (Edited 1941; 1948)

[151] Trusting in Thy Grace

AH, God! behold my grief and care. Fain would I serve Thee with a glad and cheerful countenance, but I cannot do it. However much I fight and struggle against my sadness, I am too weak for this sore conflict. Help me in my weakness, O Thou mighty God! and give me Thy Holy Spirit to refresh and comfort me in my sorrow. Amid all my fears and griefs I yet know that I am Thine in life and death, and that nothing can really part me from Thee; neither things present, nor things to come, neither trial, nor fear, nor pain. And therefore, O Lord, I will still trust in Thy grace. Thou wilt not send me away unheard. Sooner or later Thou wilt lift this burden from my heart, and put a new song in my lips; and I will praise Thy goodness, and thank and serve Thee here and for evermore. Amen.

—S. SCHERETZ, 1584-1639

[152] Thy Image Be Renewed in Us

ETERNAL Light, before whom all darkness is light, and, in comparison with whom, every other light is but darkness, may it please Thee to send forth Thy light and Thy truth, that they may lead us. Purify, we pray Thee, our souls from all impure imaginations, that Thy most beautiful and holy image may be again renewed within us, and, by contemplating Thy glorious perfections, we may feel daily improved within us that Divine similitude the perfection whereof we hope will at last make us forever happy in that full and beatific vision we aspire after. Till this most blessed day break, and the shadows fly away, let Thy Spirit be continually with us, and may we feel the powerful effects of Thy divine grace constantly directing and supporting our steps; that all our endeavors, throughout the whole remaining part of our lives, may serve to promote the honor of Thy blessed name, through Jesus Christ our Lord. Amen.

—ROBERT LEIGHTON, 1611-1684

[153] With the Trust of a Child

How shall we pray Thee,
O Lord of our life,

For those that are dearer to us than our life?

How but in laying their souls in Thy hand,
As a child his most treasured possession
In the hands of his mother, to show her his love?

Thus we bring Thee to-day these souls that we love,
And we render them gladly to Thee,
The best gift that we have.

And we pray Thee the while, with the trust of a child,
Take them and hold them Thyself;
Keeping them ever next to Thy heart.
—JOHN S. HOYLAND, 1887-1957

[154] With Kindled Affections

O ALMIGHTY God, from whom every good prayer cometh; and who pourest out on all who desire it the spirit of grace and supplication; deliver us, when we draw nigh to Thee, from coldness of heart and wanderings of mind, that with steadfast thoughts and kindled affections we may worship Thee in spirit and in truth; through Jesus Christ our Lord. Amen.

—WILLIAM BRIGHT, 1824-1901

[155] Turn My Necessities into Virtues

O ETERNAL God, sanctify my body and soul, my thoughts and my intensions, my words and actions, that whatsoever I shall think, or speak, or do, may be by me designed for the glorification of Thy Name, and, by Thy blessing, it may be effective and successful in the work of God, according as it can be capable. Lord, turn my necessities into virtue, the works of nature into the works of grace, by making them orderly, regular, temperate; and let no pride or self-seeking, no covetousness or revenge, no little ends and low imaginations, pollute my spirit, and unhallow any of my words and actions; but let my body be a servant of my spirit, and both body and spirit servants of Jesus; that, doing all things for Thy glory here, I may be partaker of Thy glory hereafter, through Jesus Christ our Lord. Amen.

—JEREMY TAYLOR, 1613-1667

[156] Thy Mercies Are Many

O SOURCE of Life and Strength! many of Thy mercies do we plainly see, and we believe in a boundless store behind. No morning stars that sing together can have deeper call than we for grateful joy. Thou hast given us a life of high vocation, and Thine own breathing in our hearts interprets for us its sacred opportunities. Thou hast cheered the way with many dear affections and glimpses of solemn beauty and everlasting truth. Not a cloud of sorrow, but Thou hast touched with glory: not a dusty atmosphere of care, but Thy light shines through! And, lest our spirits should fail before Thine unattainable perfections, Thou hast set us in the train of Thy saints who have learned to take up the cross of sacrifice. Let the time past suffice to have wrought our own will, and now make us consecrate to Thine. Amen.

—JAMES MARTINEAU, 1805-1900

[157] For the Elevation of the Mind

O GOD, Thou brilliant, eternally-shining Light! Thou hast given the external world the Light of the out-breathing of Thy Might through the rays of Thy Light, and [Thou] dost rule in all Thy Works of this world's essence by means of sun and moon. By means of these lights Thou dost generate all temporal life—all that has breath, [that] moves and lives in these lights and praises Thee in Thy Vitality! All stars receive light and shine from Thy out-poured rays. Through this light Thou adornest the earth with fair plants and flowers and [Thou] causeth all that lives and grows to rejoice. Therein dost Thou show to human beings Thy Majesty so that we may know Thy Vitality which is hidden within, and see thereby how Thou has made Thy eternal *Logos* and Activity visible, so that we may contemplate thereby Thy internal, spiritual Kingdom in which Thou dwellest in secret, and dwellest in Thy creatures and Thou workest and does all in all Thyself. . . . O Thou super-illuminated Light of the Great Mystery, give unto me the rays of Thy hidden Holiness so that I see in my light in the Light of Thy shining. . . .

O Lord! Thou all-holiest Light! Let my mind dwell in Thy forecourts so that it may rejoice in the Light which streams forth from Thee, and [let] it never again deviate from Thee, but lead it back again into the fellowship with the holy angels to which Thou hast foreordained it.

O holy Name Emmanuel, it is Thine! Do Thou with it as Thou wilt! Amen.

—JAKOB BOEHME, 1575-1624

[158] At the Lord's Table

FATHER in Heaven! As on other occasions the intercession of the congregation is that Thou wouldst comfort all them that are sick and sorrowful, so now at this hour its intercession is that to them that labor and are heavy laden Thou wouldst give rest for their souls. Oh, and yet this is hardly an intercession. Who might count himself so sound that he need only pray for others? Ah, no, every one prays on his own account that Thou wouldst give him rest for his soul. O God, to each one severally whom Thou beholdest laboring and heavy laden with the consciousness of sin, do Thou give rest for his soul.

—SÖREN KIERKEGAARD, 1813-1855

[159] Thine Example

THOU, who didst once wander on earth, leaving footprints which we should follow; Thou, who still from Thy heaven dost look down upon each wanderer, dost strengthen the weary, encourage the despondent, lead back the erring, comfort the striving; Thou who also at the end of days shalt return to judge whether each man individually has followed Thee: our God and our Saviour, let Thine example stand clearly before the eyes of our soul to disperse the mists; strengthen us that unfalteringly we may keep this before our eyes; that we by resembling and following Thee may later find the way to the judgment, for it behooves every man to be brought to the judgment, oh, but also through Thee to be brought to eternal happiness hereafter with Thee. Amen.

—SÖREN KIERKEGAARD, 1813-1855

[160] To Arise Above Despair

ETERNAL Father of humanity, forgive me for moments of despair and disillusionment. I have too frequently become so engrossed with my daily problems that I have forgotten thy majesty and grace as powers constantly working in history. Give me the persepective to remember that Jesus' era was just as dark as our own; yet in that difficult moment thou didst empower him and a small group of men to evangelize the world. Help me to be confident that thy power and mercy are eternal, accessible today to those who turn with obedience to thy will. May I share Jesus' dream of thy kingdom, knowing that thy reign is ever about me as thy gift to men of Christlike obedience. May I help my family, my friends, my enemies in their weaknesses, thus reflecting thy grace which daily supplements my human frailties. Amen.

[161] To Feel the Tragedy of the World

GREAT Guide of human destiny, I feel deeply my guilt for the tragic condition of the world. With even greater sensitivity I repent for the unchristian atmosphere of my community. If people would let Christ's spirit rule their lives, what blessed fellowship we might have in this city. May my repentance find fruition today in the graciousness I show to all men; may my words and actions strengthen the burdened, encourage the defeated, solace the grief-stricken, and enlighten the despairing. Certainly as a Christian I must do all these things if I shall be saved from the terrible sin of hypocrisy. Use me this day, O Lord, as thy emissary of thy "good news" to all men. Amen.

[162] To Keep My Values Straight

O THOU who art the great Giver of all gifts, help me to keep my values straight. I am so grateful for this marvelous universe as the setting for my life. I appreciate all things material and immaterial which nourish my existence. Men frequently place high evaluation on wealth and power; I, too, face these as my temptations. May I never let my soul be corroded by things that are temporal; rather, may I realize that wealth and power are only of value in thy universe as servants like myself use them to make this planet thy kingdom. May I have the mind of Christ as I strive with thy help to *make a life* as well as *a living*. Lend me of thy strength and grace that I may help others bear their burden throughout this day. Amon.

[163] Strength to Meet Suffering

O GOD of eternal refuge, thy mercy has been a shelter for all men in all generations—and I know it is for me. I do not ask for a life of ease; but I do want a life of dignified achievement. May I always have the courage to stand for ideals that are Christlike. In times of disappointment and anxiety may I find thy Spirit my support and help. May the experiences of Jesus during his tragic days remind me that thou art always by the side of those who battle for right, whether this battle be within one's spirit or against the foes of the external world. May I as a Christian know that trials and sufferings met with thy help not only *teach* me something but *make* me something as well. May I have an enduring confidence that thy grace will support me in every difficult situation. Amen.

[164] A Religion to Support Me

INFINITE Guide and Protector of humanity, the gamut of experience has taught me that life cannot be woven into any easy pattern. Each day brings me difficult problems to solve, trying circumstances to face, enervating tasks to perform. I need a religion which will support me in every life situation. The manner in which Jesus faced problems with courageous realism inspires me to live heroically; the strength thou gavest him for virile living intrigues me to follow his ways of making decisions; the unselfishness with which he bore the burdens of his companions shows me the secret of his divinely patterned personality. I know I cannot escape life; I possess a life and I must live it as a man. With thy help may I be determined to live like a hero in the strife—and may my heroic pattern continue to be that of Jesus Christ. Amen.

141

[165] A Religion for Troubled Times

GREAT God of comfort, I realize that I must face my world as it is made. Help me to have faith that it is the best possible world for the developing of lasting values and worthy characters. I know that the Christian life cannot be lived on easy terms; Jesus has taught me that. I also know that the greatness of my soul must be found as I appreciate the tragic sense of existence; I cannot close my eyes to the intrinsic horror of sin and evil. Yet I am confident that I can live above the corrosion of sin and the defeat of evil, for thy grace helps me. Enable me to live this day in gratitude that Jesus has so realistically and so helpfully interpreted religion, that in every troubled time men can live with purpose and courage, serenity and hope. Amen.

[166] Vision for All Men

ETERNAL God, for whom no dawn arises, and no evening sets, we look for thee to lift up thy countenance upon us and show us light. O thou that bringest deliverance to the captives and songs in the night! scatter our faithless cares to the winds. Humble our self-will beneath the cross. Speak to our conscience with no veil between, till we are wholly at one with thee. Clear, O Lord, our inward vision, that we may see through the false shows of life, and be kept quiet and true by thy great realities. Reveal to the young, thou Supreme Inspirer, what it is to live this great life of opportunity; and fill them with the pure and undefiled religion which will keep them unspotted from the world. And in the hearts of the elders, let not the fires die or their work linger, till they are overtaken by the fading light and lengthening shadows of their set time. Knowing nothing of the morrow, may we rejoice to be faithful today; gladly accepting the humblest task that waits for us by thy will, and shines with the holy light of thine approval.

—JAMES MARTINEAU, 1805-1900

[167] Quiet amid Life's Storms

ALMIGHTY God, Lord of the storm and of the calm, the vexed sea and the quiet haven, of day and night, of life and of death; grant unto us

142

so to have our hearts stayed upon thy faithfulness, thine unchanging-
ness and love, that, whatsoever betide us, however black the cloud or
dark the night, with quiet faith trusting in thee, we may look upon thee
with untroubled eye, and walking in lowliness towards thee, and in lov-
ingness towards one another, abide all storms and troubles of this mortal
life, beseeching thee that they may turn to the soul's true good; we ask
it for thy mercy's sake, shown in Jesus Christ our Lord. Amen.

—GEORGE DAWSON, 1821-1876

[168] Gratitude for God's Providence

O GOD, Giver of life and of all that makes life good, we lift our hearts
to thee and bless thy name for all that thou art, and for all that thou
bestowest upon us. We thank thee not so much for the things which we
call ours as for those things which we share with all thy children—sunshine and wind and rain and flowers and the far horizons. We give thee
thanks not that thou hast made life easy, but that thou givest us strength
equal to life's demands. We bless thee not so much for what we know,
for that is meagre, but that under the inspiration of thy Spirit we can
learn what life means and how to live. We do not thank thee for what
we are, for we are shamed as we remember our wasted talents, but we
thank thee for what in thy Providence we may be, for all that we may
yet do to retrieve the past, and for what thou canst do with us and
through us insofar as we yield our wills to thine. Accept us, Most Holy
God, as we pledge ourselves to thee, our reasonable service, to live not
for ourselves but for our brothers, and for thee, to count ourselves rich
not in what we keep but in what we share, and to strive to live in fellowship of spirit with Jesus Christ our Lord. Amen.

—MORGAN P. NOYES, 1891-

[169] Thankfulness for Everything

OUR Father, we thank thee for all the benefits we have received from
thy goodness: for our creation and preservation up to this hour; for those
who brought us into the world and have loved and nurtured us; for those
who have befriended us and made smooth the path; for thy blessed saints

143

and all the incalculable heritage of the past, which we remember today and into which we enter; for every opportunity of making beauty or of being good; for every victory gained over ourselves; for every day when we have stood in awe and sinned not; for every night when we have communed with our own heart upon our bed and been still. Most of all we thank thee for our Lord and Saviour Jesus Christ. Amen.

—ALBERT PARKER FITCH, 1877-1944

[170] Gratitude for All Experiences

WITH our whole heart we give thee thanks, Most Gracious Father, for the world in which we now struggle, suffer, and aspire, and for that better world of final achievement for which we hope; for the mercy that is new every morning, fresh every evening, and as varied as our ever-changing needs; for the gifts of faith and hope that make perpetual sunshine within us and around; for the tenderness of thy compassions in every time of our discomfiture; for the light of knowledge, the discipline of duty, the ties and obligations of kindred, and our continued fellowship with all those who were once our friends and teachers and are now with thee; for the gospel of thy Son and the new powers and hopes that are born of it; for our memories of his earthly life and our union with him in a life that is eternal; and for the assurance that his mild and gracious spirit will finally overcome all the violence of the earth, his truth deliver all souls that are in bondage, and his kingdom abide and grow and never pass away.

—HUGH CAMERON, 1854-1934

[171] A Prayer for Forgiveness

GRACIOUS Father, whose mercy is higher than the heavens, wider than our wanderings and deeper than all sin; receive back unto thyself thy bewildered and broken children. Forgive our folly and excess, our coldness to human sorrows, our envy of those who prosper and are at ease, our passion for the things of the moment that perish in the grasping, our indifference to those treasures of the spirit which are life and peace, our neglect of thy wise and gracious laws; and so change our hearts and turn all our desires unto thyself that we may love that which thou approvest, and do that which thou commandest, and with strength and resolution walk in uprightness and charity, to the serving of our brethren, and the glory of thy name.

—HUGH CAMERON, 1854-1934

[172] Confidence in God's Love

ABIDE with us, O searching and chastening Spirit of the living God, for it is evening and the day is far spent. Let the shadow of thy presence shelter us from the haste and fret of the day, and the sense of thy tranquillizing guidance give us peace and rest. From all the blunders and follies of the day, from its wandering desires and its unjust judgments; from any sense of grievance or any word of blame which has blotted the fair hours, good Lord, deliver us. May the perplexing problems and petty cares of the day relax their grasp, and the meaning of life shine through the gathering dusk like the watching stars. Lift our minds to the vision of the permanent; rescue our wills from the illusions of the day's gain or loss; that the pressure of routine may not crush the life of the spirit, or the gain of the world become the loss of the soul. May we rest tonight in the protecting shadow of thy love, and wake with new courage and hope to fulfill the duties of another day.

—FRANCIS G. PEABODY, 1847-1936

[173] Lord of the Evening Hour

LORD of the evening hour, who hast often met with us at the close of day, be our refuge now from the noise of the world and the care of our own spirits. Grant us thy peace. Let not the darkness of our ignorance and folly, of our sorrow and sin hide thee from us. Draw near to us that we may be near to thee. Speak to each of us the word that we need, and let thy word abide in us till it has wrought in us thy holy will. Quicken and refresh our hearts, renew and increase our strength, so that we may grow into the likeness of thy faithful children, and by our worship at this time be enabled better to serve thee in our daily life in the spirit of Jesus Christ our Lord. Amen.

—JOHN HUNTER, 1728-1793

145

[174] Let Us Use Our Talents Faithfully

MOST Gracious God, who art ever more ready to hear than we are to pray; who knowest our necessities before we ask and our ignorance in asking, behold us here, coming from all our various homes and works, with all our different faults and needs, asking in a common prayer for light upon our way and for peace within our hearts. And even as we come thy Spirit meets us—yes, waits for us while we are yet a long way off—waits to receive, and forgive, and bless. What is our prayer but an answer to thy call? What is our worship but the return of the wandering child back to the Father's home? Give us the listening ear; give us the responsive will; and bring such answer to each sincere and simple prayer as each one of us severally needs; giving to one of us more courage, and to another more self-restraint, and to yet another freedom from selfishness and self-interest, and to us all the inner peace of mind which the world can neither give nor take away. Here are the rich resources of our favoured lives—health, strength, youth, joy, love. Rescue us from the meagre use of thy great gifts, that at thy coming we may return thy trusts with interest. Maintain in us the fidelity of those to whom much has been given and from whom much will be required, that we may hear at last the kindly benediction, Well done, good and faithful servant! Enter into the joy of thy Lord.

—FRANCIS G. PEABODY, 1847-1936

[175] New Mercies Every Morning

FATHER, I thank thee for thy mercies which are new every morning. For the gift of sleep; for health and strength; for the vision of another day with its fresh opportunities of work and service; for all these and more than these, I thank thee. Before looking on the face of men I would look on thee, who are the health of my countenance and my God. Not without thy guidance would I go forth to meet the duties and tasks of the day. Strengthen me so that in all my work I may be faithful; amid trials, courageous; in suffering, patient; under disappointment, full of hope in thee. Grant this for thy goodness' sake. Amen.

—SAMUEL McCOMB, 1864-1938

[176] A Group of Prayers for Children

1. GRACE BEFORE BREAKFAST

Dear Father, for the happy night
We thank Thee; for its stars so bright;
And for the Mother-moon which beams
Above us with her dearest dreams.

We thank Thee for the sleep and rest
Which seemeth for our bodies best;
And for Thy shadows hovering,
And for Thy sweet winds, whispering.

We thank Thee for the dew-washed air
And for Thy loving watch and care
Which kept us through the silent night
And brought us safely to the light.

Be with us, Lord, through all this day
While we are happy at our play.
Be with us in our school and work!
May we no task or duty shirk!
Amen.

2. GRACE FOR THE NOONDAY MEAL

Dear Lord, we bow our heads to pray
At noontime of this happy day.
Thus far Thy love has kept us true
Half of this wondrous daytime through.

We thank Thee for the food we eat
And for our happy homes so sweet;
For all of those who love us so,
For all adventuring ways we go.
Amen.

3. GRACE BEFORE THE EVENING MEAL

Father, we thank Thee for this day
For food, for fun, for life, for play;
And as the evening shadows fall,
We bring to Thee, dear Lord, our all;
And as we pray, we ask Thy grace
Upon this happy, happy place.
Amen.
—WILLIAM L. STIDGER, 1885-1949

[177] Before Any New Study

ALMIGHTY God, in whose hands are all the powers of man; who givest understanding, and takest it away; who, as it seemeth good unto Thee, enlightenest the thoughts of the simple, and darkenest the meditations of the wise, be present with me in my studies and enquiries.

Grant, O Lord, that I may not lavish away the life which Thou hast given me on useless trifles, nor waste it in vain searches after things which Thou hast hidden from me.

Enable me, by thy Holy Spirit, so to shun sloth and negligence, that every day may discharge part of the task which Thou hast allotted me; and so further with thy help that labour which, without thy help, must be ineffectual, that I may obtain, in all my undertakings, such success as will most promote thy glory, and the salvation of my own soul, for the sake of Jesus Christ. Amen.

—SAMUEL JOHNSON, 1709-1784

[178] God Abides in Our Grief

ALL you who mourn the loss of loved ones, and, at this hour, remember the sweet companionship and the cherished hopes that have passed away with them, give ear to the word of comfort spoken in the name of God. Only the body has died and has been laid in the dust. The spirit lives in the shelter of God's love and mercy. Our loved ones continue, also, in the remembrance of those to whom they were precious. Their deeds of lovingkindness, the true and beautiful words they spoke are treasured up as incentives to conduct by which the living honor the dead. And when we ask in our grief: Whence shall come our help and our comfort? then in the strength of faith let us answer with the Psalmist: My help cometh from God. He will not forsake us nor leave us in our grief. Upon Him we cast our burden and He will grant us strength according to the days He has apportioned to us. All life comes from Him; all souls are in His keeping. Come then, and in the midst of sympathizing fellow-worshipers, rise and hallow the name of God.

—THE UNION PRAYERBOOK FOR JEWISH WORSHIP (Edited 1941; 1948)

[179] The Companion of My Pilgrimage

THOU, Lord, art the companion of my pilgrimage; wheresoever I go Thine eyes are always upon me. Now with Thee seeing is motion. Therefore Thou movest with me and never ceasest from motion so long as I move. If I am at rest, there Thou art with me also. If I ascend, Thou ascendest, if I descend, Thou descendest; whithersoever I turn me, there Thou art. Nor dost Thou desert me in the day of trouble; as often as I call upon Thee, Thou art near. For to call upon Thee is to turn unto Thee, and Thou canst not fail him that turneth unto Thee, nor could any turn unto Thee wert not Thou already at hand. Thou art present before I turn unto Thee. For, unless Thou were present and didst entreat me, I should know naught at all of Thee, and how could I turn unto Thee whom I knew not at all?

Thou, then, my God, art He who beholdeth all things. And with Thee to behold is to work. So Thou workest all things. Therefore not unto us, O Lord, not unto us, but unto Thy great Name . . . I will sing glory for ever.

—NICHOLAS OF CUSA, 1401-1464

[180] A Morning Prayer

BLESSED be Thou, most gracious God, that again Thou hast brought light out of darkness and caused the morning to appear! Blessed be Thou that Thou dost send me forth, in health and vigour, to the duties and doings of another day! Go with me, I beseech Thee, through all the sunlit hours, and so protect me from every evil way that, when evening comes, I need not hide my head in shame.

O Thou who hast so graciously called me to be Thy servant, I would hold myself in readiness to-day for Thy least word of command. Give me the spirit, I pray Thee, to keep myself in continual training for the punctual fulfilment of Thy most holy will.

Let me keep the edges of my mind keen:

Let me keep my thinking straight and true:

Let me keep my passions in control:

Let me keep my will active:

Let me keep my body fit and healthy:

Let me remember Him whose meat it was to do the will of Him that sent Him.

149

O Lord of the vineyard, I beg Thy blessing upon all who truly desire to serve Thee by being diligent and faithful in their several callings, bearing their due share of the world's burden, and going about their daily tasks in all simplicity and uprightness of heart.

For all who tend flocks or till the soil:
For all who work in factories or in mines:
For all who buy and sell in the market-place:
For all who labour with their brains:
For all who labour with their pens:
For all who tend the hearth:

Dear Lord, I pray.

In Thy great mercy save us all from the temptations that do severally beset us, and bring us to everlasting life, by the power of the Holy Cross. Amen.

—JOHN BAILLIE, 1886-

[181] The Joy in Suffering

O MY God, my God, unhappy and tormented was my childhood, full of torments my youth. I have lamented, I have sighed, and I have wept. Yet I thank Thee, not as the wise Sovereign; no, no, I thank Thee, the one who art infinite love, for having acted thus! Man has before him a life of thirty, forty, perhaps seventy years; in Thy love Thou hast prevented me from buying for this sum just the little sweets of the kind for which I would have no memory in eternity, or which I would even recall for my eternal torment—as having bought the worthless.

Thou hast obliged me (and there were also many moments in which Thou hast spoken with kindness but of the same thing, not that I should escape the suffering but that it was even Thy love which placed me in these sufferings). Thou hast obliged me to buy these sufferings: blessed. For each suffering thus bought is the communion in suffering with Thee, and is forever and forever an eternal acquisition, for one remembers only one's suffering.

—SÖREN KIERKEGAARD, 1813-1855

[182] Have then a Little Patience

FATHER in Heaven! Show unto us a little patience; for we often intend in all sincerity to commune with Thee and yet we speak in such a foolish fashion. Sometimes, when we judge that what has come to us is good, we do not have enough words to thank Thee; just as a mistaken child is thankful for having gotten his own way. Sometimes things go so badly that we call upon Thee; we even complain and cry unto Thee; just as an unreasoning child fears what would do him good. Oh, but if we are so childish how far from being true children of Thine who art our true Father, ah, as if an animal would pretend to have man as a father. How childish we are and how little our proposals and our language resemble the language which we ought to use with Thee, we understand at least that it ought not to be thus and that we ought to be otherwise. Have then a little patience with us.

—SÖREN KIERKEGAARD, 1813-1855

[183] Draw Near to Me, O God

FATHER in Heaven! Avert Thy countenance from me no longer, let it once again shine upon me so that I may walk in Thy path, and not lose myself further and further away from Thee, where Thy voice can no longer reach me. O, let Thy voice come unto me, be heard by me even though it overtake me with terror on the wrong path, where I live secluded and alone, as though sick and besmirched, far from communion with Thee and mankind. Thou, my Lord Jesus Christ, Thou who camest into the world in order to save those who were lost, Thou who didst leave the ninety and nine sheep in order to look for the lost one, look Thou for me in the path of my errors, where I hide myself from Thee and from mankind, Thou the good shepherd let me hear Thy gentle voice, let me know it, let me follow it! Thou Holy Spirit, come before me with inexpressible sighs, pray for me as Abraham prayed for depraved Sodom, if there be only one pure thought, only one better feeling in me, that the time of trial may be prolonged for the barren tree, O Holy Spirit, Thou dost bear again those who are already dead, who dost give youth to the old, renew my heart and create in me a new heart, Thou who with motherly care dost protect everything in which there is still a spark of life.

—SÖREN KIERKEGAARD, 1813-1855

[184] A Prayer Against Hypocrisy

O GOD, whose Spirit searcheth all things, and whose love beareth all things, encourage us to draw near to Thee in sincerity and in truth. Save us from a worship of the lips while our hearts are far away. Save us from the useless labour of attempting to conceal ourselves from Thee who searchest the heart.

Enable us to lay aside all those cloaks and disguises which we wear in the light of day and here to bare ourselves, with all our weakness, disease and sin, naked to Thy sight.

Make us strong enough to bear the vision of the truth, and to have done with all falsehood, pretence, and hypocrisy, so that we may see things as they are, and fear no more. . . . And may we have the grace of gratitude, and the desire to dedicate ourselves to Thee. Amen.

—W. E. ORCHARD, 1877-1955

[185] Twenty-eight Days After Wife's Death

O LORD, our heavenly Father, almighty and most merciful God, in whose hands are life and death, who givest and takest away, castest down and raisest up, look with mercy on the affliction of thy unworthy servant, turn away thine anger from me, and speak peace to my troubled soul. Grant me the assistance and comfort of thy Holy Spirit, that I may remember with thankfulness the blessings so long enjoyed by me in the society of my departed wife; make me so to think on her precepts and example, that I may imitate whatever was in her life acceptable in thy sight, and avoid all by which she offended Thee. Forgive me, O merciful Lord, all my sins, and enable me to begin and perfect that reformation which I promised her, and to persevere in that resolution, which she implored Thee to continue, in the purposes which I recorded in thy sight, when she lay dead before me, in obedience to thy laws, and faith in thy word. And now, O Lord, release me from my sorrow, fill me with just hopes, true faith, and holy consolations, and enable me to do my duty in that state of life to which Thou hast been pleased to call me, without disturbance from fruitless grief, or tumultuous imaginations; that in all my thoughts, words, and actions, I may glorify thy Holy Name, and finally obtain, what I hope thou hast granted to thy departed servant, everlasting joy and felicity, through our Lord Jesus Christ. Amen.

—SAMUEL JOHNSON, 1709-1784

[186] To Face Life Without Fear

GRANT unto us, Almighty God, that, when our vision fails, and our understanding is darkened; when the ways of life seem hard, and the brightness of life is gone, to us grant the wisdom that deepens faith when the sight is dim, and enlarges trust when the understanding is not clear. And whensoever Thy ways in nature or in the soul are hard to be understood, then may our quiet confidence, our patient trust, our loving faith in Thee be great, and as children knowing that they are loved, cared for, guarded, kept, may we with a quiet mind at all times put our trust in the unseen God. So may we face life without fear, and death without fainting; and, whatsoever may be in the life to come, give us confident hope that whatsoever is best for us both here and hereafter is Thy good pleasure, and will be Thy law. Amen.

—GEORGE DAWSON, 1821-1876

[187] A Consecration of Talents

O ETERNAL God, who hast created me to do the work of God after the manner of men, and to serve Thee in this generation, and according to my capacities; give me Thy grace that I may be a prudent spender of my time, so as I may best prevent or resist all temptation, and be profitable to the Christian commonwealth; and, by discharging all my duty, may glorify Thy name. Take from me all slothfulness, and give me a diligent and an active spirit, and wisdom to choose my employment; that I may do works proportionable to my person, and to the dignity of a Christian, and may fill up all the spaces of my time with actions of religion and charity; improving my talent intrusted to me by Thee, my Lord, that I may enter into the joy of the Lord, to partake of Thy eternal felicities, even for Thy mercy's sake. Amen.

—JEREMY TAYLOR, 1613-1667

[188] A Thanksgiving Prayer

O GIVER of every gift, we remember the spirit of our Pilgrim forefathers, which caused them to give thanks for thy guidance amid the bleakness

153

and hunger of the Plymouth colony. We recognize the part that belief in thy laws has played in the building of America, and we also praise thee for what life holds for us today. We praise thee for seed-time and harvest, for all the provisions nature makes for those who labor with intelligence.

We thank thee for this vast land given to us as an inheritance, for our fathers who established its communities, for those who have toiled and sacrificed for human freedom and just government. We praise thee for patriarchs, prophets, pioneers, scientists, teachers, and public servants; for all who have resisted falsehood and upheld the right; for all who have overcome backwardness and despair, and pushed forward to new horizons.

Almighty God, bless our country with sound learning, honorable industry, and pure manners. Save us from violence, discord, and confusion; from pride and arrogance; and from every evil way. Guide those to whom public responsibilities are committed. Give them wisdom and moral courage. Grant that the leaders of our nation may seek the guidance of thy spirit.

Help us all as fellow Americans to see clearly, to decide justly, and to act with united strength in the cause of freedom and fraternity. Amen.

—ROBERT M. BARTLETT, 1898-

[189] The Ascending Trail

I BOW before thee, O unseen spirit, whom men call God. Thou art from everlasting to everlasting, and thy years fail not. Of old hast thou laid the foundations of the earth. In thy sight a thousand years are but a watch in the night. O divine power who hast proved to be the abiding place of all generations, I realize as I pray that I am part of an infinite world, that I am capable of achievements not yet realized. O thou who dost live beyond change and confusion, ever greater than my thoughts, ever higher than my hopes, ever more steadfast than my loyalties, I come to thee, believing that thou art a friend closer to me than breathing, and nearer than hands and feet. . . .

Eternal God, the beginning and the end of existence is to know thee. The career of man is one long quest for thee. In the morning of life, may I train my mind to think thy thoughts after thee. As I journey onward, may I climb each day a little higher along the ascending trail that leads to knowledge of thee, until I stand at last upon the summit and achieve the fulfilment of myself. Amen.

—Robert M. Bartlett, 1898-

[190] Good Friday

O Father of love and compassion, we pray today for all those who suffer; for the hungry, weary multitudes of the earth; for those who bear the pain of sickness and the anguish of grief. We pray for the unemployed, the homeless, the destitute; for those who are overworked, downtrodden, and in despair. O God of mercy, grant that we may behold today the eternal sufferer on his cross, waiting for us to liberate him by breaking the chains of evil that enslave mankind.

On a storm-swept hill, long ago, Jesus made clear the way of love to men. Forgive us our failure to follow his ideals. On this day the vision of his noble spirit and long-suffering love steals over us, and we desire to begin a new life of comradeship with him, who made this holy hour to be remembered through the centuries. Quicken our hearts, that we may heed our brothers' cry in need, and labor valiantly to free them from pain and death.

Help us to hold fast to his way of life regardless of the cost; and if suffering comes to us, may we bear it bravely, knowing that nothing can ever separate us from thy love. When our strength is spent, help us to remember that thy everlasting arms are underneath us and that the Good Shepherd walks beside us, cheering our way. Amen.

—Robert M. Bartlett, 1898-

[191] Teach Us to Learn from Christ

O God our Father: Forgive us that we do not clearly understand how to walk in the footsteps of Christ, though with our lips we name His name. We take Thy name upon our lips in prayer, and do not deeply grasp His teachings. We confess our easy-going indifference. We confess that because our lives are not filled with the conscious desire to save others, we have not perceived that Christ, the Christ who was worthy to be the Son of God, this Christ who saves us, is offering his blood to wipe away

155

the stains which come from the gaping wounds of the hearts of men. Teach us the many things we should learn from the example of Christ. O reveal to us now, with radiant clearness, the Christ who passed through the death upon the Cross in order to redeem us. When we are sad, when we are criticized by others unkindly, when our hearts are burdened with greed, teach us to fix our eyes upon the God-like figure of Christ, who refused to depend upon violence or force, or to return evil for evil. Lead us forward upon our path, we pray, in the name of our Savior. Amen.

—TOYOHIKO KAGAWA, 1888-1960

[192] Guidance in a Time of Economic Change

O GOD, our Father: We seek Thy guidance in this time of great economic change. We confess the sins of our age: that there is struggle between the capitalists and the proletariat in our society today; that there is strife between the peoples of different nations. The poor are wandering about our streets, and social work and social movements are powerless to help them. In truth, our hearts are filled with shame at the plight in which we find ourselves.

Teach us to meditate upon the life of Christ, and to remember how he threw his life away for the race of men. As we contemplate his passion and the blood which he shed, may Thy Spirit work deeply in our hearts. Strengthen us that we may live lives worth while, be it in ever so small a way. Inspired by the love of Christ, teach us to fling aside all desire for selfish advantage and for group privilege. Do Thou teach us, O Christ, to take up the Cross and to serve society. . . . Amen.

—TOYOHIKO KAGAWA, 1888-1960

[193] To Carry Others' Burdens

HEAVENLY FATHER: Teach us of the privileged classes, whose lives are filled with every blessing, to take a step forward into the road of redemptive love. Although Jesus himself was without sin, he took the faults of men upon himself, and carried the Cross of redemptive love. We have not sincerely undertaken the life of faith. We idle our days away in listlessness. We are unconscious or only half-conscience of life's chal-

156

lenge. Awaken us, O God, that we may with sincerity carry the burdens of others. Grant that we may not be content to live empty lives, seeking only the pleasure that each day brings. Cause us to advance to the Cross. All society lies under a shadow, and we are apprehensive over the future of Japan. Our consciences are clouded. Awake us, O God, to our responsibility for sufferers in the depths of misery. Inspire us to undertake to save them, in the Spirit of Jesus, till at length all mankind will join in singing praises to Thy name. And this I pray in the name of our Lord Jesus. Amen.

—TOYOHIKO KAGAWA, 1888-1960

[194] Save Us from Pride

O THOU who transcendest all thought of Thee as the heavens are higher than the earth; we acknowledge that we cannot search Thee out to perfection, but we thank Thee that Thou, the Invisible, comest to us in the things that are seen; that Thy exceeding glory is shadowed in the flower that blooms for a day, in the light that fades; that Thine infinite love has been incarnate in lowly human life; and that Thy presence surrounds all our ignorance, Thy holiness our sin, Thy peace our unrest.

Give us that lowly heart which is the only temple that can contain the infinite. Save us from the presumption that prides itself on a knowledge which is not ours, and from the hypocrisy and carelessness which professes an ignorance which Thy manifestation has made for ever impossible. Save us from calling ourselves by a name that Thou alone canst wear, and from despising the image of Thyself Thou has formed us to bear, and grant that knowledge of Thee revealed in Jesus Christ which is our eternal life. Amen.

—W. E. ORCHARD, 1877-1955

[195] Elgin Cathedral Epitaph

> Here lie I, Martin Elginbrodde:
> Hae mercy on my soul, Lord God,
> As I would do, were I Lord God
> And Ye were Martin Elginbrodde.

157

[196] The Art of Patience

LORD, teach me the art of patience whilst I am well, and give me the use of it when I am sick. In that day either lighten my burden or strengthen my back. Make me, who so often in my health have discovered my weakness presuming on my own strength, to be strong in my sickness when I solely rely on Thy assistance.

—THOMAS FULLER, 1608-1661

[197] Prayer for Generosity

Teach us, good Lord, to serve Thee as Thou deservest:
To give and not to count the cost;
To fight and not to heed the wounds;
To toil and not to seek for rest;
To labour and not to ask for any reward
Save that of knowing that we do Thy will.

—IGNATIUS OF LOYOLA, 1491-1556

[198] Be Thou a Strong Tower of Defence

O MERCIFUL God, be Thou unto me a strong tower of defence, I humbly entreat Thee. Give me grace to await Thy leisure, and patiently to bear what Thou doest unto me; nothing doubting or mistrusting Thy goodness towards me, for Thou knowest what is good for me better than I do. Therefore do with me in all things what Thou wilt; only arm me, I beseech Thee, with Thine armour, that I may stand fast; above all things, taking to me the shield of faith; praying always that I may refer myself wholly to Thy will, abiding Thy pleasure, and comforting myself in those troubles which it shall please Thee to send me, seeing such troubles are profitable for me; and I am assuredly persuaded that all Thou doest cannot but be well; and unto Thee be all honour and glory.

—LADY JANE GREY, 1537-1554

[199] Queen Elizabeth's Prayer

O LORD God everlasting, Which reignest over the kingdoms of men . . .
so teach me, I humbly beseech Thee, Thy word, and so strengthen me
with Thy grace that I may feed Thy people with a faithful and a true
heart, and rule them prudently with power. O Lord, Thou hast set me
on high. My flesh is frail and weak. If I therefore at any time forget Thee,
touch my heart, O Lord, that I may again remember Thee. If I swell
against Thee, pluck me down in my own conceit. . . . I acknowledge, O
my King, without Thee my throne is unstable, my seat unsure, my kingdom tottering, my life uncertain. I see all things in this life subject to
mutability, nothing to continue still at one stay. . . . Create therefore in
me, O Lord, a new heart, and so renew my spirit that Thy law may be my
study, Thy truth my delight, Thy church my care, Thy people my crown,
Thy righteousness my pleasure, Thy service my government; so shall this
my kingdom through Thee be established with peace.

1533-1603

[200] God Is a Resting Place

LIKE pillow to tired head, like light to watching eyes, like wine to fainting heart, be Thou our God to us this night.

Wearied by the conflict of life, worn by the burden of the day, we
seek Thee as our resting place. May Thy eternal calm descend upon our
troubled spirits and give us all Thy peace. Amid the treacherous sands
of time Thou standest still, the Rock of Ages. In life's desert places Thou
art a spring whose waters never fail.

We turn from our perplexities, our imperfections, and our sins to Thine
infinite perfection, goodness and beauty; like men who turn from dusty
toil to cleansing streams, like those who raise their eyes from the city's
foul and narrow streets to snow-clad mountains and the light of stars.

Appear to our waiting eyes, welcome us with outstretched arms, clasp
us to Thy heart. Amen.

—W. E. ORCHARD, 1877-1955

[201] To Face the Years with Courage

O LORD, I shut out the din and fret the littleness of things that I may feel myself alone with Thee in the silence. As a child yields itself to loving arms, I yield myself to Thee, asking for nothing, complaining about nothing. What if my labor is hard, what if my lot is humble, what if my dreams turn into futile tears, if only there is the peace of Thy nearness in my heart. There comes to me in the stillness, despite the terror and tumult of life, a trust in a goodness that nourishes the roots of the grass-blade, that glows in the flaming star, and attains fulfillment in the soul of man. How healing and strengthening is this communion with Thee, O God! If only I could always abide in it! But I must go forth again to the struggle for daily bread, to the restlessness of desire and the fear of pain, to the disillusionment of dreams that never come true. Let me not go forth alone, O God. Abide Thou deep in the solitude of my heart, that I may trust in Thee and be unafraid in the face of the inscrutable years, and see that everything happens for the best. Amen.

—THE UNION PRAYERBOOK FOR JEWISH WORSHIP (Edited 1941; 1948)

[202] I Need Thy Light to Guide

Oh blessed Lord! How much I need
Thy Light to guide me on my way!
So many hands, that, without heed,
Still touch Thy wounds and make them bleed,
So many feet that day by day
Still wander from Thy fold astray!
Feeble at best is my endeavour!
I see but cannot reach the height
That lies for ever in the Light;
And yet for ever and for ever,
When seeming just within my grasp,
I feel my feeble hands unclasp,
And sink discouraged into night;—
For Thine own purpose Thou has sent
The strife and the discouragement.

  —HENRY WADSWORTH LONGFELLOW, 1807-1882

[203] To Play the Man

THE day returns and brings us the petty round of irritating concerns and duties. Help us to play the man, help us to perform them with laughter and kind faces; let cheerfulness abound with industry. Give us to go blithely on our business all this day, bring us to our resting beds weary and content and undishonored; and grant us in the end the gift of sleep. Amen.

—ROBERT LOUIS STEVENSON, 1850-1894

[204] Faithfulness in All Duties

O LORD, our Guide even unto death, grant us, I pray thee, grace to follow thee whithersoever thou goest. In little daily duties to which thou callest us, bow down our wills to simple obedience, patience under pain or provocation, strict truthfulness of word and manner, humility, kindness. In great acts of duty or perfection if thou shouldest call us to them, uplift us to self-sacrifice, heroic courage, laying down of life for thy truth's sake or for a brother. Amen.

—CHRISTINA G. ROSSETTI, 1830-1894

[205] A Prayer for Renewal

GIVE us, O Lord, purity of lips, clean and innocent hearts, and rectitude of action; give us humility, patience, self-control, prudence, justice, and courage; give us the spirit of wisdom and understanding, the spirit of counsel and strength, the spirit of knowledge and godliness, and of thy fear; make us ever to seek thy face with all our heart, all our soul, all our mind; grant us to have a contrite and humbled heart in thy presence, to prefer nothing to thy love. Have mercy upon us, we humbly beseech thee; through Jesus our Lord. Amen.

—GALLICAN SACRAMENTARY, A.D. 800

161

[206] Be All to All

WE beseech thee, O Lord, remember all for good; have mercy upon all, O
God. Remember every soul who, being in any affliction, trouble, or agony,
stands in need of thy mercy and help, all who are in necessity, or distress,
all who love or hate us. Thou, O Lord, art the Helper of the helpless, the
Hope of the hopeless, the Saviour of them who are tossed with tempests,
the Haven of them who sail; be thou All to all. The glorious majesty of
the Lord our God be upon us; prosper thou the work of our hands upon
us, O prosper thou our handiwork! Lord, be thou within us, to strengthen
us; without us, to keep us; above us, to protect us; beneath us, to uphold
us; before us, to direct us; behind us, to keep us from straying; round
about us, to defend us. Blessed be thou, O Lord our Father, for ever and
ever. Amen.

—LANCELOT ANDREWES, 1555-1626

[207] Strong to Endure

WE beseech thee, Lord, to behold us with favor. Be patient still; suffer
us a while longer to endure, and (if it may be) help us to do better. Bless
to us our extraordinary mercies. Be with our friends; be with ourselves.
Go with each of us to rest; if any awake, temper to them the dark hours
of watching; and when the day returns to us, call us up with morning
faces, and with morning hearts—eager to labor—eager to be happy, if
happiness should be our portion—and if the day be marked for sorrow—
strong to endure it.

—ROBERT LOUIS STEVENSON, 1850-1894

[208] A Petition in Time of War

ALMIGHTY God, who art the Father of our spirits and the Guardian of
our lives, we pray Thee for comfort and courage in this hour. We know
that Thou art ever with us, for we cannot be where Thou art not. In the
labors of the day as in the watches of the night, on sea and land and in
the air, in far countries, among strange peoples, Thy presence is known,

and Thy blessing, like the sun and rain, a gift from out Thy hand. So we do take heart in every lot, and fear not the peril of any hour. . . .

We pray Thee for our country, that she may be ever true to the ideals of liberty which we have been summoned to serve and save. Guard her shores from every foe, her people from undue suffering and loss, her rulers from lust of power and dominion. Grant this nation, in this hour of her travail, a new birth of freedom, that government of the people, for the people, and by the people may not perish from the earth.

And we pray, O God, for peace, for reconciliation, for brotherhood. Speed, O speed, the coming of the day when war and rumors of war shall be no more, and all men be happy in love one for another and for Thy Kingdom. Yet if the time be still delayed and the woe grievous, we would bow unto Thy holy will, and grant Thy judgments true and righteous altogether. For Thy name's sake, O God, Amen!

—JOHN HAYNES HOLMES, 1879-

[209] A Prayer for Our Country in Wartime

GRACIOUS God, Father of all men, we turn to Thee to pray for our stricken world. As nations fight and Thy children strive to slay each other we are grateful for the ties that unite those who think of Thee as their Common Father. We can thank Thee for every longing for a better world, and we know that such a world is possible only because men believe in a spiritual purpose in our universe, a far-off divine event to which the whole creation moves. May that be the goal of all our fighting and striving!

We thank Thee for our country and the idealism that persists in our dreams of a more democratic society. We want our country to aid in the creation of a better world, and we desire here for all our people in the United States a nobler and a better life. Take away our selfishness and forgive us the wrongs we have done to others in our land. . . . As members of Thy family on earth give us truly a co-operative spirit! We ask this in the name of Thy Son and our Elder Brother, Jesus Christ. Amen.

—IVAN LEE HOLT, 1886-

[210] A Prayer for Courage in Time of War

GOD of our Fathers, we stand before Thee in an hour of turmoil and strife. Our souls are bared before Thee in the commonness of experience which engulfs us all. Our nation has summoned us to defend its life and ideals, and our hearts are joined in prayer for the homes we love, for the labors we follow and for the land of our allegiance. . . .

Now we stand at the threshold of a new experience. Drawn to the service of our beloved country, we face unknown trials and dangers. We pray Thee, Giver of life and Source of love, to keep our hearts clean and our spirits exalted. Help us to be servants of that ideal which made our nation the bulwark of liberty on earth. Inspire us to know the meaning of sacrifice on behalf of the democratic way of life. Stir us to constant recognition of our duty to preserve the last best hope on earth. Give us the vision of the world that can and shall be built on the ashes of disappointment and on the ruins of withered hopes. Imbue us with respect for humanity that we remain to resist cruelty and tyranny wherever they may abide. . . . May our labors be fruitful in the building of a peace born of wider understanding and greater trust of the children of men. Establish Thou the work of our hands, yea, the work of our hands establish Thou it.

—CHARLES E. SHULMAN, 1900-

[211] Amid Time of Struggle

WE thank Thee, our Father, for the impulse to love that stirs deeply within the human heart and for the objects which thou hast provided which we can truly and constantly love: our families and friends, our associates and fellows, our schools and churches, our villages and cities and open fields, our broad free land where our lot is cast. These all move us to affection and to grateful thanksgiving. We thank thee also for the ideals we love and cherish: truth and gentleness, freedom and law, honor and tolerance, hospitality and hard work. Help us, we beseech thee, in times when some of these precious things are scorned or forgotten or the object of the destroyer's fury, to remember them as thy gifts to us and to dedicate our lives for their preservation . . . .

To this good end do thou preserve in us the sense of thyself amid the human contacts that surround us; give us a ready response to the things

164

that make for peace within the world. . . . Bless those who are dear to us and hasten the day of glad reunion and peaceful living. And against all that life may bring to us, keep us clean in body and mind, clear in vision and purpose, and courageous to do whatever the day demands. Teach unto us . . . and help us all, in thy good time, to walk together therein, through Jesus Christ our Lord. Amen.

—EDWIN McNEILL POTEAT, 1892-1950

[212] For World Brotherhood

FATHER of all mankind . . . . Thou knowest the inarticulate yearnings of my heart. Thou, in thine infinite wisdom, art aware of the unanswered questions in my mind. Illuminate my inner darkness. Help me to perceive the truth in the midst of the confused counsels of men. Give me courage to obey the truth as it is revealed to me.

I do not know what lies ahead on the long, long trail. But I believe Thou wilt be there. Help me to play the man in every situation. When danger threatens, may I not waver. When temptation assails, give me strength to resist. When loneliness overtakes me, grant me the vivid sense of Thy presence. . . .

Help us all to unite in building a world where a just and durable peace shall be the heritage of all mankind.

—ALBERT EDWARD DAY, 1884-

[213] To Be a Christian in Time of Turmoil

O GOD, I come to you because I am your child. You have created the world by your power and You are constantly sustaining and renewing it by divine wisdom and love. So also, I believe, You have created me. And I continue to live because, day by day, You are upholding me and renewing my life just as you do all the rest of Your creation.

Strengthen and sustain me with this faith in time of turmoil. O eternal and ever-loving Father, help me to realize that You are my refuge, and that underneath me, and all whom I hold dear, are Your everlasting arms.

O God, help me to be honest with myself, my friends, and most of all with You. May I never call good, evil; or evil, good. Keep me straight and true as a carpenter's square or a mason's plumbline. And, if I do wrong, may I be brave enough to tell You about it promptly and ask for Your forgiveness. May I never try to fool myself—or You! . . .

Amid all the monotony and routine of life, make me always be a good comrade, a reliable friend and a true sportsman, who tries to play the game of life clean and fair with all whom I may meet. When weariness or discouragement, loneliness or fear, make me glum and down-hearted, bring to my remembrance Jesus Christ who was a man of sorrows and acquainted with grief, but who rose triumphant over defeat and death. I would put all my trust in Him as Master of my soul, my Helper and Deliverer in every need. And so it is in His dear name I pray. Amen.

—ALBERT W. PALMER, 1879-1954

[214] To Live with Faith, Hope, and Courage

O GOD, Father of all mankind, in these days when society is divided, nation against nation, people against people, keep us ever mindful of the bonds of fellowship which bind us all into one great family. Let no differences or divisions of race, creed, or nationality sunder our sense of kinship with Thee and with one another. In the face of uncertainty and darkness, help us to live with faith and hope and courage. Though we are beset on every side, let us not despair. Though temptations surround us, keep us strong in Thy presence. Make us sensitive to our share in the sin and suffering of the world, that with repentant hearts and contrite spirits, our feet may be set upon the roads of service and sacrifice, of reconciliation and redemption. May the failures of the past be an incentive to a finer future and a more Christian order. Make us grateful for the many blessings which Thou hast given us, and grant that we may show forth our thankfulness not only by our words, but by our lives. All of which we ask through Him Who is the Giver of all good things, the Lord and Father of mankind. Amen.

—W. APPLETON LAWRENCE, 1889-

[215] God the Source of Hope

ETERNAL God, our heavenly Father, from whom our spirits come and to whom they shall return, lift us, we pray thee, to thy presence.

166

Thou art the source of our faith and the ground of our hope.

Thou art the strength that gives us courage and the courage that gives us strength.

When we offend against thy holy laws and suffer the consequences of our folly, thou art the spirit that disturbs us and the mercy that restores us.

When we loyally undertake to do thy will, thou art the light that guides us and the power that upholds us.

When our work on earth is done, thou art the resurrection and the life everlasting.

O God most merciful and gracious, we who are weary and heavy-laden would find rest in thee; we who have sinned would obtain thy forgiveness, thy healing, and thy peace; we who are confused and sorely tempted would be guided by thy wisdom and fortified by thy righteousness; we who are anxious for the morrow would know that thou art with us and that thy grace is sufficient for us. . . . Amen.

—ERNEST FREMONT TITTLE, 1885-1949

[216] To Face Every Experience with God

ALMIGHTY God, Who hast made the world and all that is in it, create in me, I humbly pray, a clean heart and renew a right spirit within me.

I am not my own, for I am Thine. Therefore help me inwardly that I may relax my own desires and let Thy wisdom and will control my doings. Deliver me from the futile effort to find in myself, my own strength, or my own wisdom any haven of final refuge, but teach me evermore to give the rule and government of all my life to Thee. Be pleased to go before me: I shall follow. . . .

Give me quietness of spirit in face of all the chances whereto my present life is subject. Give me a mind so framed that, whatsoever happens, I may neither sorrow at my own lot or envy that of others. In the midst even of extremes of danger, help me to be sensible of Thy fatherly tenderness. Since I know all has been ordered of Thee, teach me to take whatever befalls me with a well-pleased and ready will, looking to see Thine own purposes fully wrought out from any happening. Amen.

—DOUGLAS HORTON, 1891-

[217] For Employers

WE invoke thy grace and wisdom, O Lord, upon all men of good will who employ and control the labor of men. . . . When they are tempted to follow the ruthless ways of others, and to sacrifice human health and life for profit, do thou strengthen their will in the hour of need. . . . May they not sin against Christ by using the bodies and souls of men as mere tools to make things, forgetting the human hearts and the longings of these their brothers. Raise up among us employers who shall be makers of men as well as of goods.

—WALTER RAUSCHENBUSCH, 1861-1918

[218] For Workingmen

O GOD, thou mightiest worker of the universe, source of all strength and author of all unity, we pray thee for our brothers, the industrial workers of the nation. As their work binds them together in common toil and danger, may their hearts be knit together in a strong sense of their common interests and to fulfil the law of Christ by bearing the common burdens. Grant the organizations of labor quiet patience and prudence in all disputes. . . . Bless all classes of our nation, and build up for the republic of the future a great body of workers, strong of limb, clear of mind, fair in temper, glad to labor, conscious of their worth, and striving together for the final brotherhood of all men.

—WALTER RAUSCHENBUSCH, 1861-1918

[219] Canticle of the Creatures

O MOST high, almighty, good Lord God, to Thee belong praise, glory, honour, and all blessing!

Praised be my Lord God with all His creatures; and specially our brother the sun, who brings us the day, and who brings us the light; fair is he, and shining with a very great splendour: O Lord, to us he signifies Thee!

Praised be my Lord for our sister the moon, and for the stars, the which He has set clear and lovely in heaven.

168

Praised be my Lord for our brother the wind, and for air and cloud, calms and all weather, by the which Thou upholdest in life all creatures.

Praised be my Lord for our sister water, who is very serviceable unto us, and humble, and precious, and clean.

Praised be my Lord for our brother fire, through whom Thou givest us light in the darkness; and he is bright, and pleasant, and very mighty, and strong.

Praised be my Lord for our mother the earth, the which doth sustain us and keep us, and bringeth forth divers fruits, and flowers of many colours, and grass.

Praised be my Lord for all those who pardon one another for His love's sake and who endure weakness and tribulation; blessed are they who peaceably shall endure, for Thou, O most Highest, shalt give them a crown!

Praised be my Lord for our sister, the death of the body, from whom no man escapeth. Woe to him who dieth in mortal sin! Blessed are they who are found walking by Thy most holy will, for the second death shall have no power to do them harm.

Praise ye, and bless ye the Lord, and give thanks unto Him, and serve Him with great humility.

—Francis of Assisi, 1182-1226
[tr. by Matthew Arnold]

[220] Let Every Heart Burn

O God, who art to be found by those who truly seek Thee, known by those who love, seen by those whose heart is pure; Thy Spirit possesses all things, speaks in the holy dawn, calls in the quiet even, broods on the deep, and dwells in the heart of man.

Forgive us if we, made to commune with Thee, whose lives were ordered to walk with Thee, have grown insensible to Thy presence, have rested in the things that appear, grown careless of the eternal and the holy. Send now some word of Thine to make a highway to our hearts, and Thyself draw near. Shut us in gathered here, in with Thyself, alone, until every heart burns and each spirit moves toward Thee. May the Spirit of Jesus come upon us and make us at home with Thee. Amen.

—W. E. Orchard, 1877-1955

[221] Prayer for Courage

LET me not pray to be sheltered from dangers but to be fearless in facing them. Let me not beg for the stilling of my pain but for the heart to conquer it. Let me not look for allies in life's battle-field, but to my own strength. Let me not crave in anxious fear to be saved, but hope for the patience to win my freedom. Grant me that I may not be a coward, feeling your mercy in my success alone; but let me find the grasp of your hand in my failure.

—RABINDRANATH TAGORE, 1861-1941

[222] Prayer for Strength

THIS is my prayer to Thee, my Lord—Strike, strike at the root of penury in my heart. Give me the strength lightly to bear my joys and sorrows. Give me the strength to make my love fruitful in service. Give me the strength never to disown the poor or bend my knees before insolent might. Give me the strength to raise my mind above daily trifles. And give me the strength to surrender my strength to Thy will with love.

—RABINDRANATH TAGORE, 1861-1941

[223] Saint Francis' Prayer

LORD, make me an instrument of Thy peace. Where there is hate, may I bring love; where offense, may I bring pardon; may I bring union in place of discord; truth, replacing error; faith, where once there was doubt; hope, for despair; light, where was darkness, joy to replace sadness. Make me not to so crave to be loved as to love. Help me to learn that in giving I may receive; in forgetting self, I may find life eternal.

—FRANCIS OF ASSISI, 1182-1226

[224] Help Us Be Unafraid

O THOU who givest meaning to the strivings of men, attune our hearts for communion with Thee. How often, when everything else fails us, do we yearn for Thee. In the stillness of the night, in the press of the crowd, in the agony of inner conflict, we bow our heads, and lo, Thou art in our hearts and we are at peace. We know not, O Lord, whether the gifts for which we ask are for our good, whether our trials and tribulations may not be blessings in disguise, whether even the fragment of our shattered hopes and love may not minister to the upbuilding of other lives and the fulfillment of Thine unfathomable plan. So we do not pray unto Thee to make our lives easy, to give us happiness without alloy. Rather do we pray Thee to aid us to be uncomplaining and unafraid. Teach us to face life with faith and courage that we may see the blessings hidden away even in its discords and struggles. Help us to wrest victory from the discipline of pain. . . . Praised be Thou, O Lord, the stay and trust of the righteous.

—THE UNION PRAYERBOOK FOR JEWISH WORSHIP (Edited 1941; 1948)

[225] The Cross Brings Meaning to Life

OUR God, who art the Father of our spirits, when evening falls and strange feelings, ancient fears, obstinate questionings, rise within us, we turn to Thee, who alone holdest the secret of Thine own creation.

We believe some kindly purpose lies beyond our coming into the world: not chance, nor fate, nor punishment can explain life; but only love. We feel sure of this because of Thy word in our hearts, and because of Thy Word made flesh.

We have stood before a lonely cross whereon one died, despised and rejected of men, and there we have learned how pain and death need bring no defeat to Thy purposes, and hold no contradiction of Thy love.

Thou hast placed within our trembling hands the strands of life whose issues are in eternity. How shall we live aright; we who are sinful, weak, wilful? Be very merciful to Thy children, Father. The lessons of life are difficult unless one interpret to us. Give us to-night Thine interpretation of all that we are, and are destined yet to be. So shall we realize Thy salvation and be glad in Thee all our days. Amen.

—W. E. ORCHARD, 1877-1955

171

[226] For All Laborers

O GOD, Thou mightiest Worker of the universe, Source of all strength and Author of all unity, we pray Thee for our brothers the industrial workers of the nation. As their work binds them together in toil and danger, may their hearts be knit together in a strong sense of their common interests and so fulfil the law of Christ by bearing the common burdens. Grant the organizations of labour quiet patience and prudence in all disputes. Raise up leaders of able mind and large heart, and give them grace to follow wise counsel. Bless all classes of our nation and build up a great body of workers strong of limb, clear of mind, glad to labour, striving together for the final Brotherhood of all men; through Jesus Christ our Lord. Amen.

—WALTER RAUSCHENBUSCH, 1861-1918

[227] Gratitude for God's Mercies

WE thank Thee, O Lord our Lord, for our being, our life, our gift of reason; for our nurture, our preservation and guidance; for our education, civil rights and religious privileges; for Thy gifts of grace, of nature, of this world; for our redemption, regeneration, and instruction in the Christian Faith; for our calling, recalling, and our manifold renewed recallings for Thy forbearance and long suffering, Thy prolonged forbearance many a time and many a year. For all the benefits we have received, and all the undertakings wherein we have prospered; for any good we may have done; for the use of the blessing of this life; for Thy promise, and our hope of the enjoyment of good things to come; for good and honest parents, gentle teachers, benefactors ever to be remembered, congenial companions, intelligent hearers, sincere friends, faithful servants; for all who have profited us by their writings, sermons, conversations, prayers, examples, reproofs, injuries. For all these, and also for all other mercies, known and unknown, open and secret, remembered by us or now forgotten, kindnesses received by us willingly or even against our will. We praise Thee, we bless Thee, we thank Thee, and will praise and bless and thank Thee all the days of our life; through Jesus Christ our Lord. Amen.

—LANCELOT ANDREWES, 1555-1626

172

[228] A Petition for All Who Are Afflicted

ALMIGHTY God, our Heavenly Father, Who lovest all and forgettest none, we bring to Thee our supplications for all Thy creatures and all Thy children. For all whom we love and for whom we watch and care. For all who have blessed us with kindness and led us with patience, restored us with their sympathy and help.

We remember before Thee all on whom hast laid the cross of suffering, the sick in body and the weak in mind. All who have been bereaved of relations or friends, all who are troubled by the suffering or sin of those they love; all who have met with worldly loss, that in the dark and cloudy day they may find assurance and peace in Thee. We pray for all who are absorbed in their own grief, that they may be raised to share the sorrows of their brethren, and know the secret and blessed fellowship of the Cross. For all who are lonely and sad in the midst of others' joys, that they may know God as their Friend and Comforter. Remember, O Lord, the aged and infirm, all who are growing weary with the journey of life, all who are passing through the valley of shadows, that they may find that Christ the risen of the dead is with them, and that there is light at evening time.

O God our Father, hear our intercessions, answer them according to Thy will, and make us the channels of Thine infinite pity and love, for the sake of Jesus Christ Thy Son our Saviour and Redeemer. Amen.

—JOHN HUNTER, 1728-1793

[229] God Our Only Saviour

O LORD, our only Saviour, we cannot bear alone our load of responsibility; up-bear us under it. We look without seeing unless Thou purge our sight; grant us sight. We read without comprehending, unless Thou open our understanding; give us intelligence. Nothing can we do unless Thou prosper the work of our hands upon us; "O prosper Thou our handiwork." We are weak; out of weakness make us strong. We are in peril of death; come and heal us. We believe; help Thou our unbelief. We hope; let us not be disappointed of our hope. We love; grant us to love much, to love ever more and more, to love all and most of all to love Thee. Grant this, we humbly beseech Thee, for the sake of Christ Jesus our Lord. Amen.

—CHRISTINA G. ROSSETTI, 1830-1894

173

[230] A Prayer at Night

O GOD, Who never sleepest, and art never weary, have mercy upon those who watch to-night; on the sentry, that he may be alert; on those who command, that they may be strengthened with counsel; on the sick, that they may obtain sleep; on the wounded, that they may find ease; on the faint-hearted, that they may hope again; on the light-hearted, lest they forget Thee; on the dying, that they may find peace; on the sinful, that they may turn again. And save us, O good Lord. Amen.

—W. C. E. NEWBOLT, 1862-1938

[231] To Serve Others

MOST merciful Father, forgive me if I have made the lot of my fellow men more difficult through my indifference to their needs. I regret that I have sometimes been so concerned with my own narrow interests that I have forgotten my role as a friend to those less fortunate than I. May I remember that the greatest of all Christians is a servant, and that in helping to bear the burdens of others I comply with the Christian law of love. May thy mercy lend me strength to volunteer for others' crosses; may the unselfish example of Christ intrigue me to alleviate the evils about me which mar thy kingdom's arrival. When this earthly pilgrimage of mine is over I want to reflect on my life as one well spent. May this day bring thee no disappointment in me as thy co-operative servant. Amen.

[232] To See Life as an Adventure

O THOU who art the loving Protector of humanity, may I be aware this day that thou art with me in every thought and act. As thy Spirit didst abide with me through the silent hours of the night, so art thou consciously with me through the activities of my waking hours. Throughout this life of mine may Christ's experience of thy immanence remind me that thou art always my support in times of difficulty. May I grow in spiritual sensitivity to thy grace as the continuous supplement to my human frailties. As thy grace adds wonder and abundant meaning to

174

my present years, may I be further assured that this life of mine will cherish the adventure of eternal life with thee. May I live this day with such significance that its values may contribute to thy eternal purpose. Amen.

[233] O Infinite Love

THOU loving Father, everything goes wrong for me and yet Thou art love. I have even failed in holding fast to this—that Thou art love, and yet Thou art love. Wherever I turn, the only thing that I cannot do without is that Thou art love, and that is why, even when I have not held fast to the faith that Thou art love, I believe that Thou dost permit through love that it should be so, O Infinite Love.

— SÖREN KIERKEGAARD, 1813-1855

[234] The New Year

ANOTHER year has passed, O Heavenly Father! We thank Thee that it was a time of grace, and we are not terrified by the thought that it was also a time for which we shall render an account; for we trust in Thy mercy. The New Year confronts us with its demands; and though we cannot enter upon it without humility and concern, because we cannot and will not forget the lusts of the eye that ensnared us, the sweets of revenge that seduced us, the wrath that made us irreconcilable, the coldness of heart in which we fled from Thee, yet we do not enter it altogether empty-handed. For we take with us the memory of fearful doubts which were set at rest, of anxieties which were solaced, of the downcast mind which was cheered and strengthened, of the glad hope which was not put to shame. Aye, and when in our melancholy moods we seek strength and encouragement in the thought of the great men, Thy chosen instruments, who in sharp trials and profound anxieties kept their souls free, their courage unbroken, the heavens open above them, then we also wish to add to theirs our testimony, convinced that even if our courage is but discouragement in comparison with theirs, and our strength weakness, nevertheless, Thou art ever the same, the same mighty God who tires the spirits of men in combat, the same Father without whose knowledge no sparrow falls to the ground. Amen.

—SÖREN KIERKEGAARD, 1813-1855

[235] For All Who Toil

O GOD, our Heavenly Father, we beseech Thee to hear us on behalf of all those who live by strength of arm or skill of hand. For men who face peril. For women who suffer pain. For those who till the earth; for those who tend machinery. For those whose business is in the deep waters, for sailors and seafarers. For those who work in offices and warehouses, for those who buy and sell. For those who labour at furnaces and in factories. For those who toil in mines. For those who keep house, for those who train children. For all who control, rule, or employ. For all who are poor, and broken and oppressed. For all whose labour is without hope; for all whose labour is without honour. For all whose labour is without interest. For those who have too little leisure. For those who are underpaid. We pray for all women-workers. We pray for all those who work in dangerous trades. For those who cannot find work, for those who have no home. For all prisoners and outcasts. For all who are sick, hungry, or destitute. We pray, O Father, for all men everywhere, that it may please Thee to comfort, sustain, protect and support these, and all others for whom we desire to pray, through Jesus Christ our Lord. Amen.

—PERCY DEARMER, 1867-1936

[236] A Prayer for Renewal

WARM our cold hearts, Lord, we beseech Thee. Take away all that hinders us from giving ourselves to Thee. Mould us according to Thine own image. Give us grace to obey Thee in all things, and ever to follow Thy gracious leading. Make us this day to be kind to our fellow-men, to be gentle and unselfish, careful to hurt no one by word or deed, but anxious to do good to all, and make others happy. O Lord, forgive the sins of our tempers. Pardon all our hasty words and unchristian thoughts. Make us watchful, that we offend not with our tongue. Give us a meek and a

176

loving spirit, which is in Thy sight of great price. We would not live unto our selves, but unto Thee. Keep us from sin this day, and all that may offend Thee; for Jesus Christ's sake. Amen.

—ASHTON OXENDEN, 1808-1892

[237] For Some Hard Task

O FATHER, this day may bring some hard task to our life, or some hard trial to our love. We may grow weary, or sad, or hopeless in our lot. But, Father, our whole life until now has been one great proof of Thy care. Bread has come for our bodies, thoughts to our mind, love to our heart, and all from Thee. So help us, we implore Thee, while we stand still on this side of all that the day may bring, to resolve that we will trust Thee this day to shine into any gloom of the mind, to stand by us in any trial of our love, and to give us rest in Thy good time as we need. May this day be full of a power that shall bring us near to Thee, and make us more like Thee; and, O God, may we so trust Thee this day, that when the day is done our trust shall be firmer than ever. Then, when our last day comes and our work is done, may we trust Thee in death and for ever, in the spirit of Jesus Christ our Lord. Amen.

—ROBERT COLLYER, 1823-1912

[238] Consider Life's Earthly Pilgrimage

O LORD our God, and God of our fathers, Thou hast placed us upon this earth and hast appointed us to do Thy will. But we follow too often our evil inclination and transgress Thy laws. In Thy gracious love, Thou hast given us the Sabbath, that we pause in our striving after worldly goods and seek the treasures of the spirit which consecrate life unto Thee. And this Sabbath of Repentance admonishes us to turn from the pursuit of life's vanities. It bids us consider well our earthly pilgrimage and measure the deeds of the past year in the light of what we might have accomplished, had we given ourselves wholly unto Thee. We are overcome with shame and self-reproach as we realize wherein we have fallen short. Truly, O God, we know our weakness, and feel humbled and chastened. . . . May this day summon our energies to the fulfillment of

177

the divine plan of our life, and may it bring to our souls that inner peace in which alone the voice of Thy spirit is heard. Be Thou with us, O God, and receive us in Thy boundless love for Thou art our hope and support. Amen.

—THE UNION PRAYERBOOK FOR JEWISH WORSHIP (Edited 1941; 1948)

[239] God Is Known in Goodness

O LORD, how can we know Thee? Where can we find Thee? Thou art as close to us as breathing and yet art farther than the farthermost star. Thou art as mysterious as the vast solitudes of the night and yet as familiar to us as the light of the sun. To the seer of old Thou didst say: Thou canst not see my face, but I will make all My goodness pass before Thee. Even so does Thy goodness pass before us in the realm of nature and in the varied experiences of our lives. When justice burns like a flaming fire within us, when love evokes willing sacrifices from us, when, to the last full measure of selfless devotion, we proclaim our belief in the ultimate triumph of truth and righteousness, do we not bow before the vision of Thy goodness? Thou livest within our hearts, as Thou dost pervade the world, and we through righteousness behold Thy presence.

—THE UNION PRAYERBOOK FOR JEWISH WORSHIP (Edited 1941; 1948)

[240] Wisdom in Praying

> O God, grant us the serenity to accept
> What cannot be changed;
> The courage to change what can be changed,
> And wisdom to know one from the other. Amen.
>
> —REINHOLD NIEBUHR, 1892-

[241] The Living Present

O GOD in whose eternal wisdom alone is comprehended the mystery of Time, we thank Thee for the Past because Thou hast forgiven it: we

178

thank Thee for the Future because Thou hast hidden it: we thank Thee for the Present because Thou art wholly present in it, to meet us with Thy creative, redemptive, and sanctifying power, if we will awake from all dreams of past and future to live in Thy instant reality. Amen.

—GERALD HEARD, 1889-

[242] Eternity in the Heart of Man

ALMIGHTY God, our Father, who hast planted eternity in the heart of man and hast ordained that he should not find rest amid the things of time and sense: open to us, we pray Thee, the gates of that invisible realm wherein Thou dwellest, and grant that we may feel Thy greatness flow round about our incompleteness; round our restlessness Thy rest. Deliver us from bondage to sin and fear, and enable us, by Thy grace, to face life with the calm assurance of those whose confidence is in Thee. Thou art our mighty Helper amid all the perils of our earthly way. Hear us for Thy mercy's sake. Amen.

—JAMES D. MORRISON, 1893-1950

[243] Strength for Another Day

O GOD, give me strength to live another day. Let me not turn coward before its difficulties or prove recreant to its duties. Let me not lose faith in my fellow man. Keep me sweet and sound of heart, in spite of ingratitude, treachery, or meanness. Preserve me from minding little stings or giving them. Help me to keep my heart clean and to live honestly. Inspire me with the spirit of joy and gladness, and make me a cup of strength to suffering souls. Amen.

—PHILLIPS BROOKS, 1835-1893

[244] Guide Me in My Reading

LORD, let me never slight the meaning nor the moral of anything I read. Make me respect my mind so much that I dare not read what has no

179

meaning or moral. Help me to choose with equal care my friends and my books, because they are both for life. Show me that as in a river, so in reading, the depths hold more of strength and beauty than the shallows. Teach me to value art without being blind to thought. Keep me from caring more for much reading than for careful reading; for books than the Bible. Give me an ideal that will let me read only the best, and when that is done, stop me. Repay me with power to teach others, and then help me to say from a disciplined mind a grateful Amen.

—CHARLES LAMB, 1775-1834

[245] Love that Passeth Knowledge

O LOVE that passeth knowledge, come into my heart with all Thy fullness, that my heart may be made gentle with Thy gentleness. Grant me to bear others' burdens that I may cease to live for myself. Come Thou in that I may cease to be my own. Let me share with Thee in the bearing of the sin and sorrow of the vast world, let me take up crosses of the laboring and the heavy-laden. Fill me with Thyself that I may become the servant of humanity.

—GEORGE MATHESON, 1842-1906

[246] May Our Souls Be Responsive

O GOD, may our souls be responsive to the realities and to the mysteries of the ongoing life in the church. This life comes from afar, down through the ages of faith and struggle; it gathers force as the cloud of witnesses increases. Thou hast sent prophets, apostles, martyrs, heroes, and humble saints, whose influence make light to shine in earthly darkness, and enlarges the kingdom of heaven within us. Help us to cultivate with intelligence and use the good gifts we have received; and may we offer them with some increasement of understanding sacrifice and fidelity for those who come after us. Amen.

—EDWARD SCRIBNER AMES, 1870-1958

[247] A Prayer of Penitence

O GOD, when we review our lives we repent of them. We have so often been guilty of pettiness; we have let the moment obscure the hour, the hour the day, the day the year, the year the lifetime, the lifetime eternity. We have become excited over little things. We have permitted anger over insignificant matters. We have become absorbed in adventures which ended in dust. We have pursued fleeting fantasies of imagination. Forgive us. Create within us new hearts. Lend us the blessed influences of Thy divine Spirit to make us worthy of the tragic hour and competent for its responsibilities.

—ALBERT E. DAY, 1884-

DEVOTIONAL WRITINGS

 WHICH SPEAK TO OUR DAILYNEEDS

[248] Saints Are "The Salt of the Earth"

CHURCH history is full of numerous Christians who have been "the salt of the earth." In the third century Cyprian guided the Christians of North Africa through the persecutions of the Roman rulers Decius and Valerian. Benedict of Nursia in the sixth century, through his development of a realistic monastic system, created a means by which Christian values were preserved during the Dark Ages. In the sixteenth century Martin Luther brought back the Bible as the center of Christian religious authority. The teachings of this book have added zest to rich spiritual living. Lancelot Andrewes in seventeenth-century England, amid the turbulences of King James I, wrote his *Private Devotions,* a devotional classic which is esteemed by some as the purest insight into the repentant soul of man. In the seventeenth century George Fox, a lay leather worker who became a religious reformer, added savor to his age in England and began the Quaker movement. John Wesley, as he preached to thousands of people in eighteenth-century England, added a new vitality to the villages of England. Cardinal John Henry Newman said that where Wesley had once visited towns in England, the children were better-mannered, the homes better-kept, the families as a whole more happy. All these Christian reformers have been "the salt of the earth."

One needs only to call the names of modern Christians to realize how twentieth-century disciples continue to be "the salt of the earth": Edith Cavell as a nurse in Europe; Jane Addams working among the under-

185

privileged in Hull House, Chicago; Albert Schweitzer as a medical missionary in equatorial South Africa; Frank Laubach teaching languages to the illiterates on the island of Mindanao; Charles F. Andrews as a Christian teacher in India; Rudolf Otto as a great teacher of the "holiness of God" in Marburg University, Germany; Rufus Jones, the Quaker, as chairman of the American Friends Committee, lending its aid to sufferers throughout the world.

[249] What Is a Saint?

THE life of a saintly person is conditioned in the following ways:

1. His life is imbued with a deep love of the Christian religion as a way of "feeling at home" in the universe.

2. He lives with a radiance because his spirit is rooted in God's Spirit. "A saint is a person who has quit worrying about himself" because his life is centered in God. With Jakob Böhme he says, "Though my head and my hand be at labor, yet doth my heart dwell in God."

3. He starts each day with these words: "May the image of Christ radiate through me this day in each life situation."

4. He asks that God use him as an instrument of His love to bear the burdens of his fellow men. Like Francis of Assisi, the saint loves "not humanity but men."

5. He believes that before God's kingdom can arrive in society, it must first begin in him.

6. He has humility, caused by his belief that life is too much trouble unless he can live for something that is big. And most of all, his life is lost in the bigness of God.

7. He feels that every person—regardless of color, race, creed or nation—is a person in whom lie the possibilities of becoming a saint. With Robert Southwell he says, "Not where I breathe but where I love, I live."

8. He desires to use the results of prayer and devotion to better the world.

9. He believes that the two great secrets for becoming a saint lie in "the imitation of Christ" and "the practice of the presence of God."

10. His daily preparation for sainthood is in these words:

> By all means use some time to be alone.
> Salute thyself; see what thy soul doth wear.
> Dare to look into thy chest; for 'tis thy own.

[250] Saints Are Not Necessarily Geniuses

As we look over Christian history, we see that the making of an apostle may be in a vacillating Peter; a mystical-minded John; an authoritarian Jewish law-giver, Paul; strong, passionate, willful dispositions like those of Tertullian, Augustine, and Pascal; eclectic, balanced, rational natures like Clement of Alexandria, and Origen, Aquinas and Erasmus; poets and minnesingers like Francis of Assisi and Jacopone de Todi, Henry Suso, Thomas Traherne and Francis Thompson; difficult personalities with naturally fragile and often disrupted psycho-physical dispositions, such as those of Catherine of Genoa, Theresa of Avila, or Sören Kierkegaard; a mother of many children and an eminently practical administrator like Bridget of Sweden; a German cobbler, Boehme; an English leather-worker, Fox; a New Jersey tailor, Woolman; an illiterate French peasant who could not pass his theological examinations and was so particularly deficient in moral theology that it was thought wise for years not to trust him to hear confessions, the Curé of Ars. This is what the apostle means when he says that the Christian religion is not for geniuses or specialists of people of one peculiar temperament or class or taste or capacity, but is for all. What you bring does not matter, provided you bring it all.

—Douglas V. Steere, 1901-

[251] God and Liberty

While Benjamin Franklin was seeking French support for the American Revolution, the aged Voltaire returned to Paris after an absence of many years. The American representative called to pay his respects to the man all France was acclaiming, taking with him his grandson, who was serving as his secretary. The most memorable words uttered in that meeting of the two famed philosophers were in the blessing Voltaire gave to young Franklin. Placing his hands on the youth's head he spoke: "My child, God and liberty! Recollect those two words."

[252] The Secret of Sainthood

[The saints] always seemed to hit the mark; every bit of their life *told;* their simplest actions had a distinction, an exquisiteness which suggested

187

the artist. The reason is not far to seek. Their sainthood lay in their habit of referring the smallest actions to God. They lived in God; they acted from a pure motive of love towards God. They were as free from self-regard as from slavery to the good opinion of others. God saw and God rewarded: what else needed they? . . . Hence the inalienable dignity of these meek, quiet figures that seem to produce such marvellous effects with such humble materials.

—EMILY HERMAN, 1876-1923

[253] Reverence for Life Is Ethical Mysticism

ANY profound world-view is mysticism, in that it brings men into a spiritual relation with the Infinite. The world-view of Reverence for Life is ethical mysticism. It allows union with the infinite to be realized by ethical action. This ethical mysticism originates in logical thinking. If our will-to-live begins to think about itself and the world, we come to experience the life of the world, so far as it comes within our reach, in our own life, and to devote our will-to-live to the infinite will-to-live through the deeds we do. Rational thinking, if it goes deep, ends of necessity in the non-rational of mysticism. It has, of course, to deal with life and the world, both of which are non-rational entities.

In the world the infinite will-to-live reveals itself to us as will-to-create, and this is full of dark and painful riddles for us; in ourselves it is revealed as will-to-love, which will through us remove the dilemma (*Selbstentzweiung*) of the will-to-live.

—ALBERT SCHWEITZER, 1875-

[254] Reflections of Fenelon

1. ON THE FAULTS OF OTHERS

Bear ye one another's burdens, and so fulfil the law of Christ. Gal. vi. 2. CHARITY does not demand of us that we should not see the faults of others; we must, in that case, shut our eyes. But it commands us to avoid attending unnecessarily to them, and that we be not blind to the good, while we are so clear-sighted to the evil that exists. We must remem-

188

ber, too, God's continual kindness to the most worthless creature and think how many causes we have to think ill of ourselves; and finally we must consider that charity embraces the very lowest human being. It acknowledges that in the sight of God the contempt that we indulge for others has in its very nature a harshness and arrogance opposed to the spirit of Jesus Christ. The true Christian is not insensible to what is contemptible, but he bears with it.

Because others are weak, should we be less careful to give them their due? You who complain so much of what others make you suffer, do you think that you cause others no pain? You who are so annoyed at your neighbor's defects, are you perfect?

How astonished you would be, if those whom you cavil at should make all the comments that they might upon you. But even if the whole world were to bear testimony in your favor, God, who knows all, who has seen all your faults, could confound you with a word; and does it never come into your mind to fear, lest he should demand of you why you had exercised toward your brother a little of that mercy which He who is your Master so abundantly bestows upon you?

2. ON THE RIGHT EMPLOYMENT OF TIME

Let us do good as we have opportunity. Gal. vi. 10.
The night cometh, when no man can work. John ix.4.

Time is precious, but we do not comprehend all its value. We shall know it only when it will no longer be of any advantage to us. Our friends make demands upon it, as if it were nothing, and we bestow it in the same way. Often it is a burden to us. We know not what to do with it. A day will come when a single quarter of an hour may appear of more worth to us than the riches of the whole world. God who is so free and liberal in his bounty to us in everything else, teaches us by the wise economy of His providence how careful we should be of the use of time, for He gives us but one instant, and withdraws that as He gives us a second, while He retains the third in His own hands, leaving us in entire uncertainty whether it will ever be ours. . . .

Thus let us spend our days, redeeming the time, by quitting vain amusements, useless correspondences, those weak outpourings of the heart that are only modifications of self-love, and conversations that dissipate the mind and lead to no good. Thus we shall find time to serve God; and there is none well employed that is not devoted to Him.

3. I SLEEP, BUT MY HEART WAKETH

We sleep in peace in the arms of God, when we yield ourselves up to His providence, in a delightful consciousness of his tender mercies;

189

no more restless uncertainties, no more anxious desires, no more impatience at the place we are in; for it is God who has put us there and who holds us in His arms. Can we be unsafe where He has placed us, and where He watches over us as a parent watches a child? This confiding repose, in which earthly care sleeps, is the true vigilance of the heart; yielding itself up to God, with no other support than Him, it thus watches while we sleep. This is the love of Him, that will not sleep even in death.

—FRANÇOIS DE FÉNELON, 1651-1715

[255] Death's Illumination of Life

WALT WHITMAN was attending a funeral one day. Just ahead of him a girl of fourteen was standing before the open casket as though she were transfixed. Walt Whitman put his arm on her shoulder and spoke to her. "You don't understand that, do you?" he asked gently. And as she dully answered, "No," Whitman added, "Neither do I," and they moved on together.

Before another's death and its meaning the fellowship of the living, when they are honest, cannot do other than confess to each other their bewilderment. Running through all the emotions of irreparable loss, of loneliness, of fear, of relief, of outraged resentment, or of resignation, there is and there must be this common note of mystery, "I do not understand." . . .

Death illuminates life. Before the prospect of its own death this *Me* finds itself dynamically searched. (1) It finds itself groping to see if it has found a ground or a medium that gives some evidence that it will carry the *Me* in this moment of extremity. What have been its past experiences of being sustained through the drastic change that assaulted and threatened to consume the *Me*? (2) How has this *Me* been assisted in a grasp of the ground and core of its nature by the situations that have not only threatened to consume, but to individuate it, situations like the prospect of my own death, that have demanded an unequivocal choice from it, situations that have planted themselves on my threshold and refused to be dismissed by the appearance of a butler, uniformed in a conventional response, but that have kept rapping insistently at that door for the master himself to appear? (3) in the course of these encounters with life, has the Me known what it is, not alone to be sustained through change and to answer in person the summons to individuation? Has it also known a qualitative drawing that satisfies its deepest yearn-

190

ing, that raises up that which is good in it and yet at the same stroke inflicts the pain of pains, as it strikes at sin in the life? (4) And finally by confronting my personal death and discovering the ground and meaning of true self-abandonment, am I brought to discern the difference between much of the contemporary manic flight into acts of service, and what appears to be the recklessly careless unconcern for life or death of those mature ones who, having faced and known the meaning of death, then reveal a broad freedom to pour themselves out in redemptive acts for others? What, then, is death's illumination of life in these four areas?

If a consideration of the meaning of its own personal death can wring answers to these questions from its experience, the *Me* will confront death not with an answer, for that would lift the curtain, but with what is still more important—a faith and a faith-born courage in the final leap as well as a heightening of each hour and day of the life that precedes it. . . .

What is this death which I confront, and what will it do to me? My own death means a major crisis, a major change, a major transformation. . . .

Death means that I must go through the needle's eye, and that most, if not all, of what I have come to identify as my permanent possessions will be stripped from me.

—DOUGLAS V. STEERE, 1901-

[256] The Steps of Prayer

WE are now ready to take the actual steps of prayer, and there are about nine of them.

First, decide what you really want. The "you" is important. It must not be a vagrant part of you wandering into the prayer hour with no intention of committing yourself to your prayer request. You cannot pray with a part of yourself and expect God to answer, for he hears what the whole of you is saying. . . .

St. Augustine, before he became a saint, used to pray, "O God, make me pure, but not now." . . . Perhaps you are willing that you pray with the whole "you," but the other "you" is not co-operative. Then tell God you are willing to be made willing. . . .

Second, decide whether the thing you want is a Christian thing. God has shown us in Christ what the divine character is like. God is Christlike. He can only act in a Christ-like way. He cannot answer a prayer that would not fit in with his character. . . .

Let us sit down and ask about all our prayers: "Is the thing I want a Christian thing?" And remember that, if it is not a Christian thing, it would do us no good if we got it, for only the Christian thing is the thing that is good for us. Ask God to cleanse your prayers as well as you. . . .

Third, write it down. The writing of the prayer will probably help you in self-committal. For, if you write it, you will probably mean it. Committing a thing to writing is almost destiny to me; I can hardly change it afterward. The writing of it will also save you from hazy indefiniteness. . . . There will come a time, of course, when you may not need to write things down, for they will have written themselves in you. . . .

Fourth, still the mind. The stilling of the mind is a step in receptivity. Prayer is pure receptivity in the first stage. "As many as *received* him, to them gave he power." If you come to God all tense, you can get little. . . .

Receptivity is the first law of the spiritual life. It is the first law of all life. An organism can give out as much as it takes in and no more. If it hasn't learned to receive, it hasn't learned to live. The radiant soul mentioned above says: "God has done more for me in this one year that I have been receptive than I have done for myself in all the years of my life. The stupidity of people who live in a shell!" . . .

The stilling of the mind reminds you not of your pitiful little store, but of the fact that you are now harnessing yourself to God's illimitable fullness. . . .

Now you are ready for the *fifth* step: *Talk with God about it.* Note I say, "Talk with God," not "Talk to God," for it is a two-way conversation. And the most vital part may be, not what you will say to God, but what God will say to you. For God wants not merely to answer your prayer. . . .

When you talk with God about it, set the prayer in the light of that general purpose of God to make you the best instrument of his purpose he can make of you. He may have to say a lesser "no," in order to a higher "yes." . . .

There is a *sixth* step: *Promise God what you will do to make this prayer come true.* Since the conversation is a two-way affair, the accomplishment is also two-way. You and God answer it together.

At this point be silent to hear God again, and see if he makes any suggestions to you about your part in answering the prayer. If definite suggestions come to you, then promise that you will carry them out. . . .

Seventh: Do everything loving that comes to your mind about it! This step is important, for it is a cleansing and clarifying step. The word "loving" is important. It is the password to find the source of the suggestions that come to your mind. If the suggestion is not loving, it is probably from your subconscious mind, and not from the Spirit. The first

192

fruit of the Spirit is "love," and if the suggestion does not fit in with love then don't do it. Wait for the suggestion that does fit in.

If the word "loving" is important, so is the word "do." . . .

Eighth: Thank God for answering in his own way. God will answer that prayer. No prayers are unanswered. But he may answer "no," as well as "yes." "No" is an answer, and it may really be next in order leading on to a higher "yes."

Moreover, the answer may be delayed in order to toughen your fibre. The very persistence in asking for something over a long period may be one of the most character-toughening processes imaginable.

There is a *ninth* step: *Release the whole prayer from your conscious thinking.* Don't keep the prayer at the center of your conscious thinking. It may become an anxiety-center. Let it drop down into the subconscious mind and let it work at that greater depth. Then there will be an undertone of prayer in all you do, but there will be no tense anxiety. Dismissing it from the conscious mind is an act of faith that, having committed it to God you leave it in his hands, believing he will do the best thing possible. . . .

—E. Stanley Jones, 1884-

[257] The Practice of the Presence of God

In a conversation some days since with a person of piety, he told me the spiritual life was a life of grace, which begins with servile fear, which is increased by hope of eternal life, and which is consummated by pure love; that each of these states had its different stages, by which one arrives at last at that blessed consummation.

I have not followed all these methods. On the contrary, from I know not what instincts, I found they discouraged me. This was the reason why, at my entrance into religion, I took a resolution to give myself up to God, as the best return I could make for His love, and, for the love of Him, to renounce all besides.

For the first year I commonly employed myself during the time set apart for devotion with the thought of death, judgment, heaven, hell, and my sins. Thus I continued some years, applying my mind carefully the rest of the day, and even in the midst of my business, *to the presence of God,* whom I considered always as *with* me, often as *in* me.

At length I came insensibly to do the same thing during my set time of prayer, which caused in me great delight and consolation. This practice produced in me so high an esteem for God that *faith* alone was capable to satisfy me in that point.

Such was my beginning, and yet I must tell you that for the first ten years I suffered much. . . .

Ever since that time I walk before God simply, in faith, with humility and with love, and I apply myself diligently to do nothing and think nothing which may displease Him. I hope that when I have done what I can, He will do with me what He pleases.

As for what passes in me at present, I cannot express it. I have no pain or difficulty about my state, because I have no will but that of God, which I endeavor to accomplish in all things, and to which I am so resigned that I would not take up a straw from the ground against His order, or from any other motive but purely that of love to Him.

—NICHOLAS HERMAN [BROTHER LAWRENCE], 1611-1691

[258] Your Life Is Hid

Col. 3:3

ONLY one-eighth of the mass bulk of icebergs is visible; all the rest is under water. This is what makes them so formidable to navigators, this is what makes their strength. In the same way the life of a Christian should in large part be hidden: it is from what one does not see that its force is drawn.

The stability of a house cannot be gauged from its outward appearance; it is secured by its invisible foundations. When a storm comes some humble dwelling may stand while palaces crumble. The same way with every spiritual edifice: it is not a question of shining and dazzling people, but of being firmly founded, of having a "life hid with Christ in God."

This hidden life is made up of what you bring each day to your Master: mostly your tears and your troubles, the defeats and the ruins of your outer structures. These are by no means first-rate materials and the hours that you spend alone with your God often are miserable. What counts is that you seek his presence, far from prying eyes; while you groan he builds patiently in you, secretly, the indispensable foundations.

Outwardly you may remain very much like the person you were before, or like those around you. You will appear to be a peaceful, honest man, with nothing to distinguish you from the crowd. It will need the blows of the storm, the clash against the obstacle, to reveal to others and

194

to yourself your mysterious firmness—that hidden life which no one suspected.

—PHILIPPE VERNIER, 1909-

[259] Open Toward God and Wide Awake

April 22, 1930

THE "experiment" is interesting, although I am not very successful, thus far. The idea of God slips out of my sight for I suppose two thirds of every day, thus far. This morning I started out fresh, by finding a rich experience of God in the sunrise. Then I tried to let Him control my hands while I was shaving and dressing and eating breakfast. Now I am trying to let God control my hands as I pound the typewriter keys. If I could keep this morning up I should have a far higher average today than I have had for some time.

This afternoon as I look at the people teeming about me, and then think of God's point of view, I feel that this mighty stretch of time in which He has been pushing men upward is to continue for many more millions of years. We are yet to become what the spiritual giants have been and more than many of them were. Here the selection favors those who keep themselves wide open toward God and wide awake. Our possibilities are perhaps not limitless, but they are at least infinitely above our present possibilities of imagination.

There is nothing that we can do excepting to throw ourselves open to God. There is, there must be, so much more in Him than He can give us, because we are so sleepy and because our capacity is so pitifully small. It ought to be tremendously helpful to be able to acquire the habit of reaching out strongly after God's thoughts, and to ask, "God, what have you to put into my mind now if only I can be large enough?" That waiting, eager attitude ought to give God the chance he needs. I am finding every day that the best of the five or six ways in which I try to keep contact with God is for me to *wait for his thoughts, to ask him to speak.*

—FRANK C. LAUBACH, 1884-

[260] Prayer Should Undergird Every Moment

AT first the practice of inward prayer is a process of alternation of attention between outer things and the Inner Light. Preoccupation with either brings the loss of the other. Yet what is sought is not alternation but simultaneity, worship undergirding every moment, living prayer, the continuous current and background of all moments of life. Long practice indeed is needed before alternation yields to concurrent immersion in both levels at once. The "plateaus in the learning curve" are so long, and many falter and give up, assenting to alternation as the best that they can do. And no doubt in His graciousness God gives us His gifts, even in intermittent communion, and touches us into flame, far beyond our achievements and deserts. But the hunger of the committed one is for unbroken communion and adoration, and we may be sure He longs for us to find it and supplements our weakness. For our quest is of His initiation, and is carried forward in His tender power and completed by His grace.

—THOMAS R. KELLY, 1893-1941

[261] Pastor Oberlin's Artistry of Tithing

My dear friend,

You ask me for some explanation respecting the different tithes which God has commanded me to pay. I will tell you how I manage. I endeavor to devote three tithes of all that I earn, of all that I receive, and of all my revenue, of whatever name or nature it may be, to his service or to useful objects.

For this purpose I keep three boxes; the first for the first tithe; the second for the second; and the third box for the third tithe.

When I cannot pay ready money all at once, I mark how much I owe upon a bit of paper, which I put into the box; and when, on the contrary, a demand occurs which ought to be defrayed by one of the three allotments, and there is not sufficient money deposited, I advance the sum, and make the box my debtor, by marking upon it how much it owes me.

By this means I am always able to assist in my public or charitable undertaking; and as God has himself declared that "it is more blessed to give than to receive," I look upon this regular disbursement of part of my property rather in the light of a privilege than a burden.

The first of the afore-mentioned boxes contains a deposit for the worship of God.

I devote the contents of this box to the building and repairing of churches and schoolrooms; the support of conductrices; and the purchase of Bibles and pious books; in short, to any thing connected with divine worship, or the extension of the knowledge of our Redeemer's kingdom.

My parishioners are at liberty to recall from this tithe any present that either generosity, or the supposition that I expected it, may have induced them to make me.

The second box contains tithes for useful purposes.

I employ this tithe for a variety of purposes: —

1. For the improvement of the roads to the churches and schools.
2. For the schoolmasters' salaries.
3. For all works of public utility.
4. For the little expenses incurred by my becoming godfather.
5. For Sunday dinners to my poor people of the other villages. (*My parishioners might add to this catalogue.*)
6. For the churchwardens. (*For whether they do their duty voluntarily from love to God, or make a claim upon me, I always pay them well.*)
7. For expenses incurred among the peasantry of Belmont, Foudai, and Zolbach.
8. For what the poor of Waldbach expend, by inviting the poor of the other villages to come and see them.
9. For the repairing of injuries.

The third box contains tithes for the poor. (That is, it contains the third tithe every three years, or the thirtieth every year.)

I devote the contents of this box to the service of the poor; to the compensation of losses occasioned by fire; to wood, flannel, and bread, for those who stand in need, etc. etc.

—JOHN FREDERIC OBERLIN, 1740-1826

[262] Meditations of Katherine Mansfield

1. THE SOLITARY PERSON ALWAYS ACTS

NOVEMBER, 1921. Coleridge on Hamlet. "He plays that subtle trick of pretending to act only when he is very near being what he acts."

. . . So do we all begin by acting and the nearer we are to what we would be the more perfect our *disguise*. Finally there comes the moment when *we are no longer acting;* it may even catch us by surprise. We may look in amazement at our no longer borrowed plumage. The two have merged; that which we put on has joined that which was; acting has become action. The soul has accepted this livery for its own after a time of trying on and approving.

To act . . . to see ourselves in the part—to make a larger gesture than would be ours in life—to declaim, to pronounce, to even exaggerate, to persuade ourselves (?) or others (?) to put ourselves in heart? To do more than is necessary in order that we may accomplish ce qu'il faut.

And then Hamlet is lonely. The solitary person always acts.

2. MEDITATION, A CURE FOR A SICK MIND

January 26, 1922. I am sure that meditation is the cure for the sickness of my mind, i.e. its lack of control. I have a terribly sensitive mind which receives every impression, and that is the reason why I am so carried away and borne under.

3. LAUGH AT OURSELVES

October 1922. *Important.* When we can begin to take our failures non-seriously, it means we are ceasing to be afraid of them. It is of immense importance to learn to *laugh at ourselves.* What Shestov calls "a touch of easy familiarity and derision" has its value.

To be wildly enthusiastic, or deadly serious—both are wrong. Both pass. One must keep ever present a sense of humour. It depends entirely on yourself how much you see or hear or understand. But the sense of humour I have found of use in every single occasion of my life. . . .

4. FORGET YOURSELF

October, 1921. I wonder why it should be so very difficult to be humble. I do not think I am a good writer; I realize my faults better than anyone else could realize them. I know exactly where I fail. And yet, when I have finished a story and before I have begun another, I catch myself *preening* my feathers. It is disheartening. There seems to be some bad old pride in my heart; a root of it that puts out a thick shoot on the slightest provocation. . . . This interferes very much with work. One can't be calm, clear, good as one must be, while it goes on. I look at the mountains, I try to pray and I think of something *clever*. It's a kind of excitement within, which shouldn't be there. Calm yourself. Clear yourself. And anything that I write in this mood will be no good; it will be full of *sediment*. If I were well, I would go off by myself somewhere and

198

sit under a tree. One must learn, one must practice, to *forget* oneself. . . .

To go to Sierre, if it goes on like this . . . or to—or to—

5. LONGING FOR SOMETHING

November 24. These last days I have been awfully rebellious. Longing for something. I feel uprooted, I want things that J. can so easily do with out, that aren't natural to him. I long for them. But then, stronger than all these desires, is the other, which is to *make good* before I do anything else. The sooner the books are written, the sooner I shall be well, the sooner my wishes will be in sight of fulfilment. That is sober truth, of course. As a pure matter of fact I consider this enforced confinement here as God-given. But, on the other hand, I must make the most of it quickly. It is not unlimited any more than anything else is. Oh, why—oh, why isn't anything unlimited? Why am I troubled every single day of my life by the nearness of death and its inevitability? I am really diseased on that point. And I can't speak of it. If I tell J. it makes him unhappy. If I don't tell him, it leaves me to fight it. I am tired of the battle. No one knows how tired.

To-night, when the evening-star shone through the side-window and the mountains were so lovely, I sat there thinking of death. Of all there was to do—of Life, which is so lovely—and of the fact that my body is a prison. But this state of mind is *evil*. It is only by acknowledging that I, being what I am, had to suffer *this* in order to do the work I am here to perform. It is only by acknowledging it, by being thankful that work was not taken away from me, that I shall recover. I am weak where I must be strong.

6. SUFFERING IS BOUNDLESS

I should like this to be accepted as my confession. There is no limit to human suffering. When one thinks: "Now I have touched the bottom of the sea—now I can go no deeper," one goes deeper. And so it is for ever. I thought last year in Italy, any shadow more would be death. But this year has been so much more terrible that I think with affection of the Casetta! Suffering is boundless, it is eternity. One pang is eternal torment. Physical suffering is—child's play. To have one's breast crushed by a great stone—one could laugh!

I do not want to die without leaving a record of my belief that suffering can be overcome. For I do believe it. What must one do? There is no question of what is called "passing beyond it." This is false.

One must submit. Do not resist. Take it. Be overwhelmed. Accept it fully. Make it part of life.

Everything in life that we really accept undergoes a change. So suffer-

199

ing must become Love. This is the mystery. This is what I must do. I must pass from personal love to greater love. I must give to the whole of life what I gave to one. The present agony will pass—if it doesn't kill. It won't last. Now I am like a man who has had his heart torn out—but—bear it—bear it! As in the physical world, so in the spiritual world, pain does not last forever. It is only so terribly acute now. It is as though a ghastly accident had happened. If I can cease reliving all the shock and horror of it, cease going over it, I will get stronger. . . .

Life is a mystery. The fearful pain will fade. I must turn to work. I must put my agony into something, change it. "Sorrow shall be changed into joy."

It is to lose oneself more utterly, to love more deeply, to feel oneself part of life—not separate.

Oh Life! accept me—make me worthy—teach me.

—KATHERINE MANSFIELD, 1888-1923

[263] Pages from the Journal of Andre Maurois

1. A RESOLVE TO WORK

New York, January 1st.

EACH year, on this day of beginning, like Buster Brown I make my resolutions: To work, work, and work. To refuse "jobs" in order to write—not great books (that is not within my province to decide)—but at least the best I am able to conceive. To live as much as possible in the country, where the length of each day is doubled. Aside from moments of action, to view these times not as an instrument of moral torture but rather as an illusion to be described. To forbid myself to suffer over imaginary or fugitive ills while so many suffer from real and irremediable evils. To be in all things accurate and just. . . . But what is the use of setting down resolutions? One must live them.

2. IN PRAISE OF WILLIAM ALLEN WHITE

January 17th.

Wrote an article for *Victoire* on William Allen White. I knew him well when we were both members of the Book-of-the-Month Club committee. He was extremely fine. The open candor of his glance, the kindliness on his lean face, the serious air touched with humor—all united to compel and hold friendship. Add that Mrs. White, or, as their friends familiarly called her, Sallie White, had the same characteristics and the same charm, and one begins to understand the magic influence of the Whites.

Nevertheless it is a sort of miracle that the editor in chief of the Emporia *Gazette,* a local newspaper published in a town of thirty thousand inhabitants, should have become the most influential editorial writer of the United States, without ever having left Emporia or the *Gazette.*

Fortunes were offered him to come to work on some of the New York newspapers. He had the good sense to refuse and to remain faithful to the *Gazette.* Whence came this grandeur of wisdom which made him the Franklin of our age? He wrote books, excellent ones (historical studies, political works, biographies), but his daily editorial remained the fixed center of his life. He passionately loved his journalist's trade and strove to pursue it as a good writer, which he was by nature. He had tacked on the walls some *Counsels* on style which were his reporters' Bible. The only day I read them to Georges Duhamel, who was enchanted with them, for he attaches as much importance as White to the perfection of a text. In general White asked that his editors be economical of adverbs and adjectives, that they avoid clichés both in word and in attitude, and above all that hypothesis never be substituted for fact. "Don't guess. Verify. . . . Don't judge. Instruct. . . . Whatever your subject, answer the questions. *Who? What? When? Where? Why?* and *How?*"

White had the highest conception of a journalist's duty toward the community he serves: "The editorial policy of a newspaper should combine three things: intelligence, courage, and kindness." He believed besides that a newspaper has authority only if it reflects the personality of a man. In a small city such as Emporia, every reader, glancing through his paper, must hear the voice of the writer and envision his smile. His follies, his family life, his friendship must come to be part of the community's life.

Thus it came about that William Allen White wrote his finest article, an article which is included in all the anthologies, the day after the funeral of his daughter, Mary White, killed at seventeen by a horseback-riding accident. That morning he said to his wife who, like himself, had not slept:

"Get dressed, Sallie. Now we must go down to the paper and take care of Mary."

She answered, "I couldn't, Will. . . . I can't."

"But you must, my dear. We've always done everything together. I need you."

Arriving at the newspaper offices, he closed the door of his office, began to write, and passed the copy, page by page, to his wife.

"Yes, that's very good," she said. "But, Will, don't forget to say . . ."

"Now you see how I need you, Sallie." [See article 25 "Mary White"]

201

William Allen White himself died under a wintry sun in January, 1944. I had seen him a few months earlier at the University of Kansas, weary, aged, but still gay and charming. His friend Henry Haskell of the Kansas City *Star* shared the meal with us. It was he who, upon White's death, remembered that White had been the first to bring America to the realization that this was *her* war.

From all over the world, great men sent telegrams voicing their sorrow: President Roosevelt, Anthony Eden, Lord Halifax. From East to West, by airplane and by train, innumerable friends hastened to Emporia. The service was precisely the same as Mary White's: First Corinthians, Moonlight Sonata. After the service a little Negro boy was heard to ask, "Why so many flowers?"

"Because he was a very great man," a little white boy answered him.

He was indeed a very great man, a man who understood that true greatness is composed of the simplest ingredients: love of country, of a city, of a family, of a profession.

3. AN ARTIST WRITES FOR HIMSELF

February 6th.

"Why should I write for posterity?" Byron asked. "Nobody does." And how would one go about writing for posterity? The most brilliant achievement will in time be limited by the evolution of the language and the death of civilization. Three thousand years have passed over Homer's ashes? . . . Yes, I know. But wait four thousand, a hundred thousand years, and Homer himself will be forgotten. And even if he were not, wait a billion years and all life will have disappeared from this planet. Why this will to endure in a universe where all things pass, a universe which will one day cease to exist? . . . The truth is that an artist writes for himself, for a self that seems eternal and, indeed, *is* eternal, for no man knows of his own end.

—ANDRÉ MAUROIS, 1885-

[264] Letters of Baron Von Hugel to Father Tyrrell

1. LIVE, TRUST, AND WAIT

4 Holford Road: Aug. 19, 1900.

WITH your sensitive nature and delicate health, and immense need of indefinite activity and self-communication, a long course of silence and repression would be too painfully trying to yourself, for me to be able to bear to think of it as probable. I rather love to remember that all may still be better, much sooner, and in other ways and by other instruments, than we, in our blindness, can guess or foresee. And you have the quality which is as real an advantage, in the long run, with, I think, almost all others, as it is the one refuge throughout life for oneself. I am thinking, of course, of your spiritual-mindedness, which is every bit as marked a feature of yours as breadth of sympathy or freshness of thought. And already years ago Duchesne said to me, and I have so often found him right, in the lives of my various friends and in my own: "Work away in utter sincerity and open-mindedness; lead as deep and devoted a spiritual life as you can; renounce, from the first and every day, every hope or wish for more than toleration; and then, with those three activities and dispositions, trust and wait, with indomitable patience and humility, to be tolerated and excused. You will find that, if only you have patience and magnanimity enough to wait so long, and to work so hard, and to put up with, apparently, such a small result,—*that* result will not fail you: you will be put up with not more, not one inch more: but *that* much, you will achieve."

2. THE VALUE OF BATTLING AND TOILING

14 Via Veneto, Rome: Dec. 18-20, 1901.

It is so long since I managed to write to you, and my life has been so full of new-old experiences, labour and battle since I left Airolo, that I hardly know how to begin, or how to tell you one tithe of all I would like to say. What a grand and entrancing fact it is, to be sure, this unspeakable richness of the soul's life; so that, even in the midst of much sinfulness and of many actual faults, and of much trial and trouble, one would not only not, in one's sane and sober moments, have an end of living and of being, but one would not exchange one's poor life of toil, of giving (or at least of trying to give) all, and thus gaining something for the Church and her future and everything for oneself, for all the sleepy, vegetating existences in the world. And I am having the strange, very sobering impression that God is deigning somehow to use me,—me, in my measure, along with others who can and do do more, and much more, —towards making, not simply registering, history. And, dear me, what a costing process *that* is! . . .

I can't help hoping now, more strongly than at first, that the result of the whole will be a living organism, something that will be able to enter into other minds and hearts, and grow and bring fruit there. Certainly the effect upon myself is being considerable: I have become

203

a good bit more of a person, please God, of the right, the spiritual-humble sort, by battling and toiling with and in and over these great realities and problems.

3. ONLY WE CAN HARM OURSELVES

Nov. 15, 1907.

My dearest Friend,—I do indeed feel keenly the ungenerous, indeed unjust, character of that circular of the Bishop,—especially as coming in answer to that grandly straight, strong and loyal letter of yours to him; and I do not wonder a bit that you thought it right, indeed necessary, to print and circulate that letter of yours. No doubt that act of his will distinctly increase the number of those, especially among the Clergy, who feel with us. Your cousin is so tactful and worldly wise a man, that I feel quite comfortable over anything that has thus his full study and approbation. . . .

Perhaps the ideal, all-round man should be able to hate and pursue destructively, with the same directness and fulness, with which he would love and construct. *Perhaps,* though I am far from sure even of this. But I am very sure that, in any case, George Tyrrell is not that kind of man. A dominant hatred and determination to destroy even a set of men or an institution predominantly evil: such a disposition would, the writer of this scribble is absolutely certain, shrivel up and evaporate all the true power, all the deep glorious helpfulness of G. T., long before he had done any serious execution upon those his enemies. May G. T. keep realising this, and that we have no opponents who can do us or our cause much harm, except in this our temptation, our weakness, which might drive us into such sterilising negation and feverish hate. . . .

Devoted old friend,

4. CONTEMPLATION AND INNER JOY

March 25, 1908.

As to yourself. I feel very happy and confident in the conviction that this obscurity will pass by, and will leave a certain grand poignancy and rich spirituality of tone,—I mean something more so even than ever before. Thus it has been with Eucken. When I first got to know him, he was just returning from greater fog and darkness than you are likely to traverse; indeed, he had recently been all but entirely negative, I mean, quite explicitly so. And look at him now, with a grandly massive, joyous faith.—I see clearly that, over and above the intrinsic difficulties, two circumstances are added on for you, which greatly intensify each one of those trials. For one thing, our theologians, the official ones, have, during these 4 centuries, steadily allowed the accounts to accumulate unpaid, unsorted, unacknowledged. What wonder, then, that we are overwhelmed in this the day of long-deferred reckoning? We are thus required to face and to get through the arrears of some 12 generations.—And then your own temperament, on one of its two sides, adds greatly to the difficulty. For was there ever a more sensitively swift and absolute mind than yours? . . . But I pray and hope the day may soon return when your *other side,* the deep mystical, contemplative habit and attrait will again be so powerfully waked up and nurtured, that you will regain a grand steadiness of foundation, and in your very feeling as to the depths of life and of religion. *With* that, you will be great; without that, very unhappy. [These letters relate to the modernist controversy.]

—BARON FRIEDRICH VON HÜGEL, 1852-1925

[265] Evaluations of Life from Amiel's "Journal"

1. ONE THING NEEDFUL—TO POSSESS GOD

Berlin, 16th July 1848.—THERE is but one thing needful—to possess God. All our senses, all our powers of mind and soul, all our external resources, are so many ways of approaching the Divinity, so many modes of tasting and of adoring God. We must learn to detach ourselves from all that is capable of being lost, to bind ourselves absolutely only to what is absolute and eternal, and to enjoy the rest as a loan, a usufruct. . . . To adore, to understand, to receive, to feel, to give, to act: there is my law, my duty, my happiness, my heaven. Let come what come will— even death. Only be at peace with self, live in the presence of God, in communion with Him, and leave the guidance of existence to those universal powers against whom thou canst do nothing!—If death gives me time, so much the better. If its summons is near, so much the better still; if a half-death overtake me, still so much the better, for so the path of success is closed to me only that I may find opening before me the path of heroism, of moral greatness and resignation. Every life has its potentiality of greatness, and as it is impossible to be outside God, the best is consciously to dwell in Him.

2. PUT AWAY PERSONAL AMBITION

Recognise your place; let the living live; and you, gather together your thoughts, leave behind you a legacy of feeling and ideas; you will be most useful so. Renounce yourself, accept the cup given you, with its honey and its gall, as it comes. Bring God down into your heart. Embalm your soul in Him now, make within you a temple for the Holy Spirit; be diligent in good works, make others happier and better.

Put personal ambition away from you, and then you will find consolation in living or in dying, whatever may happen to you.

3. SLEEP IS THE MYSTERY OF LIFE

20th March 1853.—I sat up alone; two or three times I paid a visit to the children's room. It seemed to me, young mothers, that I understood you!—Sleep is the mystery of life; there is a profound charm in this darkness broken by the tranquil light of the nightlamp, and in this silence measured by the rhythmic breathings of two young sleeping creatures. It was brought home to me that I was looking on at a marvellous operation of nature, and I watched it in no profane spirit. I sat silently listening, a moved and hushed spectator of this poetry of the cradle, this ancient and ever new benediction of the family, this symbol of creation sleeping under the wing of God, of our consciousness withdrawing into the shade that it may rest from the burden of thought, and of the tomb, that divine bed, where the soul in its turn rests from life.— To sleep is to strain and purify our emotions, to deposit the mud of life, to calm the fever of the soul, to return into the bosom of maternal nature, thence to re-issue, healed and strong. Sleep is a sort of innocence and purification. Blessed be He who gave it to the poor sons of men as the sure and faithful companion of life, our daily healer ond consoler.

4. IN CHIEF MATTERS—ALONE

27th October 1856.—In all the chief matters of life we are alone, and our true history is scarcely ever deciphered by others. The chief part of the drama is a monologue, or rather an intimate debate between God, our conscience, and ourselves. Tears, griefs, depressions, deceptions, irritations, good and evil thoughts, decisions, uncertainties, deliberations, —all these belong to our secret, and are almost all incommunicable and intransmissible, even when we try to speak of them, and even when we write them down.

5. THE WORTH OF MYSTICISM

17th March 1861.—This afternoon a homicidal languor seized hold upon me—disgust, weariness of life, mortal sadness. I wandered out into the churchyard, hoping to find quiet and peace there, and so to reconcile myself with duty. Vain dream! The place of rest itself had become inhospitable. Workmen were stripping and carrying away the turf, the trees were dry, the wind cold, the sky gray—something arid, irreverent, and prosaic dishonoured the resting-place of the dead. I was struck with something wanting in our national feeling,—respect for the dead, the poetry of the tomb, the piety of memory. Our churches are too little open; our churchyards too much. The result in both cases is the same. The tortured and trembling heart which seeks, outside the scene of its daily miseries, to find some place where it may pray in peace, or pour out its grief before God, or meditate in the presence of eternal things, with us has nowhere to go. Our Church ignores these wants of the soul instead of divining and meeting them. She shows very little compassionate care for her children, very little wise consideration for the more delicate griefs, and no intuition of the deeper mysteries of tenderness, no religious suavity. Under a pretext of spirituality we are always checking legitimate aspirations. We have lost the mystical sense; and what is religion without mysticism?—A rose without perfume.

6. THE SADNESS OF "TOO LATE"

What a stab there is in those words, *thou hast been!* when the sense of them becomes absolutely clear to us. One feels oneself sinking gradually into one's grave, and the past tense sounds the knell of our illusions as to ourselves. What is past is past: gray hairs will never become black curls again; the forces, the gifts, the attractions of youth, have vanished with our young days.

How hard it is to grow old, when we have missed our life, when we have neither the crown of completed manhood nor of fatherhood! How sad it is to feel the mind declining before it has done its work, and the body growing weaker before it has seen itself renewed in those who might close our eyes and honour our name!—The tragic solemnity of existence strikes us with terrible force, on that morning when we wake to find the mournful word *too late* ringing in our ears! 'Too late, the sand is turned, the hour is past! Thy harvest is unreaped—too late! Thou has been dreaming, forgetting, sleeping—so much the worse! Every man rewards or punishes himself. To whom or of whom wouldst thou complain?'—Alas!

—HENRI AMIEL, 1821-1881

[266] From "The Journals of André Gide"

1. REFLECTIONS OF A WRITER

3 September, 1937

THE great secret of Stendhal, his great shrewdness, consisted in writing *at once*. His thought charged with emotion remains as lively, as fresh in color as the newly developed butterfly that the collector has surprised as it was coming out of the cocoon. Whence that element of alertness and spontaneity, of incongruity, of suddenness and nakedness, that always delights us anew in his style. It would seem that his thought does not take time to put on its shoes before beginning to run. This ought to serve as a good example; or rather: I ought to follow his good example more often. One is lost when one hesitates. The work of translating, for this, does a disservice. Dealing with someone else's thought, it is important to warm it, to clothe it, and one goes seeking the best words, the best turn of expression; one becomes convinced that there are twenty ways of saying anything whatever and that one of them is preferable to all the others. One gets into that bad habit of dissociating form from content, the emotion and the expression of the emotion from the thought, which ought to remain inseparable.

For instance, I should like to say just now that: "If others wrote less, I should have more enjoyment in writing." . . . Well, I've said it! Why should I look for anything better than this sentence? It is the first one that came to mind; it expresses my thought perfectly. But my mind goes over it again and again, examines, criticizes it, and tries to perform upon it that little operation of weathering, of destruction, that it is better to leave to time, which will take care of it. And in saying this I myself fall into that fault with which I am reproaching others.

2. FEAR OF DEATH

13 July, 1930

The closer I approach death, the weaker becomes fear of death. I hold that fear in great scorn as soon as I feel it being played up, as soon as the artist yields to it and delights in it. It has always seemed to me that the first virtue of man was knowing how to face death; and it is a lamentable thing to see it less feared by very young men than by those who ought to be, if not tired of life, at least, having lived, resigned to death.

3. FATIGUE IS OLD AGE

21 January, 1929

What I call "fatigue" is old age, and nothing can rest one from it, but death.

Of all this "bad because contrary to nature" what is the worse? To refuse oneself to pleasures as a young man or, as an old man, to still seek them? There is a certain felicity of the flesh that the aging body pursues, and ever more uselessly, if it has not been sated with them in youth. Too chaste an adolescence makes for a dissolute old age. It is doubtless easier to give up something one has known than something one imagines. It is not what one has done that one regrets here; but rather what one has not done and might have done. And one's regret even takes on the somber color of repentance.

It seems to me that here too what most induces me to renunciation are aesthetic reasons. Old hands soil, it seems, what they caress; but they too have their beauty when they are joined in prayer. Young hands are made for caresses and the sheathing of love; it is a pity to make them join too soon. Yes, that gesture of prayer simulates the mystic embrace of the impalpable after loving arms have closed on the flight of reality and on absence.

—ANDRÉ GIDE, 1869-1949

[267] Wisdom from the "Diary of a Dean"

1. PAULA'S ILLNESS AND DEATH

November 13—I PREACHED in the cathedral at Worcester.

At this date began the great sorrow of our life in London. Our two little girls were with their grandparents at Oxford, and attended a day school or kindergarten conducted by our friends the Miss Owens. On our way back from Worcester we found Paula looking so terribly ill that we took her back to London to see Dr. Still, the famous children's doctor. He confirmed our worst fears. The dear child is suffering from diabetes, and he thinks the end may come in about three weeks. Sir Sydney Beauchamp, who saw her next day, thinks there may be a temporary improvement, but gives no hope of recovery. We are to have two nurses. She lived for more than a year, with no suffering apart from the starvation diet which was then the rule in these cases. At the end of 1922 the new insulin treatment was tried, but either it was too late or the proper method had not been discovered. To our great grief Sir Sydney Beauchamp was run over and killed on his way back from our house. Dr. Still most generously attended Paula till the end.

I wrote a short memoir of my little daughter, of which 50,000 copies were sold. It helped many other parents who have had the same sorrow. When I think of that dear child, as I do every day, it is not with sorrow but with wonder and deep reverence, for I have been privileged to know one of God's saints. "In a short time she fulfilled a long time, for her soul was dear to God." The text that was most often in her mind, for she knew her condition, was "Though I walk through the valley of the shadow of death I will fear no evil, for Thou art with me." But I often thought of the words of Julian of Norwich, the medieval mystic, "To me was shown no higher stature than childhood." Her little brother said to her, "Paula, I wish you would get better." She replied, "No, Richard, you must not say that. God has let me be with you for a whole year, and it has been the happiest year of my life." Just before the end she said, "I want my flowers to be put on the soldiers' monument at Westminster; that will be my Good Friday penance." But there were no more penances for her. On Maundy Thursday she became unconscious and passed away.

2. LOVE IS STRONGER THAN DEATH

In the short memorial which I wrote of my little daughter Paula (*Personal Religion and the Life of Devotion*, tenth impression 1933, Longmans) I said, "Bereavement is the deepest initiation into the mysteries of human life, an initiation more searching and profound than even happy love. Love remembered and consecrated by grief belongs more clearly than the happy intercourse of friends, to the eternal world; it has proved itself stronger than death. Bereavement is the sharpest challenge to our trust in God; if faith can overcome this, there is no mountain which it cannot remove. And faith can overcome it. It brings the eternal world more near to us and makes it seem more real. It is not that we look forward to anything remotely resembling Ezekiel's vision of the valley of dry bones, still less could we find any comfort from the pathetic illusions of modern necromancy. These fancies have nothing to do with our hope of immortality, which would be in no way strengthened by such support. Rather does pure affection, so remembered and so consecrated, carry us beyond the bourne of time and place altogether. It transports us into a purer air, where all that has been, is, and will be lives together in its true being, meaning, and value, before the throne of God. The souls of the righteous are in the hands of God, and what is dear to Him will never be plucked out of the land of the living."

So I wrote long ago. It will be plain that by eternal life I do not mean merely survival in time. The future has not been revealed to us. In this region we can only see as in a mirror, by means of symbols. But God has revealed Himself as love; and "we know that we have passed from death unto life, because we love the brethren."

—W. R. Inge, 1860-1954

[268] Christian Perfection as Defined by John Wesley

In the year 1764, upon a review of the whole subject, I wrote down the sum of what I had observed in the following short propositions:

(1) There is such a thing as perfection; for it is again and again mentioned in Scripture.

(2) It is not so early as justification; for justified persons are to "go on unto perfection," (Heb. vi, 1).

(3) It is not so late as death; for St. Paul speaks of living men that were perfect, (Phil. iii, 15.)

(4) It is not absolute. Absolute perfection belongs not to man, nor to angels, but to God alone.

(5) It does not make a man infallible; none is infallible while he remains in the body.

(6) Is it sinless? It is not worth while to contend for a term. It is "salvation from sin."

(7) It is "perfect love," 1 John iv, 18. This is the essence of it; its properties or inseparable fruits, are, rejoicing evermore, praying without ceasing, and in everything giving thanks, (1 Thess. v, 16,) etc.

(8) It is improvable. It is so far from lying in an indivisible point, from being incapable of increase, that one perfected in love may grow in grace far swifter than he did before.

(9) It is amissible, capable of being lost; of which we have numerous instances. But we were not thoroughly convinced of this till five or six years ago.

(10) It is constantly both preceded and followed by a gradual work.

(11) But is it in itself instantaneous or not? In examining this, let us go on step by step.

An instantaneous change has been wrought in some believers: none can deny this.

Since that change, they enjoy perfect love; they feel this, and this alone; they "rejoice evermore, pray without ceasing, and in every thing give thanks." Now, this is all I mean by perfection; therefore, these are witnesses of the perfection which I preach.

—John Wesley, 1703-1791

[269] Meditations from Channing

1. EVERY MAN IS A THINKER

EVERY man is to be a student, a thinker. This does not mean that he is to shut himself within four walls, and bend body and mind over books. Men thought before books were written, and some of the greatest thinkers never entered what we call a study. Nature, Scripture, society, and life, present perpetual subjects for thought; and the man who collects, concentrates, employs his faculties on any of these subjects for the purpose of getting the truth, is so far a student, a thinker, a philosopher, and is rising to the dignity of a man. It is time that we should cease to limit to professed scholars the title of thinkers, philosophers. Whoever seeks truth with an earnest mind, no matter when or how, belongs to the school of intellectual men.

2. GOD IS WITHIN ME

Your faith has met unusual trials, and . . . you ask me for thoughts which may strengthen you. Your experience of life and of God's goodness is a far better teacher than any suggestions of a fellowbeing. The thought on which I delight to dwell, as I advance in life, is that God is within me—always present to my soul, to teach, to rebuke, to aid, to bless—that he truly desires my salvation from all inward evils, that he is ever ready to give his spirit, that there is no part of my lot which may not carry me forward to perfection, and that outward things are of little or no moment, provided this great work of God goes on within. The body and the world vanish more and more, and the soul, the immortal principle, made to bear God's image, to partake of his truth, goodness, purity, and happiness, comes out to my consciousness more and more distinctly; and in feeling God's intimate presence with this, to enlighten, quicken, and save, I find strength, and hope, and peace.

3. IT TAKES COURAGE TO PRAISE

To me it requires more courage to praise than to reprove. The meanness of flattery is so great, that I am anxious to avoid not only the thing

212

itself, but its appearance. A letter of compliment, which I feel to be due, is to me the most difficult composition. I often err in this respect. I know from my own experience that there are those who need the encouragement of praise. There are more than is thought, who feel the burden of human imperfection too sorely, who receive strength from approbation. I shrink from saying to those even all that I think. Happy they, who, from just confidence in right action, and from the habit of carrying out their convictions, need little foreign support!

4. DEATH IS A SOLEMN TEACHER

We sometimes speak as if the child, dying so early, had accomplished no purpose; but we err. The child did much. How much has it done for you all! How much warmth it has shed through your hearts! How many holy feelings it has awakened! How much happiness it has given! What a lovely image it has left behind! and what a new bond has it formed between you and the future world! Is all this nothing? Have we no cause to thank God for every pure being he has revealed and endeared to us? Let us weep for the departed, but let not the sense of loss make us forget how much has been given, and what a precious hope is left. So unwise and so unthankful a grief would show that we needed it. If we have not faith enough to strengthen and comfort us under the loss of a friend, then it is time that the friend was taken. We have not learned wisdom from the gift. We need another school, that of its loss.

. . . Death is a solemn teacher; but who of us can dispense with its lessons? What other teacher can so disenchant the world, so expand our views, give such convictions of immortality, so spiritualize our minds, so prostrate us with a sense of dependence and unworthiness before God?

—WILLIAM ELLERY CHANNING, 1780-1842

[270] Self-Reflections of John Henry Newman

1. WORK WHILE IT IS YET DAY

Wednesday February 21, 1827

MUCH has happened in the past year (1826) to make me conceited and vain. My pupils have, or I take care to fancy they have, a high opinion of me. I do not actually desire men's good opinion; I am not quite disappointed when I am overlooked; but "mihi plaudo ipse domi." It is self esteem. I am not straight forward in speech, I exaggerate, misrepresent. I am becoming somewhat worldly; thoughts about livings, the Provost-ship, promotions &c come before my mind. I am not remiss in private prayer, and reading the Scriptures. I *do* struggle against this, but *how* difficult it is! At home at Christmas I was very self willed, harsh, proud, ill tempered.

I am not aware of any Christian grace I have grown in, except it be that I have a conviction of the value of time, and the necessity of working while it is yet day. . . .

My present duties I see; what I shall be, I know not. This, thank God, I have, viz a recklessness of tomorrow, an utter thoughtlessness how I am to live and to be supported years hence. I beg He may employ me as may best subserve His purposes of good to mankind.

2. SELF-LOVE: MAN'S SOVEREIGN SIN

1 Day. Saturday April 8. ON the end of man.

Exercise 1. ½ past 4—5½ a.m. The hour has gone so wonderfully quick that I thought it was only the ½ hour, when the clock (which I had put on to accommodate my commencement) struck the end of it. I thought it was not half over, and have been puzzled, & for a moment disconcerted thinking I must have been wrong—but I certainly was not. Yet I have not been able to realize God's Presence duly the whole time. Yet it has been very pleasant to me; and especially, when the hour was gone, I felt joyful and grateful that it had seemed so short against my fears beforehand. . . .

The thoughts that struck me most were,—that God put it into my heart, when 5 or 6 years old, to ask *what* and *why* I was, yet now I am forty two, and have never answered it in *my conduct;* that if disobedience is *against nature,* I am, in the sight of Angels, like some odious *monster* which people put out of sight; that I have acted hardly ever for God's glory, that my motive in all my exertions during the last 10 years, has been the pleasure of energizing intellectually, as if my talents were given me to play a game with, (and hence I care as little about the event as one does about a game); that it is fearful to think how little I have used my gifts in God's service; that I have used them for myself. Hence that Selflove in one shape or another, e.g. vanity, desire of the good opinion of friends, &c. have been my motive; and that possibly it is *the* sovereign sin in my heart; and that therefore it will be well (1) to make it the subject of the Particular Examen.

At the end I solemnly gave myself up to God to do what He would with me—to make me what He would—to put what He would upon me.

214

3. GOD WILL NOT FAIL US NOW

August 30, 1874

I have so depressing a feeling that I have done nothing through my long life—and especially that now I am doing nothing at all. Anglicans indeed rather think more of what I have written than they did, if I may judge from letters I receive—but, as to Catholics, they would not deny that I have done some good service towards bringing Anglicans into the Church, nay am perhaps doing so still; but, as to the great controversies of the day, about the divinity of Christianity &c, they think I am passe—at least this, (perhaps rather,) that I have taken a wrong line in respect to them. At least I think the Jesuits do. They would think my line too free and sceptical, that I made too many admissions &c. On the contrary I *cannot* at all go along with them—and, since they have such enormous influence just now, and are so intolerant in their views, this is pretty much the same as saying that I have not taken, and do not take, what would popularly be called the Catholic line. . . .

But then I think—what is this to me? God will provide—He knows what is best. Is He less careful for the Church, less able to defend it than I am? Why need I fash myself about it? What am I? my time is out. I am passe—I may have done something in my day—but I can do nothing now. It is the turn of others. And if things seem done clumsily, my business is, not to criticize, but to have faith in God. The 130th Psalm is the Psalm that suits me—alas! we never read it in the office. . . . It is enough for me to prepare for death—for, as it would appear, nothing else awaits me—there is nothing else to do.

And He Who has been with me so marvellously all through my life, will not fail me now, I know—though I have no claim upon Him, . . . I certainly feel much weaker and less capable [corrected from "more incapable"] than I was—and whether this will not rapidly increase upon me, or not, how can I tell? I must give up the thought of the next generation, and think of myself.

—JOHN HENRY NEWMAN, 1801-1890

[271] Rules for Employing Our Time

1. IN the morning, when you awake, accustom yourself to *think first upon God*, or something in order to His service; and at night also, let Him close thine eyes: and let your sleep be necessary and healthful, not

215

idle and expensive of time, beyond the needs and conveniences of nature; and sometimes be curious to see the preparation which the sun makes, when he is coming forth from his chambers of the east. . . .

2. Let all the *intervals* or void spaces of time be employed in prayers, reading, meditating, works of nature, recreation, charity, friendliness and neighbourhood, and means of spiritual and corporal health; ever remembering so to work in our calling, as not to neglect the work of our high calling; but to begin and end the day with God, with such forms of devotion as shall be proper to our necessities.

3. The resting days of Christians, and *festivals* of the Church, must, in no sense, be days of idleness; for it is better to plough upon holy days, than to do nothing, or to do viciously; but let them be spent in the works of the day, that is, of religion and charity, according to the rules appointed. . . .

4. In the midst of the works of thy calling, often retire to God in *short prayers* and *ejaculations;* and these may make up the want of those larger portions of time, which, it may be, thou desirest for devotion, and in which thou thinkest other persons have advantage of thee: for so thou reconcilest thy outward work and thy inward calling, the Church and the Commonwealth, the employment of thy body and the interest of thy soul: for be sure, that God is present at thy breathings and hearty sighings of prayer, as soon as at the longer offices of less busied persons. . . .

5. Let your employment be *fitted to your person and calling.* Some there are that employ their time in affairs infinitely below the dignity of their person; and being called by God or by the republic to help to bear great burdens, and to judge a people, do enfeeble their understandings and disable their persons by sordid and brutish business. Thus Nero went up and down Greece, and challenged the fiddlers at their trade. Aeropus, a Macedonian king, made lanterns. Harcatius, the king of Parthia, was a mole-catcher; and Biantes, the Lydian, filed needles. He that is appointed to minister in holy things must not suffer secular affairs and sordid arts to eat up great portions of his employment; a clergyman must not keep a tavern, nor a judge be an innkeeper. . . .

6. Let *women of noble birth and great fortunes* do the same things in their proportions and capacities; nurse their children, look to the affairs of the house, visit poor cottages, and relieve their necessities; be courteous to the neighbourhood, learn in silence of their husbands or their spiritual guides, read good books, pray often and speak little, and "learn to do good works for necessary uses. . . ."

7. Let all persons of all conditions avoid all *delicacy or niceness in their clothing or diet,* because such softness engages them upon great mis-

spendings of their time, while they dress and comb out all their opportunities of their morning devotion, and half the day's severity, and sleep out the care and provision for their souls.

8. Let every one of every condition avoid *curiosity*, and all inquiry into things that concern them not. For all business in things that concern us not is an employing our time to no good of ours, and therefore not in order to a happy eternity. In this account our neighbours' necessities are not to be reckoned: for they concern us, as one member is concerned in the grief of another: but going from house to house, tattlers and busybodies, which are the canker and rust of idleness, as idleness is the rust of time, are reproved by the Apostle in severe language, and forbidden in order to this exercise. . . .

9. Set apart some portions of every day for *more solemn devotion* and religious employment; which be severe in observing: and if variety of employment, or prudent affairs, or civil society, press upon you, yet so order thy rule, that the necessary parts of it be not omitted; and though just occasions may make your prayers shorter, yet nothing but a violent, sudden, and impatient necessity make thee, upon any one day, wholly to omit thy morning and evening devotions; which if you be forced to make very short, you may supply and lengthen with ejaculations and short retirements in the day-time, in the midst of your employment or of your company.

10. Do not the "work of God negligently" and idly: let not thy heart be unto the world when thy hand is lifted up in prayer; and be sure to prefer an action of religion, in its place and proper season, before all worldly pleasure: letting secular things, that may be dispensed with in themselves, in these circumstances wait upon the other. Sir Thomas More being sent for by the king when he was at his prayers in public, returned answer, he would attend him when he had first performed his service to the King of kings. . . .

11. When the clock strikes, or however else you shall measure the day, it is good to say a short ejaculation every hour, that the parts and returns of devotion may be the measure of your time: and do so also in all the breaches of thy sleep; that those spaces, which have in them no direct business of the world, may be filled with religion. . . .

12. Let him that is most busied set apart some "solemn time every year," in which, for the time, quitting all worldly business, he may attend wholly to fasting and prayer, and the dressing of his soul by confessions, meditations, and attendances upon God; that he may make up his accounts, renew his vows, make amends for his carelessness, and retire back again, from the place to which levity and the vanities of

217

the world, or the opportunity of temptations, or the distraction of secular affairs, have carried him.

13. In this we shall be much assisted, and we shall find the work more easy, if, before we sleep, every night we examine the actions of the past day with a particular scrutiny, if there have been any accident extraordinary; as long discourse, a feast, much business, variety of company. If nothing but common hath happened, the less examination will suffice; only let us take care that we sleep not without such a recollection of the actions of the day.

—JEREMY TAYLOR, 1613-1667

[272] Pascal's Thoughts

1. PASCAL'S SECOND CONVERSION

As Pascal read the seventeenth chapter of the Gospel of John on the night of November 23, 1654, he received in his experience a message from God, which he wrote on a piece of paper. For the rest of his life, he wore this message sewed into his garment. The heart of the message, which was found after his death, was that the living Word and the written Word of the Bible are the same, and that it is through the Bible that God speaks His message to those in need, if they fully surrender to Christ. His "second conversion" was also partially brought about through advice he received from his sister Jacqueline, to whom he confessed his tiring of the world and its lures and who advised him that complete repentance was his only resort. The message which he wore on his garment was this:

In the year of Grace, 1654.

On Monday, 23rd of November, Feast of St. Clerment,

Pope and Martyr, and of others in the Martyrology,

Virgin of Saint Chrysogonus, Martyr; and others,

From about half past ten in the evening until about half past twelve.

FIRE

God of Abraham, God of Isaac, God of Jacob, not of the philosophers and scholars.

Certitude. Certitude. Feeling. Joy. Peace.

God of Jesus Christ.

My God and Thy God.

"Thy God shall be my God."

Forgetfulness of the world and of everything, except God.

He is to be found only by the ways taught in the Gospel.

Greatness of the soul of man.

"Righteous Father, the world hath not known Thee, but I have known Thee."

Joy, joy, joy, tears of joy.

I have fallen away from Him.

They have foresaken Me, the Fountain of living waters.

"My God, wilt Thou forsake me?"

May I not fall from Him for ever.

"This is life eternal, that they might know Thee,

The only true God, and Jesus Christ, whom Thou hast sent."

Jesus Christ.

Jesus Christ.

I have fallen away: I have fled from Him, denied Him, crucified Him.

May I not fall from Him forever,

We keep hold of Him by the ways taught in the Gospel.

Renunciation, total and sweet.

Total submission to Jesus Christ and to my director.

Eternally in joy for a day's exercise on earth.

I will not forget Thy word. Amen.

[After writing these words and sewing them on his garment, Pascal resigned himself to a life of absolute humility, vowing never to sign his name again to his writing. He secretly took the pseudonym of Monsieur de Mons, leaving Paris to reside first in Vaumurier and then in Port Royal. Later, when he wrote his *Lettres Provinciales,* his arguments against the Jesuits, he signed his name "Louis de Montalte." —T. S. K.]

2. FRIGHTENED BY THE ETERNAL SILENCE

I feel that I might not have been; for the Ego consists in my thoughts. Therefore I, who think, would not have been, if my mother had been killed before I had life. I am not then a necessary being. In the same way I am not eternal or infinite; but I see plainly that there exists in nature a necessary Being, eternal and infinite. . . .

When I see the blindness and the wretchedness of man, when I regard the whole silent universe, and man without light, left to himself, and, as it were, lost in this corner of the universe, without knowing who has put him there, what he has come to do, what will become of him at death, and incapable of all knowledge, I become terrified, like a man who should be carried in his sleep to a dreadful desert island, and should awake without knowing where he is, and without means of escape. And thereupon I wonder how people in a condition so wretched do not fall into despair. . . .

When I consider the short duration of my life, swallowed up in the eternity before and after, the little space which I fill, and even can see, engulfed in the infinite immensity of spaces of which I am ignorant, and which know me not, I am frightened, and am astonished at being here rather than there; for there is no reason why here rather than there, why now rather than then. Who has put me here? By whose order and direction have this place and time been allotted to me? . . .

The eternal silence of these infinite spaces frightens me. . . .

Why is my knowledge limited? Why my stature? Why my life to one hundred years rather than to a thousand? . . .

The last act is tragic, however happy all the rest of the play is; at the last a little earth is thrown upon our head, and that is the end forever. . . .

We are fools to depend upon the society of our fellow men. Wretched as we are, powerless as we are, they will not aid us; we shall die alone. We should therefore act if we were alone, and in that case should we build fine houses, etc. We should seek the truth without hesitation; and, if we refuse it, we show that we value the esteem of men more than the search for truth.

3. OF THE MEANS OF BELIEF

There are only three kinds of persons: those who serve God, having found Him; others who are occupied in seeking Him, not having found Him; while the remainder live without seeking Him, and without having found Him. The first are reasonable and happy, the last are foolish and unhappy; those between are unhappy and reasonable.

If we submit everything to reason, our religion will have no mysterious and supernatural element. If we offend the principles of reason, our religion will be absurd and ridiculous.

Men often take their imagination for their heart; and they believe they are converted as soon as they think of being converted.

The heart has its reasons, which reason does not know. We feel it in a thousand things. I say that the heart naturally loves the Universal Being, and also itself naturally, according as it gives itself to them; and it hardens itself against one or the other at its will. You have rejected the one, and kept the other. Is it by reason that you love yourself?

It is the heart which experiences God, and not the reason. This, then, is faith: God felt by the heart, not by the reason.

Faith is a gift of God; do not believe that we said it was a gift of

220

reasoning. Other religions do not say this of their faith. They only gave reasoning in order to arrive at it, and yet it does not bring them to it.

The knowledge of God is very far from the love of Him.

—BLAISE PASCAL, 1623-1662

[273] Charles Kingsley's Evaluation of "Theologia Germanica"

To those who really hunger and thirst after righteousness; and who therefore long to know what righteousness is, that they may copy it: To those who long to be freed, not merely from the punishment of sin after they die, but from sin itself while they live on earth; and who therefore wish to know what sin is, that they may avoid it: To those who wish to be really justified by faith, by being made just persons by faith; and who cannot satisfy either their consciences or reasons by fancying that God looks on them as right, when thy know themselves to be wrong, or that the God of truth will stoop to fictions (miscalled forensic) which would be considered false and unjust in any human court of law: To those who cannot help trusting that union with Christ must be something real and substantial, and not merely a metaphor, and a flower of rhetoric: To those, lastly, who cannot help seeing that the doctrine of Christ in every man, as the Indwelling Word of God, The Light who lights everyone who comes into the world, is no peculiar tenent of the Quakers, but one which runs through the whole of the Old and New Testaments, and without which they would both be unintelligible, just as the same doctrine runs through the whole history of the Early Church for the first two centuries, and is the only explanation of them;—To all these this noble little book will recommend itself; and may God bless the reading of it to them, and to all others no less.

—CHARLES KINGSLEY, 1819-1875

[274] Spiritual Wisdom from "Theologia Germanica"

1. ONLY SIN IS CONTRARY TO GOD

BUT what then is there which is contrary to God and hateful to Him? Nothing but sin. But what is sin? Mark this: Sin is nothing else than that the creature willeth otherwise than God willeth, and contrary to

221

Him. Each of us may see this in himself; for he who willeth otherwise than I, or whose will is contrary to mine, is my foe; but he who willeth the same as I, is my friend, and I love him. It is even so with God: and that is sin, and is contrary to God, and hateful and grievous to Him. And he who willeth, speaketh, or is silent, doeth or leaveth undone, otherwise than as I will, is contrary to me, and an offence unto me. So it is also with God: when a man willeth otherwise than God, or contrary to God, whatever he doeth or leaveth undone, in short all that proceedeth from him, is contrary to God, and is sin. And whatsoever will willeth otherwise than God, is against God's will. As Christ said: "He who is not with me is against me." Hereby may each man see plainly whether or not he be without sin, and whether or not he be committing sin, and what sin is, and how sin ought to be atoned for, and wherewith it may be healed. And this contradiction to God's will is what we call, and is, disobedience.

2. LOVE GOODNESS AS GOODNESS FOR THE SAKE OF GOODNESS

Now, wherever a man hath been made a partaker of the divine nature, in him is fulfilled the best and noblest life, and the worthiest in God's eyes, that hath been or can be. And of that eternal Love which loveth goodness as goodness and for the sake of goodness, a true, noble, Christ-like life is so greatly beloved, that it will never be forsaken or cast off. Where a man hath tasted this life, it is impossible ever to part with it, were he to live until the Judgment Day. And though he must die a thousand deaths, and though all the sufferings that ever befell all creatures could be heaped upon him, he would rather undergo them all, than fall away from this excellent life; and if he could exchange it for an angel's life, he would not.

This is our answer to the question, "If a man, by putting on Christ's life, can get nothing more than he hath already, and serve no end, what good will it do him?" This life is not chosen in order to serve any end, or to get anything by it, but for love of its nobleness, and because God loveth and esteemeth it so greatly. And whoever saith that he hath had enough of it, and may now lay it aside, hath never tasted nor known it; for he who hath truly felt or tasted it, can never give it up again. And he who hath put on the life of Christ with the intent to win or deserve aught thereby, hath taken it up as an hireling and not for love, and is altogether without it. For he who doth not take it up for love, hath none of it at all; he may dream indeed that he hath put it on, but he is deceived.

3. SELF-WILL IS THE ONLY FORBIDDEN FRUIT IN PARADISE

What is Paradise? All things that are; for all are goodly and pleasant, and therefore may fitly be called a paradise. It is said also that Paradise is an outer court of heaven. Even so this world is verily an outer court of the Eternal, or of eternity, and specially whatever in time, or any temporal things or creatures, manifesteth or remindeth us of God or eternity; for the creatures are a guide and a path unto God and eternity. Thus this world is an outer court of eternity, and therefore it may well be called a paradise, for it is such in truth. And in this Paradise, all things are lawful, save one tree and the fruits thereof. That is to say: of all things that are, nothing is forbidden and nothing is contrary to God but one thing only: that is, self-will, or to will otherwise than as the Eternal Will would have it. . . .

It is not that every work which is thus wrought is in itself contrary to the Eternal Will, but in so far as it is wrought from a different will, or otherwise than from the Eternal and Divine Will.

4. MAN IS TO ETERNAL GOODNESS AS A HAND TO A MAN

Now let us mark: Where men are enlightened with the true light, they perceive that all which they might desire or choose, is nothing to that which all creatures, as creatures, ever desired or chose or knew. Therefore they renounce all desire and choice, and commit and commend themselves and all things to the Eternal Goodness. Nevertheless, there remaineth in them a desire to go forward and get nearer to the Eternal Goodness; that is, to come to a clearer knowledge, and warmer love, and more comfortable assurance, and perfect obedience and subjection; so that every enlightened man could say: "I would fain be to the Eternal Goodness, what his own hand is to a man." And he feareth always that he is not enough so, and longeth for the salvation of all men. And such men do not call this longing their own, nor take it unto themselves, for they know well that this desire is not of man, but of the Eternal Goodness; for whatsoever is good shall no one take unto himself as his own, seeing that it belongeth to the Eternal Goodness only.

5. NOTHING BURNS IN HELL BUT SELF-WILL

Some may say: "Now since God willeth and desireth and doth the best that may be to every one, He ought so to help each man and order things for him, that they should fall out according to his will and fulfil his desires, so that one might be a pope, another a bishop, and so forth." Be assured, he who helpeth a man to his own will, helpeth him to the worst that he can. For the more a man followeth after his own self-will, and self-will groweth in him, the farther off is he from God, and true good, for nothing burneth in hell but self-will. Therefore it hath been said, "Put off thine own will, and there will be no hell." Now God is very willing to help a man and bring him to that which is best in itself and is of all things the best for man. But to this end, all self-will must depart, as we have said. And God would fain give man His help and counsel thereunto, for so long as a man is seeking his own good, he doth not seek what is best for him, and will never find it. For a man's highest good would be and truly is, that he should not seek himself nor his own things, nor he his own end in any respect, either in things spiritual or things natural, but should seek only the praise and glory of God and His holy will. This doth God teach and admonish us.

—THEOLOGIA GERMANICA

[275] Reflections on the Meaning of Jesus Christ

1. ONE SOLITARY LIFE

HERE is a man who was born in an obscure village, the child of a peasant woman. He grew up in another obscure village. He worked in a carpenter shop until he was thirty, and then for three years he was an itinerant preacher.

He never wrote a book. He never held an office. He never owned a home. He never had a family. He never went to college. He never traveled two hundred miles from the place where he was born. He never did one of the things that usually accompany greatness. . . . While still a young man, the tide of popular opinion turned against him. His friends ran away. One of them denied him. He was turned over to his enemies. He went through the mockery of a trial. He was nailed upon a cross between two thieves. His executioners gambled for the only piece of property he had on earth while he was dying—his coat. When he was dead he was taken down and laid in a borrowed grave through the pity of a friend.

Nineteen wide centuries have come and gone; today he is the centerpiece of the human race and the Leader of the column of progress.

I am far within the mark when I say that all the armies that ever marched, and all the navies that ever were built, and all the parliaments that ever sat, and all the kings that ever reigned, put together, have not affected the life of man upon this earth as powerfully as has that one solitary life.

—JAMES A. FRANCIS, 1796-1863

2. A MAN WISE IN LIFE

He was a small-town man and no world-builder. He preached the Kingdom of God, knowing God for a spirit and having an increasing realization of the kingdom as a state of being. But he had no program. He followed the inward voice, and followed it instinctively with the freedom of a river in its natural channel, with no fretting of the flesh. But where the voice left him uninformed he was simply a man from Nazareth; his social outlook was the outlook of the villager. . . .

He was a man wise in life, but unlearned. He read no books but the Scriptures, wrote nothing, took the folk way of transmitting his teaching from mouth to mouth and trusted God for the increase; and he had the folk way in his profoundest speech of identifying himself with the Power that used him. He dramatized all his relations to the Invisible. With it all he was a Jew of the circumcision. He grew up beyond Judaism as a stalk of grain from its sheath, but never out of it. Always to his death, it was there about the roots of his life.

—MARY AUSTIN, 1868-1934

3. THE GREATEST FACT ABOUT HIM

He lived in religion, and it was breath to him in the fear of God; his whole life, all his thoughts and feelings, were absorbed in the relation to God, and yet he did not talk like an enthusiast and a fanatic, who sees only one red-hot spot, and so is blind to the world and all that it contains. He spoke his message and looked at the world with a fresh and clear eye for the life, great and small, that surrounded him. He proclaimed that to gain the whole world was nothing if the soul were injured, and yet he remained kind and sympathetic to every living thing. That is the most astonishing and the greatest fact about him! . . . Yet he who had nowhere to lay his head does not speak like one who has broken with everything, or like an heroic penitent, or like an ecstatic prophet, but like a man who has rest and peace for his soul, and is able to give life and strength to others. He strikes the mightiest notes; he offers men an inexorable alternative; he leaves them no escape; and yet the strongest emotion seems to come naturally to him, and he expresses it as something natural; he clothes it in the language in which a mother speaks to her child.

—ADOLF VON HARNACK, 1851-1930

4. CHRISTIANITY BEGAN WITH THE JOINING OF HEART TO HEART

We regard the word as of pre-eminent importance. We have not heard Jesus speak. Nor do we know anyone who has heard Him. Neither our fathers nor our grandfathers wandered with Him over the hills of Galilee. For us the written word is of great weight; and of right, for it is beyond price. But there is something still more important than the written word. Did we wish, as some people unfortunately often do, to limit the sayings and the deeds, the events in those years of the Church's infancy, to what we find written down in the New Testament, as if it were a precise chronicle of all that the Christians experienced, we should go astray. And we should err still more widely if we refused to accept any testimony as to the written word in the New Testament which we cannot read in so many sentences in ecclesiastical authors. The Christian Church is more than a book. Jesus was more than a word. Jesus, the Logos, the Word, was the Life, and the Church is a living society, a living fellowship. There is something sublime in such a fellowship that passes through the ages in a living tradition. Our connection with Jesus, which reaches now over more than eighteen hundred years, does not rest upon the fact that He wrote something down, which one man and another, one after another has read and believed until this very day. So far as we know, he left no writings, no notes behind Him. We do not read that He ever told anyone to take down His words so as to give them to others in white and black. We are not told that He ever wrote or dictated even a letter. He *lived* and He spoke. Christianity began with the joining of heart to heart. Eye looked into eye. The living voice struck upon the living ear. And it is precisely such a uniting of personalities, such an action of man on man, that ever since Jesus spoke has effected the unceasing renewal of Christianity. Christianity has not grown to be what it is, has not maintained itself and enlarged itself, by reason of books being read, no, not even by reason of the Bible's being read from generation to generation. How many millions of the Christians of past days could not read! How many to-day cannot read! Christianity is first of all a life and has been passed along as life, has been lived, livingly presented from age to age. The Christian, whether a clergyman or a layman, has sought with his heart after the hearts of his fellow-men. A mother has whispered the word to her child, a friend has spoken it in the ear of his friend, a preacher has proclaimed it to his hearers, and the child, the friend, the hearers have believed and become Christians. Christianity is an uninterrupted life.

—CASPAR RENÉ GREGORY, 1846-1917

5. HIS FIGURE LAID HOLD OF MEN

Most men find in Jesus a reflection of their own ideals. Take any number of recent biographies. For Bruce Barton Jesus is a modern business man, the he-man type, an advertiser, a Rotary Club speaker, and the like. For Mary Austin he is a mystic. For Klausner and Jacobs he is a Jew. For Upton Sinclair he is a socialist. And I might go on. What is the significance of this? To me it is simply that . . . the figure of Jesus has laid hold of men. At first they thought of him as the Son of Man, then Paul thought of him more or less as the risen god of a cult of salvation, then the author of the fourth gospel identified him with the Logos, then the theologians battled for centuries as to how his nature could be both human and divine. Always he was the instrument of salvation, whether in the terms of the mysteries, in the crude barter theory of the Middle Ages, or in the atonement theory of Anselm.

—Granville Hicks, 1901-

6. freedom in his service

We cannot emphasize too strongly the fact that Christianity is a personal religion. The gateway to Christianity is not through an intricate labyrinth of dogma, but by a simple belief in the person of Christ. Leave dogma to those who enjoy it; the true Christian is simply a member of Christ's society, of his party, one of his followers. I cannot understand the nature of the Infinite Energy; but I can follow Jesus Christ, because he took the form of a young man, and we have the story of his life, actions, and words. I think he was wiser and better than Abraham Lincoln, George Washington, or Theodore Roosevelt; I find it easier to be a Christian partisan than to be a Republican or Democrat. I have more faith in the practical wisdom and knowledge of Jesus than I have in that of Julius Caesar or of any statesman, soldier or philosopher. He had more common sense than any person I ever saw, heard, or read of; he was the most independent and the most courageous individual of whom we have any record. In his service there is freedom. . . .

I want to follow the Best I know, and here it is. If any one can show me anything better, I will follow that.

—William Lyon Phelps, 1865-1943

7. napoleon's appreciation of jesus

Alexander, Caesar, Charlemagne and myself founded empires; but upon what did we rest the creations of our genius? Upon *force*. Jesus Christ alone founded his empire upon love; and at this hour millions of men would die for him.

—Napoleon Bonaparte, 1769-1821

8. more alive than ever

Modern representations of Jesus Christ have tended to portray Him as above all a Teacher, a Wise Sage who saw by unerring instinct what

227

was essential in human life and conduct. But His career was not that of a Sage. Typical teachers of mankind are Socrates and Plato, in modern times Kant and Darwin, in the East Confucius and the Buddha. All these lived long, they trained up a generation to think along the lines of their new ideas, most of them took pains to organize in some way the propagation or preservation of their philosophy. The Founders of religions, again, or of particular modes of life, such as St. Benedict, have drawn up Rules for their followers. If Moses be the legendary founder of the Israelite religion, then the Pentateuch is legitimately called the Law of Moses. Moses and Benedict both lived to a good old age, and they needed it for their work. How different was the career of Jesus, yet how marvellously influential, notwithstanding apparent failure! Therefore His special characteristic cannot have been that of the Sage, the Teacher, the Founder. It was something distinct from all these. . . .

As I once ventured to say (*Cambridge Biblical Essays,* page 198), it is not as a Philosopher but as Prometheus, that we worship Christ— the Man who came down from Heaven to give the Divine Fire. Jesus Himself once described His mission as that of a man lighting a fire, and whatever course He may have taken in doing it, it is at least certain that His fire has burned for nineteen centuries and that it is alight still. The way that the Fire was lit finds its justification in the history of the Fire.
—Francis Crawford Burkitt, 1864-1935

9. AMONG THE MIGHTY TEACHERS

For many years I have regarded Jesus of Nazareth as one among the mighty teachers that the world has had, and I say this in all humility. I claim humility for this expression because this is exactly what I feel. Of course, Christians claim a higher place for Jesus of Nazareth than I, as a non-Christian and a Hindu, am able to feel. I purposely use the word "feel" instead of "give" because I consider that neither I nor anybody else can possibly arrogate to himself the claim of *giving* a place to a great man. . . . Thus I can say that Jesus occupies in my heart the place of one of the great teachers who have made a considerable influence in my life.
—Mahatma Mohandas K. Gandhi, 1869-1948

10. WHY JESUS IS AUTHORITATIVE

The only apologetic for Jesus' teaching that I find in any way reasonable is the one which Jesus Himself propounded—experience. His way of life is not to be followed because He recommended it, or because He was virgin-born, or was a part of the Godhead, or could work miracles, or for any other reason than that experience will prove that it is a good way, none better, if one have but the understanding and tenacity of purpose to cleave to it.

—ALBERT JAY NOCK, 1902-

11. BEYOND TRAGEDY

The large, gracious carelessness of the life of Jesus is a proof of his faith in the friendliness of the universe. The tragic hero has faith, but in himself and, to a degree, in a cold world of ideals to which he stoically adheres, Jesus had faith in the universe within him: "I and my Father." There is an incident in his life which stands in striking contrast to two incidents in the tragedy of Othello. Although Othello can lightly command his friends and enemies to keep up their bright swords, or can tell them more sternly, "Were it my cue to fight I should have known it without a prompter," in a really desperate situation he seeks that "sword of Spain, the ice-brook's temper" with which to enforce his will. Jesus, taken for his life, says calmly to Peter, "Put up again thy sword into his place. . . . Thinkest thou that I cannot now pray to my Father, and He shall presently give me more than twelve legions of angels?" Othello at strongest trusted himself, at weakest his sword; Jesus trusted God. . . .

It is paradoxical that the tragic hero lives in this narrow world as though under a universal doom, while Jesus lives in the universe in an air of freedom. The explanation, perhaps, is that those who cannot live in the universe, will die in the universe, that freedom belongs only to those who can take the universe into their confidence. The tragic hero lives to die; this is the whole bent of his action. Jesus died to live—died for life; his death was a means not an end.

—JAMES McBRIDE DABBS, 1896-

12. JESUS SPEAKS TO "MODERN EMANCIPATED MAN"

"Palestine nineteen hundred years ago" raises serious objections in many minds. How can "modern emancipated man" be expected to learn from an ancient Jew who lived in one of the remote provinces of the Roman Empire? The answer is, first, that men are fundamentally alike in all lands and in all ages that are known to history. The differences are essentially superficial. The second answer is that, in nineteen hundred years, culture has not changed so greatly as moderns like to think, and that Palestine, lying between the east and the west, at the center of the ancient world, was less "provincial" than far-western Rome, or even than unique and learned Athens, for it had a much longer and more varied cultural inheritance.

In the third place, the answer is that the Hebrews represent one of

229

those phenomena which appear again and again in biological and social evolution, different as the two are in many features. A strange and as yet inexplicable combination of circumstances selects certain groups and certain individuals to make them bearers of peculiar values. As a yet undiscovered group of primates developed the human skeleton, as India developed the decimal system and Babylonia the duodecimal, as Greece developed art, science, and philosophy, and Rome business, law, government, so the Jews developed ethics and a spiritual monotheism. The problem of Jesus' place in history is therefore in part a problem for the sociologist as historian.

—CHESTER C. McCOWN, 1877-1958

13. SEEN BY FAITH ALONE

The Person of this human personality does not resemble a human being; here the humanity of Christ ceases; indeed, this Person is not historically visible at all. He can be seen by faith alone. Only to the unbelieving soul Christ says who He is. He remains completely concealed within history. Where he discloses Himself history disappears, and the Kingdom of God has begun. And when He unveils Himself He is no longer an historical personality, but the Son of God who is from everlasting to everlasting.

—EMIL BRUNNER, 1889-

14. WAS JESUS ONLY A PROPHET?

Was Jesus then only a prophet? It may be a hard saying, but after all "prophet" is only one more historical category—and Jesus was unique. In fact, on Jewish lips "prophet" was the highest possible category, next to God himself. . . . It was a far more natural, more human and more religiously significant category than the purely imaginary one of Messiah, let alone that of "Son of Man" or "Man from Heaven" in the esoteric circles of the Apocalyptists.

—FREDERICK C. GRANT, 1891-

15. JESUS, A SUPERHUMAN FOUNDER

However we interpret the personal claims attributed to Jesus, and whatever construction we put on the story of the Resurrection, one indisputable fact remains, that Christianity began with the belief in a superhuman founder . . . But in the main Christianity passed with the fourth Gospel into the wide stream of Greek thought, while bringing to that tradition its own vital contribution; henceforth we have to study the mutual assimilation of the faith of Jesus with the Idealism of Plato . . .

230

Christianity to become a world religion had to be translated into the universal and more spiritual terms of Greek intuition.

—PAUL ELMER MORE, 1864-1937

16. JESUS, UNLIKE HIS PREDECESSORS

I would venture to suggest that, through the Gospel mists and miracles, a character seems to emerge in many respects unlike that of *any* O. T or Rabbinic hero, teacher, saint . . . (Yet) the more I study the religious and ethical teaching of the Rabbis and of Jesus, the more I realize that the originalities and peculiarities of the one are complementary to the originalities and percularities of the other.

—CLAUDE G. MONTEFIORE, 1858-1938

17. JESUS, TEACHER AND PARABLE ARTIST

Jesus was not a Christian but he *became* a Christian. Jesus is for the Jewish nation, *a great teacher of morality and an artist in parable.*

—JOSEPH KLAUSNER, 1874-1958

18. JESUS, A SPIRITUAL GIFT

Jesus belonged to a general class . . . He was an itinerant preacher, and indeed one of a class typical of Galilee . . . In particular he was an itinerant preacher of eschatology . . . His vocation as the "latent Son of Man" directed him only to Israel . . . He himself is *charisma* [spiritual gift]. The Messenger is not only preacher and announcer of this kingdom, but is an integral part of the inbreaking miracle of the eschatological order itself.

—RUDOLF OTTO, 1869-1938

19. JESUS, A JEWISH RABBI

I do indeed think that we can now know almost nothing concerning the life and personality of Jesus, since the early Christian sources show no interest in either, are moreover fragmentary and often legendary . . . But if the gospel record is worthy of credence, it is at least clear that *Jesus actually lived as a Jewish rabbi.*

—RUDOLF BULTMANN, 1884-

20. ONLY A WHISPER OF HIS VOICE

It seems, then, that the form of the earthly no less than the heavenly Christ is for the most part hidden from us. For all the inestimable value of the gospels, they yield us little more than a whisper of his voice; we trace in them but the outskirts of his ways. Only when we see him

231

hereafter in his fullness shall we know him also as he was known on earth.

—ROBERT H. LIGHTFOOT, 1883-

21. MORE THAN A MARTYRED RABBI

The earliest message of the apostles was not that Jesus was a martyred rabbi who had left behind him a noble body of teaching. It was not that there had lived in Galilee an example whom all should follow. Their message was not biographical information about the Jesus whom some had known and loved. It was first of all *good news from* God. His Messiah, or Anointed One, had appeared in the person of this Jesus who had been crucified. But God had vindicated him by raising him from the dead, of which they were witnesses.

—CLARENCE T. CRAIG, 1895-1953

22. JESUS IS NEVER ANTIQUATED

The decisions at which He arrived, in their fundamental principles, hold good against all lapse of time. When moral and religious advance is made, it is not true to say that it antiquates the teaching of Jesus; on the contrary, it presents itself as a fresh unfolding of what Jesus meant. . . . When we accept His way, then we come into a position in which we can begin to see the truth of God in our own experiences as interpreted by what He said and what He was.

—CHARLES H. DODD, 1884-

23. GOD RECKONS WITH MILLENNIUMS

The Sermon on the Mount does not speak of human or worldly conditions but only of God's eternal will. . . . In spite of all differences between our time and the days of Jesus we must stand for and uphold this will of God if we believe in Christ as the Saviour. . . . God does not reckon with decades but with centuries and with millenniums.

—MARTIN DIBELIUS, 1883-1947

24. JESUS, THE LIBERATOR OF SLAVES

He was conscious of possessing within Himself the power necessary to conquer death, and to conquer it not only in Himself but in all mankind, in all people. . . . Slaves will remember the eternal name of Christ: *The Liberator*.

—DMITRI MEREJKOWSKI, 1865-1943

25. JESUS SETS OFF THE SPARK

The great faith impulse behind Christianity arose in and through Jesus of Nazareth. This event had its context in the faith of Israel, a faith granted to Israel and won by Israel through vicissitudes linked with those of all mankind in common human experience. Jesus' own life drama and the experience of his followers with him and through him released an incomparable power. This power was creative both in life and in thought. Here it was that the finger of God touched the world as though in a new day of creation. It was as though a spark had been struck between heaven and earth which gave the first community a new and blinding light on existence and which changed the face of the world. Jesus' career and teaching in that critical hour of Israel's history offered the circumstance, but it was the whole drama and fate of Jesus, read in the light of the Scriptures, which set off the spark.

—AMOS N. WILDER, 1895-

26. JESUS AS HE WAS REMEMBERED

It is Jesus as he was remembered and interpreted who is alone important for the Christian community. It is this Jesus with whom both faith and history are concerned. The perception of this fact invests the whole New Testament picture with a kind of immediate and unquestionable historical value: the event of Jesus Christ was precisely that totality of fact and meaning—of fact responded to, remembered, and interpreted—which is indubitably set forth in the New Testament (gospels and epistles) and is thus itself indubitable. We are not, therefore, under any religious or theological "pressure" to separate nicely between fact and meaning and to say exactly where one leaves off and the other begins; as a matter of fact the two are fused indissolubly. But although it is not necessary for the Christian to distinguish or identify the element of fact, it is inevitable that he shall affirm its existence: something happened.

—JOHN KNOX, 1900-

27. HE WON'T COME THAT WAY THE SECOND TIME

These gospel writers knew that Jesus was divine; they knew equally well that divinity meant superhuman power and knowledge. Thus they made Jesus over in the image of their God, and the Jesus who refused to work miracles and had no power to avoid the cross became a little-boy Superhuman, more worthy of the modern comic strips than of Christian literature.

An equally clear example of the Christian refusal to accept a carpenter

233

as a revelation of God occurred on the campus of Emory University about twenty years ago. One of my teachers was addressing a gathering of Methodist clergymen. "Suppose," he said to them, "that the Gospels are right—that a carpenter without wealth or schooling or prestige was an adequate revelation of God! Could it be that this poor man was God's Messiah? We condemn the Jews because they did not accept him, but if he came to us the same way today, would we recognize him?" Immediately an indignant preacher in the front row jumped to his feet and shouted, "But he won't come that way the second time!"

The Jews knew he would not come that way the first time! They knew the messianic prophecies as well as we do. We blame them for not seeing that the carpenter was their Messiah, but we immediately strip him of all that made him Jesus. We will not accept a carpenter as our Messiah; so we require of him that at his return he come with the power and the glory with which he did not come to Israel.

—ERNEST CADMAN COLWELL, 1901-

28. THE INTENT OF THE SERMON ON THE MOUNT

As regards the sayings of the Sermon on the Mount we may state that before Easter they were words of Jesus spoken to reveal God's will, and that after Easter these sayings were collected to be a rule of conduct for the Christian communities. During his lifetime the sayings of Jesus were intended to serve as signs of the Kingdom of Heaven. Collected and brought together in a slightly elaborated form in the summary called the Sermon on the Mount, the sayings became rules by which the Christians were to prepare themselves for the membership in that Kingdom and for a life "in Christ" meanwhile. Before Easter the simple words which we read in the Sermon on the Mount had more value than precepts of the sages, because the man who uttered them was a warrant of the Kingdom of Heaven, the personal embodiment of all faith and hope. His sayings were for his listeners a judgment and a promise in the name of God. After Easter they became the law which the heavenly Lord has given. . . .

This was the meaning of the Sermon on the Mount in the old days. For us who claim to be Christians in the present there is another question: what shall we do as Christians of today, if we want to be obedient to the Sermon on the Mount?

—MARTIN DIBELIUS, 1883-1947

29. WORTH OF MAN IN HIS DECISION

The modern conception differs fundamentally from that of Jesus, because the former assumes the *intrinsic worth of humanity,* at least of the highest and noblest in it. The highest in man, indeed, is often designated without qualification as divine. By way of contrast, the worth of a man for Jesus is not determined by his human quality or the character of his spiritual life, but simply by the decision the man makes in the here-and-now of his present life. Jesus sees man as standing here and now under the necessity of decision, with the possibility of decision through his own free act. Only what a man now does gives him his value. And this crisis of decision arises for the man because he is face to face with the coming of the Kingdom of God. Somewhat similarly one might see the essential quality of human life defined by the fact that death awaits men and by the way they allow themselves to be determined thereby. And indeed the Kingdom of God and death are alike in this— that both the Kingdom and death imply the end of earthly human existence as we know it, with its possibilities and interests. Moreover it may be said that death, like the Kingdom, is not to be considered by man as an accidental event, which sometimes will bring to an end the everyday course of life, but as the true future which confronts man and limits him in the present and puts him under the necessity of decision. Thus in either case the judgment is pronounced upon man not from the human standpoint, as if man's value were somehow immanent and securely possessed by him, but from without—according to Jesus, of course, God is the only Judge.

—D. RUDOLF BULTMANN, 1884-

30. THEY FOUND A LIVING CHRIST

The early Christians did not believe in the resurrection of Christ because they could not find his dead body. They believed because they did find a living Christ. The resurrection of Jesus did not mean the reanimation of a corpse for a brief continuation of fellowship with his friends. It meant that the new age of God had already begun. God's Messiah had been raised from the dead as the opening event in the drama of salvation.

—CLARENCE T. CRAIG, 1895-1953

31. THE STIMULUS OF CHRIST

What was it that happened to Augustine there in the garden at Milan [which stimulates him to read Paul's Letter to the Romans, with the words, "Put on the Lord Jesus Christ"]? The sensual gave way to the spiritual. The sinner became the saint. The stimulus of Christ! . . . The cavalier [Francis of Assisi] took on himself the vows of poverty and celibacy. He resolved to give his life in service. He enters the leper

235

houses, and ministers to the sufferers. He founds an order, and the Little Brothers of Francis go out to serve around the world. What happened to Francis of Assisi? The stimulus of Christ! . . . Let us visit Capetown. In his [David Livingstone's] diary, when the wife who had been so loyal and in whom his life had been centered, died in Africa, he wrote, "Oh Mary, my Mary, little did I realize I would leave you here when I brought you here." The man himself was to die kneeling beside a bed in the heart of Africa. What drove David Livingstone to his task? *The stimulus of Christ.*

—G. BROMLEY OXNAM, 1891-

[276] The Death of Socrates

SOCRATES, as interpreted by Plato in the *Dialogues,* viewed life as a prologue or rehearsal for death. All souls were of divine origin under divine guidance. Before his judges Socrates exclaimed, "Those of us who think that death is an evil are in error. . . . Wherefore, O judges, be of good cheer about death, and know this of a truth—that no evil can happen to a good man, either in life or after death." Shortly before his death Socrates further affirmed, "Fair is the prize, and the hope great! . . . I say, let a man be of good cheer about his soul, . . . who has adorned the soul in her own proper jewels, which are temperance, and justice, and courage, and nobility, and truth—in these arrayed she is ready to go on her journey . . . when her time comes." When Socrates is asked by Crito, "In what way would you have us bury you?" Socrates replies, "In any way that you like only you must get hold of me, and take care that I do not walk away from you. . . . Be of good cheer, then, my dear Crito, and say that you are burying my body only, and do with that as is usual, and as you think best."

Before Socrates raised the cup of poison to his lips he said, "I may and must pray to the gods to prosper my journey from this to the other world —may this then, which is my prayer, be granted to me." To his friends about him he said, "Be quiet then, and have patience." And then to his friend Crito he spoke his last words, "I owe a cock to Asclepius; will you remember to pay the debt?" Several moments later his friends knew that Socrates had passed from this world to the greater world. Remarks his biographer, "Such was the end of our friend, concerning whom I may truly say, that of all men of his time whom I have known, he was the wisest and the justest and the best." Was not Socrates' view of death—

236

which lent him courage, humility, sympathy, love—one of the basic factors which enriched his view of life?

[277] The Contemplation of Death Enriches Life

IT is winter, 1945. I am sitting in my office thinking about death—particularly *my* death. It brings me no sense of morbidity as I realize that my span of life on this planet will probably terminate in twenty-five years. Rather, it gives to me a drive to the worth-while things I want done—an incentive to be more kind and helpful to the people I meet, an impetus to live *this day* as though it were the last and best day of my existence. Outside it is snowing. The snowflakes are falling patiently and kindly, lodging securely on the boughs of the campus trees. Through the soft snow curtain I discern the spire of the college chapel pointing upward as though to direct my thoughts to God. The sight of the chapel reminds me of the sixteen hundred students who have walked in and out of its doors, now on the fighting fronts of the world. I realize that death to many of them at this very moment is imminent; I try to parallel their thoughts of death with mine. I conclude that many of them are weighing death in possible terms of moments, hours, days; I am weighing my death in terms of years. That is the difference. I want to live my life as courageously and dynamically in the years that lie ahead as they are forced under the expediency of war to live their lives in these tragic days. The thought of death deepens my desire to life!

I arise from my chair and say to myself, "I am not afraid of death; I believe that death is necessary in order to enrich life!"

[278] Retire into Yourself

ALTHOUGH this meditation upon mortality may soon induce in us a sense of anguish, it fortifies us in the end. Retire, reader, into yourself and imagine a slow dissolution of yourself—the light dimming about you, all things becoming dumb and soundless, enveloping you in silence, the objects that you handle crumbling away between your hands, the ground slipping from under your feet, your very memory vanishing as if in a swoon, everything melting away from you into nothingness and you your-

237

self also melting away, the very consciousness of nothingness, merely as the phantom harbourage of a shadow, not even remaining in you.

—MIGUEL DE UNAMUNO, 1864-1936

[279] We Live Always

MOST Americans are victims of wishful thinking. They believe they can avoid immortality, or that—if they must live forever—it will be some sort of "impersonal immortality"—which must mean, if it means any-thing, that their souls will be swallowed up by an oversoul, and John Smith will no longer be John Smith. The idea that death spells finis is a very comfortable one. It means that you can do what you want to while you are alive, and if you are clever enough you can have a very happy time of it, and then die before too many sorrows come your way. Sometimes I wish I could believe it is so, but I am afraid the facts are against it. Whether we like it or not, God has made us to live not seventy years—or the hundred and fifty years that modern medicine may give us—but always.

—CHAD WALSH, 1914-

[280] The Magic Key Is Prayer

IN Cologne, early in 1940, a much-beloved professor of philosophy, Peter Wust, lay dying after a long illness. His pupils sent in word to him and asked him to give them a parting message of counsel from his deepest experience of life. He sent back to them the following message:

The magic key is not reflection, as you might expect from philosopher, but it is prayer. Prayer as the most complete act of devotion makes us quiet, makes us objective. A man grows in true humanity in prayer. Prayer is the final humility of the spirit. The greatest things in existence will only be given to those who pray. In suffering one learns to pray best of all.

—DOUGLAS V. STEERE, 1901-

[281] Credo

I BELIEVE in God, who is for me spirit, love, the principle of all things.
I believe that God is in me, as I am in Him.
I believe that the true welfare of man consists in fulfilling the will of God.
I believe that from the fulfillment of the will of God there can follow nothing but that which is good for me and for all men.
I believe that the will of God is that every man should love his fellowmen, and should act toward others as he desires that they should act toward him.
I believe that the reason for life is for each of us simply to grow in love.
I believe that this growth in love will contribute more than any other force to establish the Kingdom of God on earth—
To replace a social life in which division, falsehood and violence are all-powerful, with a new order in which humanity, truth and brotherhood will reign.

—LEO TOLSTOI, 1828-1910

[282] A Lever to Move the World

IN the third century before Christ a Greek mathematician and inventor, Archimedes of Syracuse, made an interesting statement, "Give me a lever long enough, and a fulcrum strong enough, and single-handed I can move the world." In our present age of power some have similarly felt that gadgets and machines will give us the dynamic necessary to change the course of the world. In our century, however, one of our leading novelists, Joseph Conrad, penetrated the folly of Archimedes' idea: "Don't talk to me of your Archimedes' level. . . . Give me the right word and the right accent and I will move the world." Paul, in writing to the church at Corinth, believed that he had "the right word"; "The word of the cross is folly to those who are perishing, but to us who are being saved it is the power of God" (I Cor. 1:18).

[283] Lead, Kindly Light

EVERY man goes through his times of spiritual struggle, wondering if he is led by God's Spirit. John Henry Newman in his visit to Sicily in 1833 had his "dark night of the soul"; his spiritual moorings were momentarily unstable. Finally after months of spiritual torment he headed back from Sicily toward England. His ship was calmed for a week in the Straits of Bonifacio. As he sat one night in his cabin, he saw the value of his struggles; it was not for nothing that he had left England; the words of the psalmist came to his mind as true, "The Lord shall preserve thy going out and thy coming in." Then, "led by the Spirit," he wrote:

> Lead, kindly Light, amid the encircling gloom,
> Lead Thou me on!
> The night is dark, and I am far from home;
> Lead Thou me on!
> Keep Thou my feet; I do not ask to see
> The distant scene—one step enough for me.

[284] Hold Fast to God

HOLD fast to God and he will add every good thing. Seek God and you shall find him and all good with him. To the man who cleaves to God, God cleaves and adds virtue. Thus, what you have sought before, now seeks you; what you once pursued, now pursues you; what you once fled, now flees you. Everything comes to him who truly comes to God, bringing all divinity with it, while all that is strange and alien flies away.

—MEISTER ECKHART, 1260?-1328?

[285] Go to the Depths of the Soul

To get at the core of God at his greatest, one must get into the core of himself at his least, for no one can know God who has not first known himself. Go to the depths of the soul, the secret place of the Most High, to the roots, to the heights; for all that God can do is focused there.

—MEISTER ECKHART, 1260?-1328?

[286] About Disinterest

I PUT disinterest higher than love. . . . Disinterest brings God to me and I can demonstrate it this way: Everything likes its own habitat best; God's habitat is purity and unity, which are due to disinterest. Therefore God necessarily gives himself to the disinterested heart. . . . I also put disinterest above mercy, for mercy is nothing but a man's going out to the want of a fellow and the heart is disturbed by it. Disinterest, however, is exempt from this, being self-contained and allowing nothing to disturb.

—MEISTER ECKHART, 1260?-1328?

[287] Insights from the Diary of Bishop Charles H. Brent

1. ESSENTIAL HAPPINESS

1907

SENSITIVENESS is a gift not a defect. It needs training and involves suffering, but it is the handmaid of sympathy and opens all sorts of doors that otherwise would always remain closed. I think it is a good thing to learn early that no one has a right to any happiness other than that which comes from a life without reproach before God. That is an essential happiness: the rest is incidental and of no deep importance. However, this a truth that can be borne in upon us chiefly through experience.—Letter, April 27.

2. THE NEED OF COURAGE

1909

I wish to cultivate the distinctly virile in myself. I would take for my motto, "I can do all things through Christ who strengtheneth me." I need courage—courage to be unpopular if need be, to blaze a new trail for my fellows. Lord, help me to be daring.—January 1.

3. PROBLEMS SOLVE US

1914

I have come to feel that difficulty is man's best environment. Often we are not intended to solve problems with which we are confronted: they are intended to solve us. We can always challenge difficulty and cheat failure by denying it. The hardest part of life is when depression clouds one. But after a while one learns that if there is no obvious cause, accidie is most fruitful. We are in the gloom to find more of God. We come to realize, after we have patiently passed through it, that we were not unattended, and that in our hands are gleanings which, all unconsciously, we were gathering as we waited.—Letter, February 26

4. THY HAND GUIDE ME

1918

Tranquility of spirit is what I lack, O God. It is always elation (though seldom this) or timidity and apprehension and despondency. Lord, lift me clear of the pit of darkness by Thy love. If I must walk in darkness, let Thy sure hand guide me even when I think I am alone and untended. Feed my deep inner self with Thyself and Thy life.—August 26.

5. THE FLAME AND THE STARS

1926

Why should we experiment in doubtful fields when we have the sky above us as the limits of endeavor upwards? Why play with flame at the risk of being consumed, instead of playing with the stars at the risk of becoming immortal?—Notebook, February 18

6. A WHIP AND A SPUR

1929

It is a strange and interesting world, and to get at its heart we must do so with a whip for our prejudices in one hand, and a spur to our sincerity and honesty before God in the other.—Letter, January 8.

—CHARLES H. BRENT, 1862-1920

[288] Spiritual Insights of Francis of Sales

1. DEVOUT SOULS ASCEND TO GOD

As ostriches never fly, as hens fly low, heavily, and but seldom, and as eagles, doves, and swallows fly aloft, swiftly and frequently, so sinners fly not at all towards God, but lie, grovelling on earth, with only earthly objects in view. Good people, who have not as yet attained to devotion, fly towards God by their good works, but rarely, slowly and heavily;

242

but devout souls ascend to Him by more frequent, prompt, and lofty flights. In short, devotion is nothing else but that spiritual agility and vivacity by which charity works in us, or we work by her, with alacrity and affection; and as it is the business of charity to make us observe all God's commandments, generally and without exception, so it is the part of devotion to make us observe them more fully and with diligence. Wherefore he who observes not all the commandments of God cannot be esteemed either good or devout; since to be good he must be possessed of charity; and to be devout, besides charity, he must show a cheerfulness and alacrity in the performance of charitable actions.

2. WEAR A SPIRITUAL NOSEGAY

Besides all this, as I have already told you, you must gather a little nosegay of devotion. One who has been walking in a beautiful garden, departs not willingly without gathering a few flowers to smell during the remainder of the day; thus ought we, when our soul has been entertaining itself by meditating on some mystery, to select one, or two, or three of those points in which we have found most relish, and which are most proper for our advancement, to think frequently on them, and smell them as it were spiritually during the course of the day. This is to be done in the place in which we have been meditating, either remaining there in silence, or walking by ourselves for some time after.

3. RETIRE OCCASIONALLY INTO SOLITUDE

As birds have their nests on trees, to which they occasionally retire, and the deer, bushes and thickets, in which they conceal themselves and enjoy the cool shade in the heat of summer, so shall we, Philothea, choose some place every day, either on Mount Calvary, or in the wounds of our Lord, or in some other place near him, as a retreat to which we may occasionally retire to refresh and recreate ourselves amidst our exterior occupations; and there, as in a stronghold, defend ourselves against temptations. Blessed is he that can say with truth to our Lord: "Thou art my place of strength and my refuge, my defence from storms, and my shadow from the heat."—Ps. lxx. 3; xxv. 4.

Remember then, Philothea, to retire occasionally into the solitude of your heart while you are outwardly engaged in business or conversation. This mental solitude cannot be prevented by the multitude of those who surround you; for, as they are not about your heart, but your body, your heart may remain in the presence of God alone.

4. RELIGION WILL CARRY YOU THROUGH THE STORM

For as the bees, when surprised by the wind in the fields lay hold of little stones that they may be able to keep their balance in the air and not be so easily carried away by the storm, so our soul, having resolutely embraced the precious love of God remains constant in the midst of inconstancy and vicissitude of consolations and affections temporal as well as spiritual, exterior as well as interior.

—FRANCIS OF SALES, 1567-1622

[289] Disciplines from "The Imitation of Christ"

1. AGAINST THE TONGUES OF SLANDERERS

MY son, take it not grievously if some think ill of thee, and speak that which thou wouldest not willingly hear.

Thou oughtest to be the hardest judge of thyself and to think no man weaker than thyself.

If thou dost walk spiritually, thou wilt not much weigh fleeting words.

It is no small wisdom to keep silence in an evil time, and in thy heart to turn thyself to me, and not to be troubled by the judgment of men.

Let not thy peace depend on the tongues of men; for, whether they judge well of thee or ill, thou art not on that account other than thyself. Where are true peace and true glory? are they not in me?

And he that careth not to please men, nor feareth to displease them, shall enjoy much peace.

From inordinate love and vain fear ariseth all disquietness of heart and distraction of the mind.

2. OF PUTTING OUR TRUST IN GOD WHEN EVIL WORDS ARISE

My son, stand steadily, and put thy trust in me; for what are words, but words?

They fly through the air, but hurt not the rock.

If thou be guilty, see that thou be willing to amend thyself; if conscience reproach thee not, resolve to suffer willingly for God's sake.

It is but a small matter to suffer sometimes a few words, if thou hast not yet the courage to endure hard stripes.

And why do such small matters go to thy heart, but because thou art yet carnal, and regardest men more than thou oughtest?

For because thou art afraid to be despised, therefore thou art not willing to be reproved for thy faults, but seekest the shelter of excuses.

But look better into thyself, and thou shalt acknowledge that the world is yet alive in thee, and a vain desire to please men.

For when thou shunnest to be abased and reproved for thy faults, it is evident that thou art neither truly humble, nor truly dead to the world, nor the world crucified to thee.

But give diligent ear to my words, and thou shalt not regard ten thousand words spoken by men.

Behold, if all should be spoken against thee that could be most maliciously invented, what would it hurt thee, if thou sufferedst it to pass entirely away, and madest no more reckoning of it than a mote? could it pluck so much as one hair from thy head?

But he that hath no heart within him, and hath not God before his eyes, is easily moved with a word of dispraise.

Whereas he that trusteth in me, and hath no wish to trust in his own judgment, shall be free from the fear of men.

For I am the judge and the discerner of all secrets: I know how the matter was; I know him that offered the injury, and him that suffered it.

From me hath this proceeded; this hath happened by my permission, that the thoughts of many hearts might be revealed.

I shall judge the guilty, and the innocent; but by a secret judgment I would beforehand prove them both.

The testimony of men oftentimes deceiveth; but my judgment is true; it shall stand and not be overthrown.

It is commonly hidden, and not known in all respects, but to few: notwithstanding it never erreth, neither can it err, although to the eyes of the foolish it seemeth not right.

Men ought therefore to have recourse to me in every judgment, and not to lean on their own opinion.

For the just man will not be moved, whatsoever befalleth him from God: and if any unjust charge be brought against him, he will not be so much troubled.

Neither will he rejoice with a foolish exultation, if by means of others he be reasonably vindicated.

For he considereth that I am he that searcheth the heart and reins, and judgeth not according to the outside, nor according to human appearance.

For that oftentimes is my sight found worthy of blame, which in the judgment of men is thought to be commendable.

—GERHARD GROOTE, 1340-1384

[290] What Is the Dark Night?

THE experience of the dark night of the soul is a common theme in mystical literature. Not only St. John of the Cross but his teacher and comrade in spiritual reform, St. Teresa of Avila, describes with great vividness the soul's bereftness during periods of struggle to recapture the lost sense of God's nearness. Before their time, in the fourteenth century, John Tauler, St. Catherine of Siena, and Henry Suso (whose victory over it cause him to go down in history as the "Blessed Henry Suso") had to fight such darkness. In the seventeenth, George Fox's "great openings" are not to be understood with any clarity except as they are viewed against the backdrop of his great depressions, and John Bunyan had his own battles with the powers of darkness. A detailed and ingenious self-revelation is to be found in Madame Guyon's *Autobiography* and her *Spiritual Torrents*. Times of spiritual "dryness" were apparently the normal expectancy of most of the mystics, and are treated with much understanding and helpful counsel by the author of the *Imitation of Christ*. As *accidie,* or spiritual torpor, the experience was common enough to be regarded by the medieval church as one of the seven deadly sins, the deadliness of which had been obscured in translation by the colorless and inaccurate "sloth." . . .

The most characteristic note in all descriptions of this unhappy state is that of a frustrated quest for the divine Presence. One who has found in God precious companionship desires to go on to more intimate spiritual fellowship and finds, to his great dismay, that he seems to be further from God than before. To some of the mystics this experience came with sudden shock; in others there was a gradual breaking up of an earlier equilibrium, with "dry times" of increasing duration and frequency encroaching on the life of devotion and sapping its power. The resulting privation threw the soul into confusion, turmoil, and deep distress. . . .

A second and closely related characteristic is a union of self-distrust with self-condemnation. "It is an amazing thing," says Madame Guyon, "for a soul that believes herself to be advanced in the way of perfection, when she sees herself thus go to pieces all at once." St. Catherine of Siena, tormented by visions of sin that appalled her, speaks graphically of "digging up the root of self-love with the knife of self-hatred. . . ." Though this is doubtless a form of emotional insecurity not unmixed with self-pity, it is not the self-exonerating, alibi-seeking insecurity of the unregenerate.

A third dominant trait is loneliness, which means the bitterness of

246

isolation both from God and man. Bereft of divine companionship, the soul cries out for human fellowship. But this too is denied. Partly because the experience makes the sufferer irritable and "odd," partly because his increased self-centeredness makes him abnormally sensitive, his friends withdraw. They do not understand him or he them, and he suffers acutely from imagined gibes and slights. Thus he cuts himself off from fellowship just when he needs it most.

A fourth note, following inevitably from the others, is spiritual impotence. This does not mean, for the most part, yielding to overt temptation. The mystics, even in their darkest hours, were usually able to resist the devil when he came in the form of fleshly lusts. What they could not master was the temptation to spiritual weariness and discouragement. They could not rise to the challenge to "be not weary in well-doing," for the soul was already faint and saw no prospect of reaping. Almost invariably a soul caught in the "dark night" thinks that it will never emerge. . . .

Various evil moods ensue, not the least of which is the exasperation of helplessness. Teresa, saint though she was, speaks language understood by the rest of us when she says, "The devil then sends so offensive a spirit of bad temper that I think I could eat people up!" Many who record such spiritual turmoil were victims of ill health, though whether the physical accompaniment was cause or effect it is hard to say. Not infrequently there is evidence of loss of intellectual power and grasp of worldly affairs. In short, the futility which the saints feared often passed from imagination to reality as the state progressed.

—GEORGIA HARKNESS, 1891-

[291] Four Degrees of Christian Living

GHOSTLY friend in God, thou shalt well understand that I find, in my boisterous beholding, four degrees of Christian men's living, and they be these: *Common, Special, Singular,* and *Perfect.* Three of these may be begun and ended in this life; and the fourth may by grace be begun here, but it shall ever last without end in the bliss of heaven. And right as thou seest how they be set here in order, each after other, first *Common,* then *Special,* after *Singular,* and last *Perfect:* right so me thinketh that in the same order and in the same course hath our Lord of his great mercy called thee and led thee unto him by the desire of thine heart.

247

For first thou knowest well, that when thou wert living in the *common* degree of Christian men's living in company of thy worldly friends, it seemeth to me that the everlasting love of his Godhead through the which he made thee and wrought thee when thou wert nought, and then bought thee with the price of his precious blood when thou wert lost in Adam, might not suffer thee to be so far from him in form and degree of living. And therefore he kindled thy desire full graciously, and fastened by it a leash of a lovely longing, and led thee by it into a more *special* state and form of living, to be a servant of the special servants of his; where thou mightest learn to live more specially and more ghostly in his service than thou didst, or mightest do, in the common degree of living before.

And what more? Yet it seemeth that he would not leave thus lightly, for the love of his heart, the which he hath evermore had unto thee since thou wert aught. But what did he? Seest thou not how sweetly and how graciously he hath privily pulled thee to the third degree and manner of living, the which is called *singular*? In the which solitary form and manner of living thou mayest learn to lift up the foot of thy love, and to step towards that state and degree of living that is *perfect,* and the last state of all.

—THE CLOUD OF UNKNOWING (14th Century)

[292] Rest Only on God

WHAT is truly detached man's object in all things? It is to die to himself; and when he dies to himself all things die to him.

What is the least obstacle? It is a thought. What is the greatest obstacle? It is when the soul abides in the obstinacy of its self-will.

A detached man should not let any moment pass away unmarked.

A detached man should not be always looking to see what he needs, but he should be always looking to see what he can do without.

If a detached man wishes to conform himself to the truth, he must in the first place be diligent in turning inward from things of sense, for God is a spirit. Secondly, he must take note whether he has attached himself to any obstacle (i.e., anything which stands between him and God). Thirdly, he must observe whether he is his own guide in anything, owing to the sensual appetite having got the start. Fourthly, he must, in the light which fills his soul, consider the presence of the all-penetrating divine essence in him, and that he is one of its vessels.

248

The more a man turns away from himself and all created things, the more perfect are the union and bliss to which he attains.

—HEINRICH SUSO, 1300?-1366

[293] Knowledge of God

I ONCE asked a famous theologian why he did not preach the love and knowledge of God from his pulpit as he had been discoursing of them for a couple of hours with me, instead of setting forth

Doctrine hard
In which Truth shows herself as near a lie
As can comport with her divinity.

He answered that, if he were to do so, his whole congregation would be living in mortal sin before the end of the week. It is true. The work of the Church in the world is, not to teach the mysteries of life, so much as to persuade the soul to that arduous degree of purity at which God Himself becomes her teacher. The work of the Church ends when the knowledge of God begins.

—COVENTRY PATMORE, 1823-1896

[294] Resignation of Self

1. I HAVE received from Thy hands a cross of religious penitential discipline; through Thy grace I will continue to bear it till my death, never forsaking any ways to ease it by external employments, or to escape from it, and shake it off by missions, &c.

2. For Thy love, O my God, and in conformity to Thy will, I resign myself to die when, where, and in what manner Thou shalt ordain.

3. I am content to see others make a great progress in spirit, and to do more good in Thy Church than myself.

4. I renounce all satisfaction and false peace which is got by yielding to my inordinate passions, and not by resisting and mortifying them.

5. My God, till Thou hast humbled that great pride which is in me, do not spare to send me daily yet more and greater humiliations and mortifications.

6. I offer myself unto Thee, to suffer with patience and quietness

whatsoever desolations, obscurity of mind, or deadness of affections that shall befall in a spiritual course; notwithstanding all which, through Thy grace, I will never neglect a serious tendency to Thee.

7. I am content to serve Thee with those mean talents that Thou has given me.

8. I yield myself to endure all manner of injuries and contempts, and yet to be esteemed by others to be impatient and revengeful.

9. I do renounce all solicitude to please others, or to gain the affections of any one to myself.

10. I do resign myself to such painful and withal base offices as my proud and slothful nature doth abhor, whensoever obedience, charity, or Thy will shall impose them on me.

—Augustine Baker, 1575-1641

[295] Gazing on the Lord

I am not asking you at this time to fix your attention on Him, nor to engage in discursive reasonings, nor to make subtle and learned considerations. All that I request is that you direct the glance of your soul to Him. Who is there who can prevent the turning of your gaze toward our Lord, even though it be only for a moment? Is it conceivable that you can look upon the most hideous objects and still you have not the power to behold the most ineffable sight that can be imagined? If you do not find Him beautiful, you need never look upon Him again. He, however, watches you constantly. Although you have offended Him by a thousand insults and indignities, He has been patient with you. Despite your faults, He has never ceased to fix His gaze upon you. Is it too much, then, to ask that you withdraw your gaze from exterior things to contemplate Him sometimes? . . . He values your glance so highly that He will neglect no means to ingratiate Himself with you.

—Teresa of Avila, 1515-1582

[296] First Method of Prayer

The first Method of Prayer is on the Ten Commandments, and on the Seven Deadly Sins, on the Three Powers of the Soul and on the Five

Bodily Senses. This method of prayer is meant more to give form, method and exercises, how the soul may prepare itself and benefit in them, and that the prayer may be acceptable, rather than to give any form or way of praying.

The Ten Commandments

First let the equivalent of the second Addition of the Second Week be made; that is, before entering on the prayer, let the spirit rest a little, the person being seated or walking about, as may seem best to him, considering where he is going and to what. And this same addition will be made at the beginning of all Methods of Prayer.

Prayer. A Preparatory Prayer, as, for example, to ask grace of God our Lord that I may be able to know in what I have failed as to the Ten Commandments; and likewise to beg grace and help to amend in future, asking for perfect understanding of them, to keep them better and for the greater glory and praise of His Divine Majesty.

For the first Method of Prayer, it is well to consider and think on the First Commandment, how I have kept it and in what I have failed, keeping to the rule of spending the space of time one says the *Our Father* and the *Hail Mary* three times; and if in this time I find faults of mine, to ask pardon and forgiveness for them, and say an *Our Father.* Let this same method be followed on each one of the Ten Commandments.

First Note. It is to be noted that when one comes to think on a Commandment on which he finds he has no habit of sinning, it is not necessary for him to delay so much time, but according as one finds in himself that he stumbles more or less on that Commandment so he ought to keep himself more or less on the consideration and examination of it. And the same is to be observed on the Deadly Sins.

Second Note. After having finished the discussion already mentioned on all the Commandments, accusing myself on them and asking grace and help to amend hereafter, I am to finish with a Colloquy to God our Lord, according to the subject matter.

—IGNATIUS OF LOYOLA, 1491-1556

[297] Man Must Have a Cross

MAN must always have a Cross; it was necessary that Christ should suffer before He entered into His Glory. Whatever thou mayest encounter in thy inmost heart, either in seeing or tasting, let it alone, do not meddle with it, ask not what it is, but fall back upon thy nothingness.

Our Lord said: "If any man will come after Me, . . . let him take up his Cross and follow Me." It is not in comfort, but with the Cross that we must follow God. The Holy Apostle, St. Andrew, said: "I welcome thee, thou much-to-be-desired Cross, for I have longed for thee with all my heart. Take me from amongst men, and give me again to my Master." This must not take place one day and not on the next; but it must go on at all times, unceasingly; thou must ever be examining thyself in all things. . . .

St. Matthew followed God at once, and leaving all his affairs unsettled; and, if thou findest that thou hast sinned, do not make thy Cross too heavy outwardly. Leave it to truth, and be faithful and at rest; for none will be condemned except those who wantonly turn to temporal things; while to those who delight in the love of God, and think only of Him, everything will prove a discipline.

—Johannes Tauler, 1300?-1361

[298] Holy Patience

He that with steadfast humility and patience suffereth and endureth tribulation, through fervent love of God, soon shall attain great grace and virtues, and shall be lord of this world, and shall have a foretaste of the next and glorious world. Everything that a man doeth, good or evil, he doeth it unto himself; therefore, be not offended with him that doeth thee an injury, for rather oughtest thou to have humble patience with him, and only grieve within thee for his sin, taking compassion on him and praying God earnestly for him. The stronger a man is to endure and suffer patiently injuries and tribulations, for love of God, the greater is he in the sight of God, and no more; and the weaker a man is to endure pain and adversity, for love of God, the less is he in the sight of God. If any man praise thee, speaking well of thee, render thou that praise to God alone; and if any man speak evil of thee, or revile thee, aid thou him, speaking evil of thyself, and worse. . . . Much greater consolation and a more worthy thing it is to suffer injuries and revilings patiently, without murmuring, for love of God, than to feed a hundred poor folk and fast continually every day. But how shall it profit a man, or what shall it avail him, to despise himself and afflict his body with great fastings and vigils and scourgings, if he be unable to endure a small injury from his neighbours? . . . The truly humble man looketh for no reward nor merit from God, but striveth ever only how he can

252

give satisfaction in all things, owning himself God's debtor: and every good thing he hath, that, he knoweth he hath through the goodness of God, and not through any merit of his own; and every adversity he endureth, he knoweth it to be truly because of his sins.

—FRANCIS OF ASSISI, 1182-1226

[299] Of God's Work

1. GOD'S POWER IS SEEN IN ALL CREATION

ALL the works of God are unsearchable and unspeakable, no human sense can find them out; faith only takes hold of them without human power or aid. No mortal creature can comprehend God in his majesty, and therefore did he come before us in the simplest manner, and was made man, ay, sin, death, and weakness.

In all things, in the least creatures, and in their members, God's almighty power and wonderful works clearly shine. For what man, how powerful, wise, and holy soever, can make out of one fig a fig-tree, or another fig? or, out of one cherry-stone, a cherry, or a cherry-tree? or what man can know how God creates and preserves all things, and makes them grow.

Neither can we conceive how the eye sees, or how intelligible words are spoken plainly, when only the tongue moves and stirs in the mouth; all which are natural things, daily seen and acted. How then should we be able to comprehend or understand the secret counsels of God's majesty, or search them out with our human sense, reason, or understanding. Should we then admire our own wisdom? I, for my part, admit myself a fool, and yield myself captive.

—TABLE TALK

2. GOD'S BENEFITS OBSCURE OUR FAITH

God could be rich readily enough, if he were more provident, and denied us the use of his creatures; let him, for ever so short a while, keep back the sun, so that it shine not, or lock up air, water, or fire, ah! how willingly would we give all our wealth to have the use of these creatures again.

But seeing God so liberally heaps his gifts upon us, we claim them as of right; let him deny them if he dare. The unspeakable multitude of his benefits obscures the faith of believers, and much more so, that of the ungodly.

—TABLE TALK

253

3. GOD'S POWER IN OUR WEAKNESS

God very wonderfully entrusts his highest office to preachers that are themselves poor sinners who, while teaching it, very weakly follow it. Thus goes it ever with God's power in our weakness; for when he is weakest in us, then is he strongest.

—TABLE TALK

4. GOD DEALS STRANGELY WITH HIS SAINTS

God deals strangely with his saints, contrary to all human wisdom and understanding, to the end, that those who fear God and are good Christians, may learn to depend on invisible things, and through mortification may be made alive again; for God's Word is a light that shines in a dark place, as all examples of faith show. Esau was accursed, yet it went well with him; he was lord in the land, and priest in the church; but Jacob had to fly, and dwell in poverty in another country.

God deals with godly Christians much as with the ungodly, yea, and sometimes far worse. He deals with them even as a house-father with a son and a servant; he whips and beats the son much more and oftener than the servant, yet, nevertheless, he gathers for the son a treasure to inherit, while a stubborn and a disobedient servant he beats not with the rod, but thrusts out of doors, and gives him nothing of the inheritance.

—TABLE TALK

5. LEAVE ETERNITY TO GOD

As lately I lay very sick, so sick that I thought I should have left this world, many cogitations and musings had I in my weakness. Ah! thought I, what may eternity be? What joys may it have? However, I know for certain, that this eternity is ours; through Christ it is given and prepared for us, if we can but believe. There it shall be opened and revealed; here we shall not know when a second creation of the world will be, seeing we understand not the first. If I had been with God Almighty before he created the world, I could not have advised him how out of nothing to make this globe, the firmament, and that glorious sun, which in its swift course gives light to the whole earth; how, in such manner, to create man and woman, &c., all which he did for us, without our counsel. Therefore ought we justly to give him the honour, and leave to his divine power and goodness the new creation of the life to come, and not presume to speculate thereon.

—TABLE TALK
—MARTIN LUTHER, 1483-1546

[300] Grace Must Draw Us Up

GANDHI, a few days before his death, was asked by an anxious but much-tied seeker after liberation, "Is there any way without Renunciation?" "There is no way without Renunciation," he replied, and so set one more seal on the witness of every spiritual guide. The spiritual life, the way to freedom, is through a double, reciprocal process. If it is to work it must be a balanced work. Grace must draw me up. But as soon as Grace begins to pull I discover how I am tied. It is then my turn, now that Grace has given me a new superior purchase, to loose my old ties. First, of course, I loose those which prevent my responding to Grace at all. If I do that and leave specifically bad habits, then Grace draws me still further and will sustain me still further. It is then that I discover that I could obtain far further freedom and immunity from relapse if I would let Grace lift me right out of my old ruts in which my life has so long run. I must loose every adhesion that I find able to be loosed. God does not ask us to do the impossible but He does ask us to do what He has rendered it possible for us to do. And we generally don't. It is a constant reciprocation between what I find myself ready to give and God can continue giving. If I find no more need of His Graces—if I can find no more room in my life for His designs—if I am content with what He has done for me—then He can give me no more, for there is no room for His gift to come into my filled life. When young William Penn asked George Fox what he should do about wearing his sword at Court, Fox replied, "Wear it as long as Thou canst." Fox was certain that in this soul Grace was taking the place of all dependence on social respect, that the hunger for God was taking the place of all other needs. So he knew that Grace would make the sword drop off. If then we pray much, that is, if we have a constantly recurring, constantly growing longing for God, we shall, we must, discover a constantly lessening attachment to our tastes, goods, prestige. The growth of one interest is always at the atrophy-price of all the others. Attention, when it is total, is, conversely, total unawareness of any distraction, any other interest. So God weans us, gives us natural, heaven-sent opportunities to let our old tacklings drop. . . .

Certainly if we are not continually casting off these old holds, as soon as Grace has shown us that we could—the moment we know that we can depend no longer on them but on Grace—we shall make no further progress. . . .

—GERALD HEARD, 1889-

255

[301] Gateways into Holy Obedience

SOME men come into holy obedience through the gateway of profound mystical experience.

It is an overwhelming experience to fall into the hands of the living God, to be invaded to the depths of one's being by His presence, to be, without warning, wholly uprooted from all earth-born securities and assurances, and to be blown by a tempest of unbelievable power which leaves one's old proud self utterly, utterly defenseless, until one cries, "All Thy waves and thy billows are gone over me" (Ps. 42:7). Then is the soul swept into a Loving Center of ineffable sweetness, where calm and unspeakable peace and ravishing joy steal over one. And one knows now why Pascal wrote, in the center of his greatest moment, the single word, "Fire." There stands the world of struggling, sinful, earth-blinded men and nations, of plants and animals and wheeling stars of heaven, all new, all lapped in the tender, persuading Love at the Center. There stand the saints of the ages, their hearts open to view, and lo, their hearts are our heart and their hearts are the heart of the Eternal One. In awful solemnity the Holy One is over all and in all, exquisitely loving, infinitely patient, tenderly smiling. Marks of glory are upon all things, and the marks are cruciform and blood-stained. . . .

One emerges from such soul-shaking, Love-invaded times into more normal states of consciousness. But one knows ever after that the Eternal Lover of the world, the Hound of Heaven, is utterly, utterly real, and that life must henceforth be forever determined by that Real. Like Saint Augustine one asks not for greater certainty of God but only for more steadfastness in Him. There, beyond, in Him is the true Center, and we are reduced, as it were, to nothing, for He is all.

Is religion subjective? Nay, its soul is in objectivity, in an Other whose Life is our true life, whose Love is our love, whose Joy is our joy, whose Peace is our peace, whose burdens are our burdens, whose Will is our will. Self is emptied into God, and God in-fills it. In glad, amazed humility we cast on Him our little lives in trusting obedience, in erect, serene, and smiling joy. And we say, with a writer of Psalms, "Lo, I come: in the book of the law it is written of me, I delight to do Thy will, O my God" (Ps. 40:7-8). For nothing else in all of heaven or earth counts so much as His will, His slightest wish, His faintest breathing. And holy obedience sets in, sensitive as a shadow, obedient as a shadow, selfless as a shadow. Not reluctantly but with ardor one longs to follow Him the second half. Gladly, urgently, promptly one leaps to do His bidding, ready to run and not be weary and to walk and not faint. . . .

256

But the first step to the obedience is the flaming vision of the wonder of such a life, a vision which comes occasionally to us all, through biographies of the saints, through the journals of Fox and early Friends, through a life lived before our eyes, through a haunting verse of the Psalms—"Whom have I in heaven but Thee? And there is none upon earth that I desire beside Thee" (Ps. 73:25)—through meditation upon the amazing life and death of Jesus, through a flash of illumination or, in Fox's language, a great opening. But whatever the earthly history of this moment of charm, this vision of an absolutely holy life is, I am convinced, the invading, urging, inviting, persuading work of the Eternal One. It is curious that modern psychology cannot account wholly for flashes of insight of any kind, sacred or secular. It is as if a fountain of creative Mind were welling up, bubbling to expression within prepared spirits. There is an infinite fountain of lifting power, pressing within us, luring us by dazzling visions, and we can only say, The creative God comes into our souls. An increment of infinity is about us. Holy is imagination, the gateway of Reality into our hearts. The Hound of Heaven is on our track, the God of Love is wooing us to His Holy Life.

Once having the vision, the second step to holy obedience is this: Begin where you are. Obey *now*. Use what little obedience you are capable of, even if it be like a grain of mustard seed. Begin where you are. Live this present moment, this present hour as you now sit in your seats, in utter, utter submission and openness toward Him. Listen outwardly to these words, but within, behind the scenes, in the deeper levels of your lives where you are all alone with God the Loving Eternal One, keep up a silent prayer, "Open thou my life. Guide my thoughts where I dare do not let them go. But Thou darest. Thy will be done." Walk on the streets and chat with your friends. But every moment behind the scenes be in prayer, offering yourselves in continuous obedience. I find this internal continuous prayer life absolutely essential. It can be carried on day and night, in the thick of business, in home and school. Such prayer of submission can be so simple. It is well to use a single sentence, repeated over and over and over again, such as this: "Be Thou my will. Be Thou my will," or "I open all before Thee. I open all before Thee," or "See earth through heaven. See earth through heaven." This hidden prayer life can pass, in time, beyond words and phrases into mere ejaculations, "My God, my God, my Holy One, my Love," or into the adoration and submission and rejoicing and exultation and glory.

And the third step in holy obedience, or a counsel, in this: If you slip and stumble and forget God for an hour, and assert your old proud self, and rely upon your own clever wisdom, don't spend too much time in anguished regrets and self-accusations but begin again, just where you are.

Yet a fourth consideration in holy obedience is this: Don't grit your teeth and clench your fists and say, "I will." Relax. Take hands off. Submit yourself to God. Learn to live in the passive voice—a hard saying for Americans—and let life be willed through you. For "I will" spells not obedience.

—Thomas R. Kelly, 1893-1941

[302] A Serious Call to Holy Living

1. how to begin morning devotions

The first thing that you are to do, when you are upon your knees, is to shut your eyes, and with a short silence let your soul place itself in the presence of God; that is, you are to use this, or some other better method, to separate yourself from all common thoughts, and make your heart as sensible as you can of the Divine presence.

Now if this recollection of spirit is necessary,—as who can say it is not?—then how poorly must they perform their devotions, who are always in a hurry; who begin them in haste, and hardly allow themselves time to repeat their very form, with any gravity or attention! Theirs is properly saying prayers, instead of praying.

To proceed: if you were to use yourself (as far as you can) to pray always in the same place; if you were to reserve that place for devotion, and not allow yourself to do any thing common in it; if you were never to be there yourself, but in times of devotion; if any little room, or (if that cannot be) if any particular part of a room was thus used, this kind of consecration of it as a place holy unto God, would have an effect upon your mind, and dispose you to such tempers, as would very much assist your devotion. For by having a place thus sacred in your room, it would in some measure resemble a chapel or house of God. This would dispose you to be always in the spirit of religion, when you were there; and fill you with wise and holy thoughts, when you were by yourself. Your own apartment would raise in your mind such sentiments as you have when you stand near an altar; and you would be afraid of thinking or doing any thing that was foolish near that place, which is the place of prayer and holy intercourse with God.

When you begin your petitions, use such various expressions of the attributes of God, as may make you most sensible of the greatness and power of the Divine Nature.

Begin, therefore, in words like these: O Being of all beings, Fountain of all light and glory, gracious Father of men and Angels, whose universal Spirit is everywhere present, giving life, and light, and joy, to all Angels in Heaven, and all creatures upon earth, etc.

For these representations of the Divine attributes, which show us in some degree the Majesty and greatness of God, are an excellent means of raising our hearts into lively acts of worship and adoration.

2. LET THE EVENING PRAYER CONTEMPLATE DEATH

Having thus examined and confessed your sins at this hour of the evening, you must afterwards look upon yourself as still obliged to betake yourself to prayer again, just before you go to bed.

The subject that is most proper for your prayers at that time is death. Let your prayers, therefore, then be wholly upon it, reckoning upon all the dangers, uncertainties, and terrors of death; let them contain everything that can affect and awaken your mind into just apprehensions of it. Let your petitions be all for right sentiments of the approach and importance of death; and beg of God, that your mind may be possessed with such a sense of its nearness, that you may have it always in your thoughts, do everything as in sight of it, and make every day a day of preparation for it.

Represent to your imagination, that your bed is your grave; that all things are ready for your interment; that you are to have no more to do with this world; and that it will be owing to God's great mercy, if you ever see the light of the sun again, or have another day to add to your works of piety.

And then commit yourself to sleep, as into the hands of God; as one that is to have no more opportunities of doing good; but is to awake amongst spirits that are separate from the body, and waiting for the judgment of the last great day.

Such a solemn resignation of yourself into the hands of God every evening, and parting with all the world, as if you were never to see it any more, and all this in the silence and darkness of the night, is a practice that will soon have excellent effects upon your spirit.

For this time of the night is exceeding proper for such prayers and meditations; and the likeness which sleep and darkness have to death, will contribute very much to make your thoughts about it the more deep and affecting. So that I hope, you will not let a time so proper for such prayers, be ever passed over without them.

—WILLIAM LAW, 1686-1761

[303] What Then Must I Do?

LIVE AS AN "INDIVIDUAL"

THE talk asks you, then, *whether you live in such a way that you are conscious of being an "individual."* . . . Indeed it is precisely this consciousness that must be asked for. Just as if the talk could not ask in generalities, but rather asks you as an individual. Or, better still, my listener, if you would ask yourself, whether you have this consciousness, whether you are actively contemplating the occasion of this talk. For in the outside world, the crowd is busy making a noise. The one makes a noise because he heads the crowd, the many because they are members of the crowd. But the all-knowing One, who in spite of anyone is able to observe it all, does not desire the crowd. He desires the individual; He will deal only with the individual, quite unconcerned as to whether the individual be of high or low station, whether he be distinguished or wretched.

Each man himself, as an individual, should render his account to God. No third person dares venture to intrude upon this accounting between God and the individual. Yet the talk, by putting its question, dares and ought to dare, to remind man, in a way never to be forgotten, that the most ruinous evasion of all is to be hidden in the crowd in an attempt to escape God's supervision of him as an individual, in an attempt to get away from hearing God's voice as an individual. Long ago, Adam attempted this same thing when his evil conscience led him to imagine that he could hide himself among the trees. It may even be easier and more convenient, and more cowardly to hide oneself among the crowd in the hope that God should not be able to recognize one from the other. But in eternity each shall render account as an individual. That is, eternity will demand of him that he shall have lived as an individual. Eternity will draw out before his consciousness, all that he has done as an individual, he who had forgotten himself in noisy self-conceit. In eternity, he shall be brought to account strictly as an individual, he who intended to be in the crowd where there should be no such strict reckoning. Each one shall render account to God as an individual. The King shall render account as an individual; and the most wretched beggar, as an individual. No one may pride himself at being more than an individual, and no one despondently think that he is not an individual, perhaps because here in earth's busyness he had not as much as a name, but was named after a number.

For, after all, what is eternity's accounting other than that the voice of conscience is forever installed with its eternal right to be the exclusive voice? What is it other than that throughout eternity an infinite stillness reigns wherein the conscience may talk with the individual about what he, as an individual, of what he has done of Good or of evil, and about the fact that during his life he did not wish to be an individual? What is it other than that within eternity there is infinite space so that each person, as an individual, is apart with his conscience? For in eternity there is no mob pressure, no crowd, no hiding place in the crowd, as little as there are riots or street fights! Here in the temporal order conscience is prepared to make each person into an individual. But here in the temporal order, in the unrest, in the noise, in the pressure of the mob, in the crowd, in the primeval forest of evasion, alas, it is true, the calamity still happens, that someone completely stifles the voice of his conscience—his conscience, for he can never rid himself of it. It continues to belong to him, or more accurately, he continues to belong to it. Yet we are not now talking about this calamity, for even among the better persons, it happens all too readily that the voice of conscience becomes merely one voice among many. Then it follows so easily that the isolated voice of conscience (as generally happens to a solitary one) becomes overruled—by the majority. But in eternity, conscience is the only voice that is heard. It must be heard by the individual, for the individual has become the eternal echo of this voice. It must be heard. There is no place to flee from it. For in the infinite there is no place, the individual is himself the place. It must be heard. In vain the individual looks about for the crowd.

—SÖREN KIERKEGAARD, 1813-1855

[304] What Is Worship?

IT is the soul searching for its counterpart.
It is a thirsty land crying out for rain.
It is a candle in the act of being kindled.
It is a drop in quest of the ocean.
It is a man listening through a tornado for the Still Small Voice.
It is a voice in the night calling for help.
It is a sheep lost in the wilderness pleading for rescue by the Good Shepherd.
It is the same sheep nestling in the arms of the rescuer.
It is the Prodigal Son running to his Father.
It is a soul standing in awe before the mystery of the Universe.

261

It is a poet enthralled by the beauty of a sunrise.

It is a workman pausing a moment to listen to a strain of music.

It is a hungry heart seeking for love.

It is a heart of love consecrating herself to her lover.

It is Time flowing into Eternity.

It is my little self engulfed in the Universal Self.

It is a man climbing the altar stairs to God.

He who neglects Worship neglects that which separates man from the birds, the animals, the insects, the fishes.

The unworshipful man is an anthropoid with a highly devolped brain.

He may be a paragon of morality, but so are bees and ants.

He may be keenly intelligent, but so are wolves and foxes.

He may provide for his family, but so do hyenas and orangoutangs.

He may be successful in affairs, but so are beavers and muskrats.

He may be artistic, but so are birds and butterflies.

Worship is the chief concern of highly developed human beings.

A human being must be graded according to his capacity for worship.

Worship for men is what song is for a thrush, or physical beauty for a tiger, or speed for a race horse.

Worship lifts men to the next level of experience and justifies their existence as men.

Worship is Man expressing his entire personality.

To neglect Worship is to accept low-rating as a man.

To neglect Worship is to fail in life's highest function.

The neglect of Worship is psychical suicide.

Intelligent Worship is the most remarkable achievement of which a human being is capable.

The primary functions of a Church are to supply incentives for Worship and to furnish the atmosphere for Worship.

If one cannot worship in Church, the Church may be at fault or the man may be at fault.

If the Church is at fault, it will eventually perish unless it remedies the condition.

If the Man is at fault, he will dry up and become a Spiritual mummy unless he changes himself.

—DWIGHT BRADLEY, 1889-

[305] That Daily Quarter of an Hour

THAT daily quarter of an hour, for now forty years or more, I am sure has been one of the greatest sustenances and sources of calm for my life. Of course, such "reading" is hardly reading in the ordinary sense of the word at all. As well could you call the letting a very slowly dissolving lozenge melt imperceptibly in your mouth "eating." Such reading is, of course, meant as directly as possible to feed the heart, to fortify the will—to put these into contact with God—thus, by the book, to get away from the book to the realities it suggests—the longer the better. And above all, perhaps it excludes, by its very object, all criticism, all going off on one's own thoughts as, in any way, antagonistic to the book's thoughts; and this, not by any unreal (and *most dangerous* forcing of oneself to swallow, or to "like," what does not attract one's simply humble self, but (on the contrary) by a gentle passing by, by an instinctive ignoring of what does not suit one's soul. This passing by *should be without a trace of would-be objective judging;* during such reading we are out simply and solely to feed our poor soul, such as it is *hic et nunc.* . . .

I need not say that I would not restrict you to only one quarter of an hour a day. You might find two such helpful. But I would not exceed the fifteen minutes *at any one time;* you would sink to ordinary reading, if you did.

—BARON FRIEDRICH VON HÜGEL, 1852-1925

[306] Keep the Vision You Impart

Do you remember how, in Thomas Hardy's *Far from the Madding Crowd,* Gabriel Oak, that perfect shepherd, used to stand upon a hill at night and gaze into the starry sky, until he could feel this little world rolling through the immensity of space? That great vision made him a better shepherd, not a worse one. When Bathsheba's sheep over-ate themselves and got indigestion, he was the person who was sent for and knew exactly what to do. And so too it is with the teacher. If you once allowed yourself to think that your immediate job was everything, and nothing lay beyond to give it meaning, you might soon give up in disgust, when petty worries and failures overwhelmed you. But if beyond that little bit of life you can glimpse the steadfast reality of God, and feel that same living and infinite reality penetrating and moulding all souls and working through you, then you gain new heart for going on. It is towards an ever greater sense of that Eternal Reality that you want to help your pupils' souls to grow. You want them to expand and become more and more what human life is really meant to be, to move on from an existence bound down to natural things and desires, into an existence that is controlled by spiritual needs and desires. But if you are to do that successfully, you must have and keep something of the vision that you are trying to impart.

—Evelyn Underhill, 1875-1941

[307] Cure d'Ars: Patron Saint of Parish Priests

CONSIDER the Curé d'Ars, the pattern and patron saint of parish priests. There was a man of very humble origins, of very limited intellectual power, and with a minimum of education needed for his career; but with the maximum of devotedness. From the human point of view, this was his total equipment. At a very difficult moment in the history of the French Church, he was sent to a particularly hopeless village, where religion and morals had gone to seed; and there he spent his whole life. No preferment, no external help either spiritual or material, no apparent scope. Yet bit by bit, as his spiritual power developed, and the strange magnetism of a living Christianity was felt, this poor, obscure peasant priest became the conscience of France, the determining influence in thousands of lives. His church was a place of pilgrimage for a multitude of troubled souls from every part of the country. There was no reason for this except the power of God, acting through a loving and abandoned soul transformed by prayer. Not many clergy would care to tackle his average working day. The number of hours which he spent in pastoral work, or in his church—either in worship, or in ministering to those who came to him—often amounted to sixteen out of the twenty-four. So long as any one needed him, he just went on and on. But this intimidating programme, and this untiring love and care for souls, still left time for that which made it possible: the deep personal life of prayer, self-offering, communion, supplication—loving, realistic, confident intercourse with God.

—Evelyn Underhill, 1875-1941

[308] Augustine's Conversion

BUT when a profound reflection had, from the secret depths of my soul, drawn together and heaped up all my misery before the sight of my heart, there arose a mighty storm, accompanied by as mighty a shower of tears. Which, that I might pour forth fully, with its natural expressions, I stole away from Alypius; for it suggested itself to me that solitude was fitter for the business of weeping. So I retired to such a distance that even his presence could not be oppressive to me. Thus it was with me at that time, and he perceived it; for something, I believe, I had spoken, wherein the sound of my voice appeared choked with weeping, and in that state had I risen up. He then remained where we had been sitting, most completely astonished. I flung myself down, how, I know not, under a certain fig-tree, giving free course to my tears, and the streams of mine eyes gushed out, an acceptable sacrifice unto Thee. And, not indeed in these words, yet to this effect, spake I much unto Thee—"But Thou, O Lord, how long?" "How long, Lord? Wilt Thou be angry for ever? Oh, remember not against us former iniquities; for I felt that I was enthralled by them. I sent up these sorrowful cries—How long, how long? To-morrow, and to-morrow? Why not now? Why is there not this hour an end to my uncleanness?"

I was saying these things and weeping in the most bitter contrition of my heart, when, lo, I heard the voice as of a boy or girl, I know not which, coming from a neighboring house, chanting, and oft repeating, "Take up and read; take up and read." Immediately my countenance was changed, and began most earnestly to consider whether it was usual for children in any kind of game to sing such words; nor could I remember ever to have heard the like. So, restraining the torrent of my tears, I rose up, interpreting it no other way than as a command to me from Heaven to open the book, and to read the first chapter I should light upon. For I had heard of Antony, that, accidentally coming in while the gospel was being read, he received the admonition as if what was read were addressed to him, "Go and sell what thou hast, and give it to the poor, and thou shalt have treasure in heaven; and come and follow me." And by such oracle was he forthwith converted unto Thee. So quickly I returned to the place where Alypius was sitting; for there had I put down the volume of the apostles, when I rose thence. I grasped, opened, and in silence read that paragraph on which my eyes first fell—"Not in rioting and drunkenness, not in chambering and wantonness, not in strife and envying; but put ye on the Lord Jesus Christ, and make not provision for the flesh, to fulfil the lusts thereof." No further would

265

I read, nor did I need; for instantly, as the sentence ended—by a light, as it were, of security infused into my heart—all the gloom of doubt vanished away.

Closing the book, then, and putting either my finger between, or some other mark, I now with a tranquil countenance made it known to Alypius. And he thus disclosed to me what was wrought in him, which I knew not. He asked to look at what I had read. I showed him; and he looked even further than I had read, and I knew not what followed. This it was, "Him that is weak in the faith, receive ye"; which he applied to himself, and discovered to me. By this admonition was he strengthened; and by a good resolution and purpose, very much in accord with his character (in which, for the better, he was always far different from me), without any restless delay he joined me. Thence we go in to my mother. We make it known to her—she rejoices. We relate how it came to pass—she leaps for joy, and triumphs, and blesses Thee, who are able to do exceeding abundantly above all that we ask or think; for she perceived Thee to have given her more for me than she used to ask by her pitiful and most doleful groanings.

—AUGUSTINE, 354-430

[309] Thoughts on Prayer and Worship

1. *Prayer is power!* Fifteen pounds of energy will run all the machinery in the United States for one year. God's power is also accessible for the pray-er.

2. Prayer moves the hand that moves the world. Prayer lets God's spiritual laws change you; it does not change his laws.

3. On sleepless nights remember the words of Bernard of Clairvaux, "I would rather pray than sleep!"

4. Remember the weekday to keep it holy.

5. With lights out before you sleep let your last thought be, "Father into thy hands I commit my spirit."

6. Let your first prayer be in the morning, on your knees: "May today be with thy help the most wonderful day of my life!"

7. To say about eleven o'clock on Sunday morning, "It's time to go to church," is needed in every American home.

8. In *Low Prayer* you pray for yourself; in *Middle Prayer* you pray for others; in *High Prayer* you adore God out of your love for him. All three types are needed in the prayer life.

9. Nineteen million sleeping tablets are used each night in the United States; eleven million pounds of aspirin are sold yearly in our drugstores. For many, prayer can become a substitute to calm nerves and bring rest.

10. Ask God in your praying to do something *through* you rather than *for you.* Thus prayer becomes a co-operation.

[310] The Art of Waiting

To wait is not easy. It is a hard lesson to learn. In patience we are promised to possess our souls, but how few of us succeed. Our capacity for waiting shows our concrete trust in God. God's way is not our way and God's pace is not ours. The less we are willing to wait the less we believe Him. Anxiety shows itself to a great extent in restlessness. People cannot even allow the muscles of their faces or their hands to relax. Worriers rub their hands, wash their hands, fiddle with their rings or watch chains, thump cigarettes, or dawdle with anything that is handy. They must ever be doing something. They do not like to be still even in church. Prolonged silence makes them nervous. Something must happen, and if they are not causing it, they are sure that nothing is happening. . . .

Some people cannot trust themselves enough to believe that what is done well and with a good intention can be let go. They are always berating themselves for what they did or did not do and stewing over the results. They cannot wait to grow themselves and to see their work ripen. Nor can they wait to be corrected by time. They must be perfect and above blame right away. They therefore picture themselves and their work in a false light and sputter when they are not recognized or their deeds are not appreciated.

Nor can they trust others. They cannot delegate responsibility. Unless they do the thing themselves they feel that nothing will be done right; at least they cannot wait and see. Nor can they wait to let others grow. They do things for their children to get them done properly. Then they worry because they have not time for everything, because they get no rest, because their children do not mature and assume responsibility, because everyone considers them bossy and prefers for fellowship others who do not "amount to" so much as they. The world can do little with these self-serious perfectionists. They cannot know fellowship, for they trust only themselves. Other people are unreal and they cannot take time for them to show what they can do, what responsibility they can shoulder, or what capacity for growth is in them.

267

Harder still is it to wait for God. His patience seems slackness. After all, He has eternity and our concern is present time. The world is wrong and we are here to right it, and at once. The zeal of many a reformer is disguised atheism. Much desire to please others is nervous self-protection. What God wants, however, is relaxed, trustful waiting. . . .

Real waiting is also victorious waiting. We have unsolvable problems, but God has none. We have permanent problem children, but He does not. We die and do not see the fruits of our labor in this life, but God never dies and beyond this life we shall see the reward of every deed done in the body. Real waiting is victorious waiting because though our warfare seems constant the outcome is certain. . . .

Real waiting is living within the quiet joy and peace of God's own way, more natural than the return of the salmon to its breeding place or of the waterfowl to its summer nest. Such waiting is the cure for worry, for it is living within the perspective, pace, and proportion of God. Such waiting is peace and power.

Real waiting is the soul's sabbath rest amidst the unrest and confusion of the workaday world.

—NELS F. S. FERRÉ, 1908-

[311] Solitude and Silence

Let him who cannot be alone beware of community. He will only do harm to himself and to the community. Alone you stood before God when he called you; alone you had to answer that call; alone you had to struggle and pray; and alone you will die and give an account to God. You cannot escape from yourself; for God has singled you out. If you refuse to be alone you are rejecting Christ's call to you, and you can have no part in the community of those who are called. "The challenge of death comes to us all, and no one can die for another. Everyone must fight his own battle with death by himself, alone. . . . I will not be with you then, nor you with me" (Luther).

But the reverse is also true: *Let him who is not in community beware of being alone.* Into the community you were called, the call was not meant for you alone; in the community of the called you bear your cross, you struggle, you pray. You are not alone, even in death, and on the Last Day you will be only one member of the great congregation of Jesus Christ. If you scorn the fellowship of the brethren, you reject the call of Jesus Christ, and thus your solitude can only be hurtful to you. "If I die, then I am not alone in death; if I suffer they [the fellowship] suffer with me" (Luther).

We recognize, then, that only as we are within the fellowship can we be alone, and only he that is alone can live in the fellowship. Only in the fellowship do we learn to be rightly alone and only in aloneness do we learn to live rightly in the fellowship. It is not as though the one preceded the other; both begins at the same time, namely, with the call of Jesus Christ.

Each by itself has profound pitfalls and perils. One who wants fellowship without solitude plunges into the void of words and feelings, and one who seeks solitude without fellowship perishes in the abyss of vanity, self-infatuation, and despair.

—DIETRICH BONHOEFFER, 1906-1945

[312] Counsel Regarding Private Devotion

1. BE simple and direct in your secret prayer. The grace of simplicity is not to be despised in public prayer; but when we call on God in secret, any formality or elaborateness in our petitions is an offense.

2. Pray audibly. You need not lift your voice to be heard in the street, but it is vastly better to pray not merely in your thoughts but also with words. The utterance of our wants helps to define them. . . .

3. Be honest in your secret prayer. Do not express any want that you do not feel. Do not confess any fault that you do not mean to forsake. Do not keep anything back. Remember that it is He that searcheth the heart to whom you are speaking. . . .

4. Pray earnestly. The words need not be loud, but the desire should be intense. "The fervent, energetic prayer of a righteous man availeth much." "The Kingdom of heaven suffereth violence, and the violent take it by force." No listless, drowsy petitioning will serve. . . .

5. Do not mock God in your prayers. Do not beg him to come to you. You know that he is never far from any soul that seeks him. That prayer is answered before you utter it. Do not ask God to do for you that which he has expressly bidden you to do. How grossly in such prayers as these we abuse his infinite patience. . . .

6. Pray always with special reference to the needs of the day and the hour;—the warfare to be waged, the temptations to be resisted, the work to be done, the sorrow to be borne; put your life into your prayer; and let it be the most real and the most immediate business of your life.

—WALTER RAUSCHENBUSCH, 1861-1918

[313] Enlargement in Sorrow

THIS is one of the grandest testimonies ever given by man to the moral government of God. It is not a man's thanksgiving that he has been set free from suffering. It is a thanksgiving that he has been set free through suffering: "Thou hast enlarged me when I was in distress." He declares the sorrows of life to have been themselves the source of life's enlargement. And have not you and I a thousand times felt this to be true? It is written of Joseph in the dungeon that "The iron entered into his soul." We all feel that what Joseph needed for his soul was just the iron. He had seen only the glitter of the gold. He had been rejoicing in youthful dreams; and dreaming hardens the heart. He who sheds tears over a romance will not be most apt to help reality; a real sorrow will be too unpoetic for him. We need the iron to enlarge our nature. The gold is but a vision; the iron is an experience. The chain which unites me to humanity must be an iron chain. That touch of nature which makes the world akin is not joy, but sorrow; gold is partial, but iron is universal.

My soul, if thou wouldst be enlarged into human sympathy, thou must be narrowed into the limits of human suffering; Joseph's dungeon is the road to Joseph's throne. Thou canst not lift the iron load of thy brother if the iron hath not entered into thee. It is thy limit that is thine enlargement. It is the shadows of thy life that are the real fulfilment of thy dreams of glory. Murmur not at the shadows; they are better revelations than thy dreams. . . . God has enlarged thee by the binding of sorrow's chain.

—GEORGE MATHESON, 1842-1906

[314] How to Attain Steadfast Virtue

1. THE first means, which albeit seemingly the most ordinary, is in truth the hardest, is to will so to attain. But the will must be sincere, hearty, effectual, and persevering; and such a will is no common thing. . . . Do you ask God daily to confirm and strengthen your will and each day's perseverance will help forward the morrow.

2. The second means for attaining a steadfast progress in holiness, is to have a daily rule, and to observe it punctually. But it is not well to overload one's self with observances at first,—it is better to increase spiritual exercises gradually. Due regard must be had to health, age, position, and the duties entailed thereby. . . .

3. A third means is the continual recollection of God's Presence; and to this end you must firmly believe that God dwells within our hearts, and that He is to be found there by those who seek Him; that He inspires us with holy thoughts, leading us from sin to seek righteousness. We often call conscience that which is in truth God's own Voice; warning, rebuking, enlightening, directing the soul;—our part is to be attentive in listening, and steadfast in obeying this Voice. Dissipation and excitement hinder us from hearing it; it is when we are calm and still—our passions and imagination at rest—that the Voice of God fills the heart. . . .

4. The fourth means is to give a fixed daily time to God, during which His Presence is our sole occupation, and in which we listen to Him and talk with Him, not with the lips, but in the heart. This is real mental prayer. Those who are beginners in this exercise cannot do better than use *The Imitation of Christ,* pausing on each sentence and meditating upon it. At first a quarter of an hour morning and evening is enough, but you should acquire, if possible, the habit of at least half an hour's morning meditation. . . .

5. The fifth means of progress is diligently to use the means of grace which God has provided in His Church; if you use confession, guard against over-scrupulousness, but beware lest confusion be a mere formal routine, a danger to some who use it frequently. Those who aim at perfection should chiefly accuse themselves of their resistance to grace—their indulgence of self-love—their voluntary and deliberate words or deeds contrary to that aim. That Communion is unquestionably good, from which you come filled with fresh courage, and a renewed purpose of hearty faithfulness to God. . . .

6. A sixth means of progress is spiritual reading, for which a wide field is open to you. It is well to select such books as touch your heart, and rouse it to fervour. Rodriquez on *Perfection* is a useful book for beginners, and for those more advanced the *Imitation,* the works of S. Francis de Sales, Surin, and *The Lives of the Saints,* to say nothing of Holy Scripture above all. Your spiritual reading should in some respects be like a meditation, that is to say, you should watch for God's action within you, and pause when you feel your heart touched by what you read. *Always read with a view to practise.* . . .

7. The seventh means is mortification of the heart. . . .

8. An eighth means is frequent meditation on the virtues of humility and purity, taking the Blessed Virgin as an example, of whom Holy Scripture tells us that she is "blessed among women." . . .

9. Finally, it often may be very helpful to seek out some discreet spiritual adviser from whom you may receive counsel in matters which con-

cern your soul: who being himself led by God's Holy Spirit, is therefore capable of leading you in the right way.

—JEAN NICHOLAS GROU, 1731-1803

[315] In the World, Yet Not of It

JUST as the mariner should not leave the lanes of navigation and flee to the pole, so the soul should not leave the world and flee to God. To be in the world yet not of it is the worshiper's portion. He steers toward port through tempest and sunshine, his compass held steady by a power beyond the clouds and the very sun. Then at last within his soul there dawns the final stage of worship, which is fruition. Not the ecstasy of mystic communion but the fruit of the Spirit—love, joy, peace, long-suffering, gentleness, faith, meekness, temperance—is the true goal or worship. These virtues when they grow out of a life of worship have a very different inner aspect than when they are cultivated for their own sakes. Fruits grow out of the life of the organism; so the fruit of the Spirit. As is the love of human person and human person, so is the love of human person and divine person: first, contemplation of the Loved One; then revelation of the mysteries of the true nature of the Loved One; then, a communion of life; and, finally, creation of new life, "birth in beauty," as Plato calls it. This should not be taken to mean that the worship of God is merely a means to an end, a mere instrument to personal character or social sentiments or conduct; it means, rather, that, unless the end sought is one of which worship is both root and integral part, the human personality will never find its maturest fruition.

—EDGAR S. BRIGHTMAN, 1884-1953

[316] On Meeting People

ONE wayside pulpit displayed a rather startling sentence: "Remember everyone you meet is fighting for his life." Can it be true? Most people are like ourselves. What meticulously hidden struggles are we engaged in? Why is Dopey the most beloved of all the seven dwarfs? Is it because we see ourselves in his clumsiness, his eagerness to do the right

272

thing, his stupidity? He makes more mistakes than we do. How comforting to see that such as he can be attractive, lovable!

Let us learn to look on the people we meet, not as the efficient, successful people they pretend to be, but as secret and often defeated strugglers like ourselves. Let us allow God's spirit in us to go out silently to greet God's spirit in them. Let's make a short formula to use when entering a crowded bus or subway, remembering "how much each person there needs God and how much God loves each. How near He is to them, how dear they are to Him."

—MURIEL LESTER, 1883-

[317] Quietude Brings Balance into Living

WHEN I was young, as you are, and lived in England, I was very active and used to spend the day in ceaseless activities. Indeed, I would almost grudge the time that I spent in quiet and prayer and meditation. At that time, I was working among the poor in South London, and the work itself was Christ's own work; so I said to myself, "This work is surely the work of Christ. Let me do it with all my heart and take up all my time in doing it."

With this thought in my mind I used to work night and day, with hardly any pause or time for rest. In doing so, I forgot that Christ Himself went into retreat and retirement when He was working actively among the poor. But I did not realise the need of this while I was in England. Yet it was a grievous blunder. For it was causing my own character to be much too restless.

But when I came out to India, at the age of thirty-four, I noticed a great difference here between India and England. In India, I had more time for leisure and rest and prayer. But that was not all. For, from the first, I had a great friendship with a very noble Indian Christian, named Susil Kumar Rudra, and my friendship showed me how different he was from myself. How quiet he was, how patient, how gentle! His whole life was more balanced than mine! Love can notice these things very quickly. . . .

When I became at last his true friend, he used to tell me about this side of my character which he had noticed: and he would say that he was quite certain that Jesus meant us as His followers to have peace and calm, and not to be so hurried and restless and over-anxious to get things done.

Then we used to go together in the hot weather to the Himalaya Mountains and there I met Sadhu Sundar Singh. I saw his face, and it was so peaceful and full of joy. I also watched his life—how he spent long hours in prayer and meditation. He did not talk much, but he was wonderfully full of love for Christ, and I saw that he had something which I had not got and I used to question him also about it. He silently taught me in his own remarkable way—though he was very much younger than I was—how Christ brings to us this peace even in the midst of the troubled anxieties of the world around us.

Later on, I stayed at Santiniketan with Rabindranath Tagore, and even though Tagore was not a Christian he had this same calmness of spirit; and I used to watch him also and see how different he was from what I was myself. Sometimes when I got up in the night, before daybreak, I would see Tagore already seated in quiet meditation. He would remain there, silent, in the moonlight, very, very early—perhaps for two or three hours before the day's work began.

So I said to myself, "Here is something I must learn. I must come to Christ and ask Him to teach me." And then I found He was ready to teach me so kindly. . . . So, little by little, those who were my dearest friends, such as Sadhu Sundar Singh, Rudra, and Tagore all taught me, in their own way, this lesson of quietness and peace.

—Charles F. Andrews, 1871-1940

[318] Faith-knowledge and the Resurrection

"I *know* that my Redeemer liveth": "I *believe* in Jesus Christ, risen from the dead": such is the Christian's confession.

"I know" and "I believe" or "have faith"—these are not here mutually exclusive expressions. This "knowing" is not that with which scientific theory is concerned, based upon empirical sense-knowledge; it is rather *faith-knowledge,* and faith-knowledge does not rely on the evidence of the senses, but is, in the scriptural phrase, "the evidence of things not seen," that is, not presented to sense-perception; and it would lose its essential nature and be transformed into a mere sorry empirical knowledge, if it relied on any other evidence than "the witness of the Holy Spirit," which is not that of sense-experience. And so we cannot afford to account Christ's resurrection, and our own, known facts, in this lower "scientific" sense of knowledge. The simplest understanding feels this. To speak of "resurrection" is to utter a mystery, and mystery is a subject for faith, not science. And, for Christianity, how this faith itself comes to be is no less a mystery, indeed the greatest of all mysteries. But if "faith" were knowledge, directly attested by the senses or based upon the tradition of a former occurrence attested by the senses, this mystery would wholly disappear.

And so we hold that in endeavouring to account for our assurance of the Risen Christ two sorts of interpretation must be excluded, the naïvely supernaturalistic and the rationalistic. The former is that which has recourse to the "Empty Tomb." It holds that Christ's tomb was proved to be empty by the evidence of the senses, that the Risen Christ was perceived by the senses, and that the truth of the facts so certified in sense-experience was then handed down by human testimony. On this view the conviction of the resurrection was from the first not *faith,* but a piece of empirical knowledge. . . . The earliest and most authentic witness to the resurrection of Christ—that of St. Paul in 1 Cor. xv—makes no mention of the empty tomb, although there the Apostle is at pains to assemble all possible reasons for assurance in the reality of the Resurrection.

But the ordinary rationalistic interpretation is equally inadmissible. A deep "impression" of the person of Jesus had remained, so it is said, with the disciples and especially with Peter, and from this impression grew their conviction after His death, "Such a one cannot have remained dead." And this conviction, thus born in their minds, took imaginative and figurative form in visions, which must therefore be regarded as purely subjective. But this explanation is patently forced and unsatisfactory, and seems to us to miss altogether the uniqueness and coherence of the experience centering in the Resurrection. The two lines of interpretation have this in common, however: they both entirely ignore the fundamental fact about the experience, that it was a *mystery;* both agree in disregarding altogether its mystery character.

We can only get beyond the opposition between supernaturalism and rationalism by frankly recognizing that the experiences concerned with the Resurrection were *mystical experiences* and their source "the Spirit." It is only "of the Spirit" that the higher knowledge is born.

—RUDOLF OTTO, 1869-1938

[319] The Secret Garden of the Soul

EVERY soul that is truly alive has a garden of which no other holds the key; and in hours of weariness, when it is breathless with the hot race of life, and harassed by a babel of voices, it slips through the gate and walks at peace among the flowers. There is a garden of the soul also, of which that beyond the brook Kedron is the type, where Jesus walks with His disciples, and the clash of the world cannot drown the music of His voice. It was said of the garden on the farther side of Kedron that "Jesus ofttimes resorted thither with His disciples"; and when the High Priest's servants sought to convict Peter of his discipleship, they clinched their appeal with, "Did not I see thee in the garden with Him?" And still the true Christian disciple is a man of the garden. He carries with him a breath of the pure, invigorating, fragrant air that blows across the secret garden of communion. The sound of its crystal fountains is in his voice; the radiance of its sunlit flowers is mirrored in his eyes. He is not as other men are; he carries a garden in his heart, and his fellows take knowledge of him that he has been with Jesus.

In the garden of communion the clamour of the world and the contendings of the Church are alike unheard. No sound of controversy penetrates that enclosed sanctuary; no rivalries can live within its gates of peace. There the Twelve clamour no longer for the highest place in the Kingdom; there Peter steps out of the shallows of impetuosity into the clear depths of love, John unlearns on the bosom of his Lord the passion that would call down fire from heaven, and Philip's questionings are lost in a certainty deeper than that of the enquiring mind. Small wonder that the disciples loved the garden, and that disciples of all ages have been loth to exchange its sweet intimacies for the rough and irritating traffic of the open road! It belonged at once to the strength and to the weakness of mediaeval sainthood that it lingered so persistently in the garden.

—EMILY HERMAN, 1876-1923

[320] Spiritual Maxims

1. THE more we learn what humility is, the less we discover of it in ourselves.

276

2. Let no one ask a stronger mark of an excellent love to God, than that we are insensible to our own reputation.

3. Would you exert all your powers to attain Divine Union? Use all your strength for the destruction of self.

4. Faith and the cross are unseparable: the cross is the shrine of faith, and faith is the light of the cross.

5. The more the darkness of self-knowledge deepens about us, the more does the divine truth shine in the midst.

6. How rare is it to behold a soul in an absolute abandonment of selfish interests, that it may devote itself to the interests of God!

7. It is harder to die to our virtues than to our vices; but the one is just as necessary as the other for perfect union. Our attachments are the stronger as they are more spiritual. . . .

8. He who has a pure heart will never cease to pray; and he who will be constant in prayer, shall know what it is to have a pure heart. . . .

9. Self-seeking is the gate by which a soul departs from peace; and total abandonment to the will of God, that by which it returns.

10. He who has learned to seek nothing but the will of God, shall always find what he seeks.

—MADAME JEANNE GUYON, 1648-1717

[321] Maxims to Know a Simple, Humble, and True Heart

ENCOURAGE thyself to be humble, embracing tribulations as instruments of thy good; rejoice in contempt, and desire that God may be thy holy refuge, comfort, and protector. . . .

He that is taken with praise is not yet arrived at profound humility, tho he does not desire praise, nor seek it, but rather avoids it; because, to an humble heart, praises are bitter crosses, altho it be wholly quiet and immovable.

He has no internal humility who doth not abhor himself, with a mortal but withal a peaceable and quiet hatred; but he will never come to possess this treasure who has not a low and profound knowledge of his own vileness and rottenness, and misery.

He that makes excuses and replies has not a simple and humble heart, especially if he does this with his superior; because replies grow from a secret pride that reigns in the soul, and from thence proceeds the total ruin of it. . . .

So much (nay more) doth false humility displease God, as true pride does; because that is hypocrisy besides.

The truly humble man, tho everything falls out contrary to him, is neither disquieted nor afflicted by it; because he is prepared, and thinks he deserves no less. He is not disquieted under troublesome thoughts, wherewith the devil seeks to torment him, nor under temptations, tribulations, and desertions; but rather acknowledges his unworthiness, and is affected that the Lord chastises him by the devil's means, tho he be a vile instrument; all he suffers seems nothing to him, and he never doth a thing that he thinks worth any great matter.

He that is arrived at perfect and inward humility, altho he be disturbed at nothing, as one that abhors himself because he knows his imperfection in everything, his ingratitude and his misery, yet he suffers a great cross in enduring himself. This is the sign to know true humility of heart by. But the happy soul, which is gotten to this holy hatred of itself, lives overwhelmed, drowned, and swallowed up in the depths of its own nothingness, out of which the Lord raises him, by communicating divine wisdom to him, and filling him with light, peace, tranquillity, and love.

—Miguel de Molinos, 1640-1697

[322] The Lesson from the Bee

Observe the wise bee and make it your model. It dwells in a community in the midst of its companions, and it goes forth, not during the storm, but when the weather is calm and still and the sun is shining; and it flies towards all the flowers on which it can find sweetness. It does not rest on any flower, neither in its beauty nor in its sweetness, but it draws from each calix honey and wax—that is to say, the sweetness and the substance of its brightness—and it bears them back to the community in which all the bees are assembled, so that the honey and wax may profitably bear fruit.

The opened heart on which Christ, the Eternal Sun, is shining, grows and flourishes under His rays, and flows with all its inner powers into joy and sweetnesses.

Now the wise man will act like the bee, and he will fly out in order to settle with care, intelligence, and prudence on all the gifts and on all the sweetness which he has experienced, and on all the good which God has done to him; and through the rays of the sun and his own inward observation he will experience a multitude of consolations and blessings. And he will not rest on any flower of all these gifts, but, laden with gratitude and praise, he will fly back again toward the home in which he longs to dwell and rest for evermore with God.

—JAN VAN RUYSBROECK, 1293-1381

[323] The Four Degrees of Love

NEVERTHELESS, because we are carnal and are born of the concupiscence of the flesh, it follows as a necessary consequence that our desire for personal gratification, or our love should have its source in the flesh. But if it is directed according to the right order of things, advancing by its several degrees under the guidance of grace, it will at last be consummated by the spirit because; that was not first which is spiritual, but that which is natural; afterwards that which is spiritual. First, therefore, man loves himself for his own sake; for, he is flesh and he can have no taste for anything except in relation to himself. And when he sees that he cannot subsist of himself he begins to seek God through faith as something, as it were, necessary for him, and to love Him. Thus he loves God according to the second degree, but for his own sake, not for himself. But when, in truth, on account of his own necessity, he has begun to worship and come to him again and again by meditating, by reading, by prayer and by being obedient, little by little God becomes known to him through experience, in a sort of familiarity, and consequently He grows sweet; and thus by tasting how sweet is the Lord he passes to the third degree so that he loves God now, not for his own sake but for Himself. Yes, in this degree he stands still for a very long time and I know not if the fourth degree is attained in its perfection by any man in this life so that forsooth, a man loves himself only for the sake of God. If there are any who have experience of this let them declare it; to me, I confess, it seems impossible. But it will be so, beyond a doubt, when the good and faithful servant has been brought into the joy of his Lord and inebriated with the plenty of God's house. For, forgetful of himself in a wonderful way, as it were, and as if entirely freed of self he will continue on, wholly, into God, and thereafter being joined to Him he will be one spirit with Him.

—BERNARD OF CLAIRVAUX, 1090-1153

279

[324] Albert Schweitzer's Hope for Mankind

To the question whether I am a pessimist or an optimist, I answer that my knowledge is pessimistic, but my willing and hoping are optimistic.

I am pessimistic in that I experience in its full weight what we conceive to be the absence of purpose in the course of world-happenings. Only at quite rare moments have I felt really glad to be alive. I could not but feel with a sympathy full of regret all the pain that I saw around me, not only that of men but that of the whole creation. From this community of suffering I have never tried to withdraw myself. It seemed to me a matter of course that we should all take our share of the burden of pain which lies upon the world. Even while I was a boy at school it was clear to me that no explanation of the evil in the world could ever satisfy me; all explanations, I felt, ended in sophistries, and at bottom had no other object than to make it possible for men to share in the misery around them, with less keen feelings. That a thinker like Leibnitz could reach the miserable conclusion that though this world is, indeed, not good, it is the best that was possible, I have never been able to understand.

But however much concerned I was at the problem of the misery in the world, I never let myself get lost in broodings over it; I always held firmly to the thought that each one of us can do a little to bring some portion of it to an end. Thus I came gradually to rest content in the knowledge that there is only one thing we can understand about the problem, and that is that each of us has to go his own way, but as one who means to help to bring about deliverance. . . .

If men can be found who revolt against the spirit of thoughtlessness, and who are personalities sound enough and profound enough to let the ideals of ethical progress radiate from them as a force, there will start an activity of the spirit which will be strong enough to evoke a new mental and spiritual disposition in mankind.

Because I have confidence in the power of truth and of the spirit, I believe in the future of mankind. Ethical world and life-affirmation contains within itself an optimistic willing and hoping which can never be lost. It is, therefore, never afraid to face the dismal reality, and to see it as it really is.

March 7, 1931

—ALBERT SCHWEITZER, 1875-

[325] Prayer Is Power

PRAYER is not only worship; it is also an invisible emanation of man's worshiping spirit—the most powerful form of energy that one can generate. The influence of prayer on the human mind and body is as demonstrable as that of secreting glands. Its results can be measured in terms of increased physical buoyancy, greater intellectual vigor, moral stamina, and a deeper understanding of the realities underlying human relationships.

If you make a habit of sincere prayer, your life will be very noticeably and profoundly altered. Prayer stamps with its indelible mark our actions and demeanor. A tranquility of bearing, a facial and bodily repose, are observed in those whose inner lives are thus enriched. Within the depths of consciousness a flame kindles. And man sees himself. He discovers his selfishness, his silly pride, his fears, his greeds, his blunder. He develops a sense of moral obligation, intellectual humility. Thus begins a journey of the soul toward the realm of grace.

Prayer is a force as real as terrestrial gravity. As a physician, I have seen men, after all other therapy has failed, lifted out of disease and melancholy by the serene effort of prayer. It is the only power in the world that seems to overcome the so-called "laws of nature"; the occasions on which prayer has dramatically done this have been termed "miracles." But a constant, quieter miracle takes place hourly in the hearts of men and women who have discovered that prayer supplies them with a steady flow of sustaining power in their daily lives. . . .

When we pray, we link ourselves with the inexhaustible motive power that spins the universe. We ask that a part of this power be apportioned to our needs. Even in asking, our human deficiencies are filled and we arise strengthened and repaired.

—ALEXIS CARREL, 1873-1944

[326] Eros and Agape

IN contrast with *eros, agape* can be effectively illustrated by Nygren's own tabulation of opposite descriptive terms:

"Eros is a desire of good for the self.

Eros is man's effort to ascend.

Agape is self-giving.

Agape comes down from above.

Eros is man's way to God.

Eros is man's achievement, the endeavor of man to achieve salvation.

Eros is ego-centric love, a form of self-assertion of the highest, noblest, sublimest kind.

Eros seeks to gain its life, a life Divine, immortal.

Eros is a will to have and to possess, resting on a sense of need.

Eros is primarily human love, and God is the object of Eros.

Eros, when it is applied to God, is a love fashioned after the pattern of human love.

Eros is determined by and dependent on the quality of its object, its beauty and value, hence it is not spontaneous, but "caused," called forth by the value of its object.

Eros recognizes value in its object, and therefore loves it.

Agape is God's way to man.

Agape is a free gift, a salvation which is the work of Divine love.

Agape is unselfish love, which "seeketh not its own," and freely spends itself.

Agape lives by God's life, and therefore dares to "lose it."

Agape freely gives and spends, for it rests on God's own richness and fullness.

Agape is primarily God's own love, for God is Agape.

Agape, when it appears in man, is a love that takes its form from God's own love.

Agape is sovereign and independent with regard to its object, and is poured out on "the evil and the good"; hence it is spontaneous, "uncaused," and bestows itself on those who are not worthy of it.

Agape loves, and creates value in its object."

—NELS F. S. FERRÉ, 1908-

[327] Twenty Minutes of Reality

It was an ordinary March day. I am glad to think that it was. I am glad to remember that there was nothing extraordinary about the weather, nor any unusualness of setting—no flush of spring or beauty of scenery —to induce what I saw. It was, on the contrary, almost a dingy day. The branches were bare and colorless, and the occasional half-melted piles of snow were a forlorn gray rather than white. Colorless little city sparrows flew and chirped in the trees, while human beings, in no way remarkable, passed along the porch.

There was, however, a wind blowing, and if any outside thing intensified the experience it was the blowing of that wind. In every other respect it was an ordinary commonplace day. Yet here, in this everyday setting, and entirely unexpectedly (for I had never dreamed of such a thing), my eyes were opened, and for the first time in all my life I caught a glimpse of the ecstatic beauty of reality.

I cannot now recall whether the revelation came suddenly or gradually; I only remember finding myself in the very midst of those wonderful moments, beholding life for the first time in all its young intoxication of loveliness, in its unspeakable joy, beauty, and importance. I cannot say exactly what the mysterious change was. I saw no new thing, but I saw all the usual things in a miraculous new light—in what I believe is their true light. I saw for the first time how wildly beautiful and joyous, beyond any words of mine to describe, is the whole of life. Every human being moving across that porch, every sparrow that flew, every branch tossing in the wind, was caught in and was a part of the whole mad ecstasy of loveliness, of joy, of importance, of intoxication of life.

It was not that for a few keyed-up moments I *imagined* all existence as beautiful, but that my inner vision was cleared to the truth so that I *saw* the actual loveliness which is always there, but which we so rarely perceive; and I knew that every man, woman, bird, and tree, every living thing before me, was extravagantly beautiful, and extravagantly important. And as I beheld, my heart melted out of me in a rapture of love and delight. A nurse was walking past; the wind caught a strand of her hair and blew it out in a momentary gleam of sunshine, and never in my life before had I seen how beautiful beyond all belief is a woman's hair. Nor had I ever guessed how marvelous it is for a human being to walk. As for the internes in their white suits, I had never realized before the whiteness of white linen! but much more than that, I had never so much as dreamed of the mad beauty of young manhood. A little sparrow chirped and flew to a near-by branch, and I honestly believe that only "the morning stars singing together, and the sons of God shouting for joy" can in the least express the ecstasy of a bird's flight. I cannot express it, but I have seen it.

Once out of all the gray days of my life I have looked into the heart of reality; I have witnessed the truth; I have seen life as it really is—ravishingly, ecstatically, madly beautiful, and filled to overflowing with a wild joy, and a value unspeakable. For those glorified moments I was in love with every living thing before me—trees in the wind, the little birds flying, the nurses, the internes, the people who came and went. There was nothing that was alive that was not a miracle. Just to be alive was in itself a miracle. My very soul flowed out of me in a great joy.

—MARGARET PRESCOTT MONTAGUE, 1878-

283

INDEXES

 TITLES—AUTHORS—TOPICS

INDEX OF TITLES

INDEX OF AUTHORS

292

GANDHI, MAHATMA (1869-1948) Indian statesman and leader whose non-resistance helped to win freedom of India; though a Hindu, he took the Sermon on the Mount as his ethical code, 275:9

GARBEDIAN, H. GORDON (1905-) Mexican writer, author of *Albert Einstein: Maker of Universes* (1939), 00

GIDE, ANDRÉ (1869-1949) French writer and savant, best known for his journal reflections, 266:1-3

GRAHAM, FRANK (1893-) American sports columnist and writer; formerly sports editor *Look* magazine, now with the *New York Journal-American*, 39

GRANT, FREDERICK C. (1891-) American New Testament author and teacher, at Union Theological Seminary (New York City) since 1938; member of translating committee of the Revised Standard Version, 275:14

GREGORY, CASPAR RENÉ (1846-1917) American-born New Testament scholar who spent most of his teaching-writing days at Leipzig University (Germany); best known for his *The Canon and Text of the New Testament*, 275:4

GREY, LADY JANE (1537-1554) English noblewoman, great-granddaughter of Henry VII of England, executed as usurper of the crown of England; wife of Lord Guilford Dudley, 198

GROOTE, GERHARD (1340-1384) Dutch lawyer who became a lay preacher and outstanding preacher in Holland; founder of The Brethren of the Common Life; thought by some to be the author of most of *The Imitation of Christ* which Thomas à Kempis edited, 289:1-2

GROU, JEAN NICHOLAS (1731-1803) Jesuit priest and mystic, best known for his *The Hidden Life of the Soul*, 314

GUNTHER, JOHN (1901-) Political writer and correspondent whose writings are based on interviews of most of the world's leaders, and whose "Inside" books portray the events of many countries of the world, 106

GUYON, MADAME JEANNE (1648-1717) French writer on mysticism who spent much of her life in confinement because of the Church's antagonism to her religious viewpoint, 320

HARKNESS, GEORGIA (1891-) One of the world's leading women theologians and a writer of note, whose teaching in the last twenty years has

Harkness—*cont'd*
been at Garrett Biblical Institute and Pacific School of Religion, 290

HARNACK, ADOLF VON (1851-1930) One of the greatest of New Testament scholars and early church historians whose teaching was primarily at Berlin University, 275:3

HEARD, GERALD (1889-) British-born scientist and religious thinker whose writings on prayer and mysticism have given penetrating insights into the devotional life, 241, 300

HERMAN, EMILY (1876-1923) English writer and editor, wife of a Presbyterian minister, her best-known book being *The Secret Garden of the Soul and Other Devotional Studies*, 252, 319

HERMAN, NICHOLAS (1611-1691) Footman and soldier who at fifty-five joined the Barefooted Carmelites; called Brother Lawrence; the person who gave stimulation to *The Practice of the Presence of God*, 257

HICKS, GRANVILLE (1901-) American author, editor, and poet, 275:5

HOLMES, JOHN HAYNES (1879-) American Unitarian clergyman, 1907-1949 minister of the present Community Church of New York City, and now minister-emeritus; author of numerous books in religion and sociology, 98, 208

HOLMES, KENNETH (1917-) American writer, author of *Foes of the Spirit*. Article, "Just for Today," was widely read in *The American Weekly*, 58

HOLMES, OLIVER WENDELL, JR. (1841-1935) Justice of the Supreme Court, 53

HOLT, IVAN LEE (1886-) Methodist bishop, author, and former president of the Federal Council of Churches of Christ in America, 209

HOOVER, HERBERT (1874-) Thirty-first president of the United States; known for his humanitarian interests; originally trained as a mining engineer; author of numerous books and articles, 54

HORTON, DOUGLAS (1891-) American Congregationalist clergyman, formerly minister of the General Council of the Congregational Christian Churches, Dean emeritus of Harvard Divinity School, 216

HOWE, CHARLES (1661-1745) Engaged in English embassy labors, but declined appointment as ambassador; after his wife's death in 1690, he secluded himself in the country in religious meditation, 128, 148

INDEX OF TOPICS

300